FEDERAL REGULATION OF BANKING

1983-84

FEDERAL REGULATION OF BANKING
1983-84

By Carter H. Golembe
and David S. Holland

GOLEMBE
Golembe Associates, Inc.

Golembe Associates, Inc.
Suite 900-N
1800 M Street, NW
Washington, D.C. 20036

ISBN 0-9608840-1-7
Library of Congress Catalog Card No. 83-082233

Printed in the United States of America

Contents

Charts in Text

Tables in Text

Tables in Statistical Section

Preface

This 1983–84 edition of *Federal Regulation of Banking* deals with an industry in transition. Such a statement could have been made at the outset of each of the preceding editions, in 1975 and in 1981, but it would not have had quite the same significance. For the fact is that in 1983 it is becoming increasingly difficult to separate out from all financial institutions, and particularly from the body of depository institutions, those that are properly described as "banks."

The tightly compartmentalized financial system and structure put into place in the early 1930s is disappearing, at least to the extent that distinctions among institutions are defined in a functional sense. It is no longer the case that commercial banks alone have the ability to offer transaction account services to the public, a function that since the 1930s had provided the crucial distinction between these institutions and other financial institutions. Similarly, "banking services"—whether in the form of multi-purpose lending or various fee-based services—are now available from institutions that formerly specialized in just one or a few types of loans or services. And at the same time, commercial banks, often utilizing the holding company vehicle, have begun to offer services, particularly in the securities area, that had been unavailable, in most instances, from banks.

The transition now underway is far from complete. Neither law nor regulation has yet recognized, except in a marginal sense, the underlying functional changes now underway. Charters are granted by separate authorities, separate codes are amended, regulations are issued for each type of institution, and examinations are conducted as if the world is as it was. The fact that a commercial bank and savings and loan association may both make commercial loans, offer transaction accounts to the public, and provide trust services does not mean, as yet at least, that they answer to the same regulatory agencies applying the same statutes. Or put another way, there continues to be, as a matter of law and regulation, an identifiable body of institutions called banks—institutions which dominate by number and aggregate assets the total of all depository institutions.

In Chapter 1 of the 1981 edition, we noted "the possibility that future editions of this volume will be compelled to include the regulation of institutions not presently defined as 'banks.'" That time is not yet here, though the dilemma posed for the editors was real: to let the next edition wait until law and regulation catch up with reality, while our 1981 volume becomes increasingly out-of-date, or to continue to focus just on banks—commercial banks primarily but including, as in prior editions, material on savings banks where appropriate.

We have taken the latter option, with modifications. The basic revisions have been intended to incorporate in this 1983–84 edition the changes that have occurred in the regulation of banks, changes that in just two years are numerous and significant. In addition, we have added a new part, dealing with other depository and with non-depository institutions. Also, where useful and appropriate we have added to the various banking chapters information on nonbank institutions.

As with the earlier edition, our focus is primarily on the "why" and "what" of regulation. The faults or virtues of the system, and whether or not it should be drastically reformed, are matters beyond the scope of this work.

The audience for whom this book is intended consists of those persons who desire in one convenient place the essential information on federal regulation of banks, and who may want, in addition, some introductory material on the regulation of other depository institutions. It should be of special interest to students in university courses related to banking or financial institutions; to participants in educational or training programs operated by banks and other financial institutions, banker associations, and governmental agencies; and to many bank officers whose necessary preoccupation with day-to-day operations has prevented them from acquiring as complete an understanding of the federal regulatory system as would be desirable.

This book does not attempt to describe or evaluate the regulatory structures of the states, except to the extent necessary in outlining relationships and differences between state and federal regulation of banks. Nevertheless, regulation is incidental to the chartering power, and banks are chartered by the states as well as the federal government. (Federally chartered banks may be identified by the title, which will include the word "National" or "N.A.," the abbreviation for National Association.) Indeed, the large majority of banks in this country are chartered and regulated by states, although virtually all of them are subject also to some measure of federal regulation. State regulation of banks, however, is a separate subject, certainly deserving of treatment but well beyond the scope of this effort.

Because so much of the present edition continues to rely on work done on the previous editions, particularly the 1981 edition, the authors think it appropriate to include earlier contributors among those deserving thanks. A special indebtedness is due Raymond E. Hengren, former Senior Advisor to the Board of Directors of the Federal Deposit Insurance Corporation. Mr. Hengren was one of the authors of the first edition and responsible in an important way for the chapter structure, which largely survives in this volume. More generally, but for the impetus provided by the first edition, there would have been no subsequent editions of *Federal Regulation of Banking*. Thus, Mr. Hengren's contributions to this work are difficult to overestimate.

As with the two earlier editions, Lewis N. Dembitz, Senior Consulting Associate, Golembe Associates, made extensive comments and suggestions on the text. His editorial assistance was invaluable.

Other present and past members of Golembe Associates' professional staff who have made significant contributions include Richard M. M. McConnell, Max H. Kumin, Suzanne C. Hutchinson, Cynthia W. Wood, Karen Rosenquist, Janet E. Easley, Susan C. Gaw, Bruce D. McCullough, Loretta Mockler, Douglas S. Morgan, Letitia A. Pemberton, Susan C. Raynes, Warren S. Rosenthal, Richard O. Stoner, Miguel C. Thames, and James R. Walker.

Several individuals at the federal banking agencies provided comments on portions of the text of the second, or 1981, edition. At the Federal Deposit Insurance Corporation, these were Stanley C. Silverberg and Benjamin B. Christopher. And at the Office of the Comptroller of the Currency, the individuals were William A.

Longbrake, Robert R. Bench, Frank R. Carbone, Ellen S. Goldberg, Christopher James, and Steven J. Weiss.

A number of individuals at the agencies have also been helpful in providing statistical data. Three whose time and efforts call for special mention are Jack A. Pinion, Bank Information Analyst in the FDIC's Division of Management Systems and Financial Statistics, James V. Houpt, Senior Financial Analyst in the Federal Reserve Board's Division of Banking Supervision and Regulation, and Mary T. Mitchell, Associate Director of the FDIC's Division of Bank Supervision.

Rhonda J. Holland deserves a special mention for her editorial efforts on both the 1981 and the 1983–84 editions.

Finally, the production staff at Golembe Associates deserves thanks for their efforts. Those past and present members of the staff who did a significant amount of work on this project include: Gloria J. Butler, Patricia A. Ighnat, William T. Kennedy, Barbara V. Mansfield, Barbara L. Smith, Janet Y. Strain, Gloria E. Westover, Sandra L. Whittaker, and Janice L. Yohman.

Despite the numerous contributions of others, however, the authors take full responsibility for the contents of *Federal Regulation of Banking*.

July 1983

Carter H. Golembe
David S. Holland

PART I

Development of Federal Regulation of Depository Institutions

The federal government regulates depository institutions that it charters, or which have obligations insured by it, through five federal agencies. The regulatory structure in its present form was largely put into place in 1933–34, although federal involvement in banking regulation began in 1863. Some have argued that the result is a jerry-built structure, lacking symmetry and stability, while others maintain that each piece was carefully added in a consistent and logical manner. Whatever the merits of these two contentions, all would agree that the resulting structure is intricate and, to many, baffling.

In Chapter 1 the evolution of the federal regulatory structure is briefly sketched. Chapter 2 focuses on the principal bank regulatory agencies, first with respect to the jurisdictional limits assigned to each agency and to efforts at coordinating their activities, and then with respect to their internal organization. Mention is also made of other federal agencies with which the banking industry comes into contact.

1

Origins and Development

For almost a century and a half, beginning in 1791, the history of the federal government's efforts to control and regulate depository institutions related only to commercial banks. They were not the only depository institutions; mutual savings banks had appeared on the scene by the 1820s, and investment banking houses accepted deposits during much of this early period—in fact, until 1933. Commercial banks, however, were the only incorporated institutions possessing specific authority to issue currency (banknotes), which along with deposit liabilities subject to check, comprised the bulk of the nation's circulating medium. Bank liabilities continue in the 1980s to provide most of the circulating medium, though the currency function has long since been taken over by the federal government.

It is the monetary function, wherein commercial banks serve as the vehicles through which much of the nation's money supply is created and held, that accounts for the federal government's deep interest in the soundness and stability of the industry. As the primary mobilizers and allocators of credit, banks are also subject to governmental interest attached to those functions. Moreover, as time goes on, government has become increasingly concerned with the uses to which bank credit is put.

The federal government's regulatory interest in other depository institutions has developed only during the last fifty years. Some of the motives were the same, though only recently could it be said that thrift institutions have an important monetary role. As the holders of the cash resources of millions of individuals, however, these institutions have joined commercial banks as objects of federal concern and regulation.

THE EARLY YEARS, 1787–1862

For the first 75 years after the adoption of the Constitution, the regulation of banking was almost entirely a state matter. In that period of the nation's history the federal government's major involvement with banking was limited to the two Banks of the United States, each chartered for a 20-year period, from 1791 to 1811 in the case of the first Bank of the United States, and from 1816 to 1836 in the case of the second bank.

This was not, it should be stressed, a modest involvement. A plan for a "National Bank," i.e., one chartered by the federal government, was submitted by Secretary of the Treasury Alexander Hamilton to the first Congress; that plan led, in 1791, to the formation of the first Bank of the United States. At the time, there was already in operation a handful of state-chartered banks, in each of the then major cities. The new federal bank, headquartered in Philadelphia, was given a 20-year charter and an authorized capital of $10 million (immense for that time), of which the federal government itself was to subscribe $2 million while private stockholders would hold the remaining $8 million.

Mr. Hamilton believed strongly in the advantage to business of commercial banking and, in addition, viewed the new institution as an essential aid in carrying out the fiscal responsibilities of the Treasury. However, his plan for a federal bank was not easily implemented, running into a storm of opposition from agrarians and Jeffersonians, who doubted that any bank, whether state-chartered or federally chartered, could be anything but a corrupting, evil influence in the new nation. The Jeffersonians, or at least some of them, were also convinced that if there had to be banks, at least they should be state-chartered institutions.

Although there is general agreement among historians that the first Bank of the United States was capably managed and did indeed serve many of the objectives sought by Mr. Hamilton, it was nevertheless allowed to go out of existence when its charter expired in 1811. At the time of its demise, there were approximately 88 state banks. In the absence of the restraining influence of the federal institution, the number of these banks almost tripled during the following five years, reaching 246 by 1816.

Not only had the number of state banks multiplied, but the currency of the nation was in sorry condition, consisting primarily of the currency issues of such institutions. Redemption of notes in gold or silver coin had been suspended in 1814 and the Treasury encountered considerable difficulty in conducting its operations. The Jeffersonians were now in power and, in fact, it was President Madison, who earlier had doubted the constitutionality of a federal bank, who now proposed that a new federal institution be chartered. It was an interesting turn of events, with the Jeffersonians now railing against the monopoly of power by the state-chartered banks, and the Federalists, who had been the most vociferous supporters of the first Bank of the United States, now in opposition. But President Madison's proposal was adopted in 1816.

The second Bank of the United States was chartered for 20 years, but this time with a capital of $35 million as compared with the $10 million approved for its predecessor. Again, the federal government was to hold one-fifth of the stock while the remaining four-fifths was in private hands.

The federal government was therefore again involved in the banking business in 1816, but out of it once more twenty years later at the expiration of the charter of the second Bank of the United States. The history of the great conflict over whether to renew the charter, which became known as the "Bank War," is too complex to recount here in any detail. Basically, the old agrarian-Jeffersonian antipathy toward any banking, the strong opposition by state banks toward control exercised by the second Bank of the United States, and the interests of the business community in more liberal credit extension were forged by President Jackson into a coalition powerful enough to bring down the second Bank of the United States and to end federal government involvement in commercial banking for almost three decades.

One of the important issues during the "Bank War" of the 1830s was the public hostility toward banks and banking concentration, whether in public or private hands. Indeed, hostility was so intense that banking was outlawed in a few states; but such extreme animosity soon vanished. However, a significant residual of the concern over concentration was the adoption of the so-called free banking laws, establishing a system that survives today. The pioneer step in this development was taken by New York in 1838 (although Michigan had adopted a preliminary version of the New York law a year earlier), and similar laws were enacted by many other states in the following decades.

The free banking laws were intended to ensure that, instead of each bank's charter being a special legislative act, the business of banking would be open to any group of persons able to provide adequate capital and willing to subject the activities and resources of the enterprise to such supervision and control as would, it was believed, protect the funds supplied by the public. Establishment of a bank regulatory agency was a concomitant of "free banking" legislation.

Actually, regulation of banking had appeared in New York State even earlier (1829), and in a somewhat different context. In an endeavor to protect the public against the consequences of bank failures, New York established a deposit and circulating note insurance system, identified at the time as a "safety fund," with remarkable similarities to that fashioned by the federal government more than a century later. New York's insurance act made provision for the establishment of the nation's first bank regulatory department and for examination of insured banks.

Many other states in the pre-Civil War period followed the New York precedents of free banking or insurance. Thus by the middle of the nineteenth century, regulation of banks by state governments was reasonably well established. Such regulation was almost always an integral part of state legislation which authorized "free banking" or gave depositors and noteholders some protection against losses due to bank failure.

DUAL BANK CHARTERING AND REGULATION, 1863–1912

With the first and second Banks of the United States, but particularly with the latter, the federal government had begun to develop a central bank. That effort was abandoned, and the federal government returned to the banking scene in 1863 with the passage of multi-purpose legislation that included a provision for bank chartering. Banks chartered pursuant to this legislation—the National Currency Act of 1863—were authorized to issue national bank notes secured by the deposit of federal obligations with the Treasury of the United States. Thus, a new area of investment was created for the lodgment of federal securities—then urgently needed to facilitate government financing as the Civil War entered the climactic stage. In addition, the legislation provided the basis for a sound hand-to-hand currency which in a few years supplanted the diverse state bank note issues, many of which were of dubious value.

The National Bank Act of 1864 revised and strengthened the National Currency Act, but the essential features of the statute were not altered. Thus, with the passage of the National Bank Act, the Congress, in effect, ratified the decision of the states and instituted "free banking" at the national level. At the same time, following the state precedent, it established a bank regulatory agency, the Office of the Comptroller of the Currency.

In 1963, the American Bankers Association celebrated the hundredth anniversary of the "dual banking system," i.e., a system offering the option of chartering and supervision by federal or by state authorities. It is doubtful, however, that anyone in 1863 was conscious of the fact that such a system had been created. If anything, the two banking systems were at war, with each seeking the extermination of the other. State banks were furious at the appearance of the new federal institutions. For example, the New York City banks sought to keep the national banks out of the clearing house, on the ground that they were not chartered to do a legitimate banking business.

At the same time, many of the proponents of the national banking system saw it as the replacement for state banks. And in fact, in an effort to drive state-chartered banks out of business, Congress in 1865 levied a prohibitive tax on the circulating banknotes of state commercial banks. At the time it was thought that without the ability to issue such notes, a bank could not survive. The fact was that deposit banking was well along even then, and the state banks, effectively deprived of the right to issue currency, simply accelerated the development of the deposit business, substituting deposit liabilities for banknote liabilities.

By the National Bank Act the federal government was provided with comprehensive chartering authority as well as with a regulatory agency with extensive powers over its banks. Nonetheless, the growth of state banks during the latter part of the nineteenth and the early decades of the twentieth century meant that an increasing percentage of banks operated beyond the purview of federal bank regulation. For example, in 1870 there were 1,612 national banks subject to federal supervision. The number of state-chartered institutions was 325, and they held about one-tenth of all bank resources. By way of contrast, in 1910, the number of state-chartered banks substantially exceeded national banks, 17,376 to 7,138, and the state banking system comprised almost one-half of all bank assets.

FEDERAL AUTHORITY OVER BANKS EXTENDED, 1913–1956

A major extension of federal bank regulation occurred in 1913 with the passage of the Federal Reserve Act. One of the objectives, according to the preamble to that act, was "to establish a more effective supervision of banking." Although the supervisory activities in the early years of the Federal Reserve developed slowly, they now have attained a position of substantial importance in the structure of bank regulation. Likewise, in the course of time, the other objectives of the Federal Reserve have evolved so that the System is also expected to serve the much broader purpose of conducting monetary policy in such fashion as to assist in assuring a healthy economy with maximum employment, domestic price stability, and an acceptable balance in international finance. Nonetheless, the Federal Reserve's bank regulatory activities continue to be important.

The Federal Reserve Act superimposed on the then existing banking system the authority of a new federal banking agency, with the objective of bringing state banks within the ambit of federal regulation. Unfortunately, from the point of view of those who sought such an end, the attempt was not very successful. Since membership in the Federal Reserve System was required only of national banks and was voluntary for state banks, the extension of federal regulation could occur only to the extent that state banks elected to join the Federal Reserve System. At first such state banks were regulated by the Comptroller of the Currency; soon the System developed its own regulatory machinery within the Federal Reserve Banks. Nevertheless, large numbers remained outside the System, subject only to state regulation. By 1930, for example, of the 24,273 banks in the United States, there were 15,364 state banks not supervised by any federal agency.

Still another force—the phenomenon of bank failures—contributed to the next significant extension of federal regulation in the field of banking. Bank failures had plagued the nation throughout its history, and the basic trouble had not been remedied by either the National Bank Act or the Federal Reserve Act. Whenever banking difficulties became widespread, there was concern over losses by depositors as well as a recognition of the need for more effective supervision of banks. As a reflection of this concern over bank failures and depositor losses, in the early decades of this century deposit insurance systems were established by eight states, primarily in the Great Plains area. These systems resembled the pre-Civil War efforts by a few states to protect depositors and circulating note holders against losses.

Extension of federal regulatory authority to virtually all commercial banks did not occur until 1933, with enactment of the Federal Deposit Insurance law. All banks that were members of the Federal Reserve System—whether national or state—were required to have their deposits insured by the FDIC, and all other banks were free to participate in the new federal insurance program if they so chose. As expected, almost all state nonmember banks found it essential to participate and, by so doing, became subject to the regulatory authority of the Federal Deposit Insurance Corporation.

The last major step in fashioning the federal bank regulatory system occurred in 1956 with the passage of the Bank Holding Company Act. Congress in that year gave to the Federal Reserve full regulatory authority over multi-bank holding companies, and in 1970 further extended this authority to all bank holding companies, whether one-bank or multi-bank.

OTHER DEPOSITORY INSTITUTIONS

Savings banks, savings and loan associations, and credit unions, often referred to as "thrift institutions," appeared on the American financial scene at fairly early dates. Savings banks came first, organized prior to 1820 in Philadelphia, New York, and Boston. The objective of the early organizers of these institutions was to encourage thrift among the so-called "laboring poor." Savings banks were conceived of as a means of combatting pauperism; to serve as an organizer or director was often to fulfill a civic or philanthropic purpose.

Savings and loan associations were patterned after the early British building societies. The purpose was to devise a means by which members could pool savings through small, regular contributions, with each member having an opportunity (sometimes determined by lot) to borrow from the fund in order to purchase a home. The first association organized in this country was the Oxford Provident Building Association, opened in 1831 in Frankford, Pennsylvania.

Although credit unions were found in many European countries during the latter half of the 19th century (having originated in Germany about mid-century), they did not appear in this country until somewhat later. The first credit unions in the United States were organized in New Hampshire in 1908. Among the reasons for their organization was a desire to offer low income persons an alternative to usurious loan rates; many early credit unions were organized by churches.

From the beginning, savings bank liabilities were true deposits, whereas for many years the obligations of savings and loan associations and credit unions were more similar to equity interests, and were often referred to as "shares." Though stock savings banks and stock savings and loan associations were also organized in some states, the overwhelming majority of all three types of thrift institutions were, and are, mutual in form.

To the extent that any regulation at all was accorded thrift institutions, it was the states that assumed the responsibility. For mutual savings banks, Massachusetts was among the first states to take an interest in their activities, passing supervisory laws in the 1830s. New York was the first state to extend supervision to savings and loan associations, in 1879. By the turn of the century about half of the states had done so, and by 1931 all but two states had provided for some degree of regulation.

Federal supervision and regulation came to all three types of thrift institutions as a result of the financial collapse of the early 1930s. Various devices were used. Federal deposit insurance was made available to mutual savings banks from the outset (in fact, savings banks had earlier been eligible for Federal Reserve membership and several had so opted).

The offering of federal charters and the creation of a special federal insurance program for which state-chartered savings and loan associations were eligible swept the major part of the savings and loan industry into federal regulation. The Federal Home Loan Bank System was established in 1932. In 1933, in the Home Owners' Loan Act, provision was made for federal charters for savings and loan associations. Insurance came in the following year, with creation of the Federal Savings and Loan Insurance Corporation. A primary reason for the establishment of the latter organization was a fear that deposit insurance for commercial banks through the FDIC would make it impossible for associations, whether federally or state chartered, to survive. In any event, the federal insurance program for S&Ls served as a means of extending federal regulation to state-chartered S&Ls, in the same way that the FDIC served as a means of extending federal regulation to state banks.

Federal chartering of credit unions was provided for in legislation enacted in 1934. Federal insurance for credit union shares did not appear until 1970, however. Responsibility for regulating federal credit unions was passed around among various federal agencies (including the FDIC, from 1942 until 1947). The present independent agency, the National Credit Union Administration, was created in 1970. The NCUA is both the regulator for federal credit unions and the administrator for the insurance program for federal credit unions and those state credit unions with federal insurance.

Regulation of savings and loan association holding companies came later than for bank holding companies, but had many similarities to the 1956 Bank Holding Company Act. The Savings and Loan Holding Company Act was adopted in 1967 and distinguished between one-association, or unitary, and multi-association or multiple, companies. The former have substantially more leeway in the type of non-S&L activities they may conduct than do the latter.

THE RECENT DECADES

Although the regulatory structure put into place by the federal government in 1934 retains essentially the same outlines fifty years later, in mid-1983, there are increasing signs that changes in that structure, reflecting changes in the financial industry, are in the offing. Among these signs was the creation by Congress, in 1978 and in 1980, of two new coordinating bodies. In the earlier year, the Federal Financial Institutions Examination Council was established, consisting of the heads of the three banking agencies and of the Federal Home Loan Bank Board and the National Credit Union Administration. In 1980, to oversee the phase-out of interest rate ceilings on savings and time deposits, the Depository Institutions Deregulation Committee was created, consisting of the Secretary of the Treasury and the Chairmen of the Federal Reserve Board, the FDIC, the FHLBB, and the National Credit Union Administration. The Comptroller of the Currency is a non-voting member.

This seeming drift toward a full or partial consolidation of functions is of course prompted by the removal of many of the old distinctions among depository institutions. In 1980, for example, the equivalent of checking account authority—the ability to issue NOW accounts—was given to thrift institutions nationally, and reserve requirements were made applicable to all depository institutions offering such transaction accounts. In 1982, the lending and investment powers of the thrifts were substantially broadened, such that the nature of many of these institutions may become that of multi-purpose lenders and providers of financial services, rather than of specialized financial institutions.

By no means all distinctions among depository institutions have been removed, however. The powers and functions of each type of depository institution continue to be dependent to a large extent on statutes and regulations. And banks are still the predominant type of depository institution. At the end of 1982, the total assets of all depository institutions—commercial banks, savings banks, savings and loan associations, and credit unions—were $2,848.7 billion. Of this total, $2,030.2 billion, or 71.3 percent, was in commercial and mutual savings banks that were regulated by the three traditional banking agencies—the Office of the Comptroller of the Currency, the FDIC, and the Federal Reserve Board. Specifically, federal banking regulation at the end of 1982 extended: to 14,451 commercial banks, or 97.1 percent of all such banks; to 315 mutual savings banks, or 75.4 percent of all such banks; and to all companies owning or controlling one or more banks (with negligible exceptions). It is this banking regulation with which most of the chapters that follow are concerned.

NOTES

A thorough and readable account of the development of banking in the United States to the time of the Civil War is Bray Hammond's *Banks and Politics in America From the Revolution to the Civil War*, Princeton, Princeton University Press, 1957. A most important work on the history of banking is Fritz Redlich's *The Molding of American Banking*, New York and London, Johnson Reprint Corporation, 1968.

The chapter mentions the basic laws that have shaped the U.S. banking structure. The current provisions of these laws are codified principally in the following chapters of Title 12 of the U.S. Code: the National Currency Act of 1863 and the National Bank Act of 1864—Chapters 1 and 2 (see the note to §38 for a list of U.S. Code sections containing provisions of the National Bank Act); the Federal Reserve Act of 1913—Chapter 3 (see the note to §226 for a list of U.S. Code sections); the Federal Deposit Insurance Act—Chapter 16 (the Federal Deposit Insurance Corporation was created in 1933 by an addition to the Federal Reserve Act; in 1950 Congress enacted Chapter 16 to contain most of the statutory provisions concerning the FDIC and provided that these provisions were to be known as the Federal Deposit Insurance Act; see the note to §1811); and the Bank Holding Company Act—Chapter 17.

The principal laws concerning the nonbank depository institutions are codified in the following chapters and sections of Title 12: the Home Owners' Loan Act, which concerns federal savings and loan associations and federal savings banks—Chapter 12; the National Housing Act, a portion of which pertains to the Federal Savings and Loan Insurance Corporation—Chapter 13; the Savings and Loan Holding Company Act—§1730a; and the Federal Credit Union Act–Chapter 14.

For a discussion of some of the problems in tracing Congressional enactments to current law see Jonathan L. Levin's article, "In Search of the National Bank Act," *Banking Law Journal* 97 (September 1980): 741.

2

Agencies Regulating Banks

The federal bank regulatory structure, which was largely fashioned between 1863 and 1933, is distinctive in several ways. First, it divides the principal regulatory duties among three major agencies. For most regulated industries, there is a single federal agency that has the primary supervisory responsibility. Second, only one of the three federal banking agencies—the Office of the Comptroller of the Currency—is solely a regulatory body. The other two banking agencies—the Federal Reserve and the Federal Deposit Insurance Corporation—exercise important responsibilities in addition to banking regulation. While it would not be correct to characterize bank regulation as merely incidental to the monetary policy responsibilities of the Federal Reserve or to the insurance responsibilities of the FDIC, in each case the effectiveness of these agencies is determined not so much by their regulatory work as by their operations in the monetary or insurance fields respectively.

Finally, banks are not isolated from some regulation by other governmental agencies. Indeed, banks (and bank holding companies) frequently find themselves subject to the regulatory reach of federal authorities not primarily involved in banking.

The focus in this chapter is on the three federal banking agencies: the FDIC, the OCC, and the Federal Reserve Board. A section also covers several other agencies with which banks come into contact. Discussion of the agencies concerned with the activities of the nonbank depository institutions—the Federal Home Loan Bank Board and its subsidiary deposit insurer, the Federal Savings and Loan Insurance Corporation, and the National Credit Union Administration—is reserved primarily for Chapter 12, although these agencies will also appear at other points in the book.

THE BANKING AGENCIES

The federal government's initial entry into the bank regulatory business occurred with the passage of national bank legislation and the establishment of the Office of the Comptroller of the Currency in 1863. On each successive occasion when a new banking agency was created by Congress, the banks already subject to federal regulation were linked to the new agency as part of its constituency. Thus national banks, regulated by the Comptroller of the Currency, were required to become members of the Federal Reserve System

Chart 1: Distribution of Bank Regulatory Authority, December 31, 1982

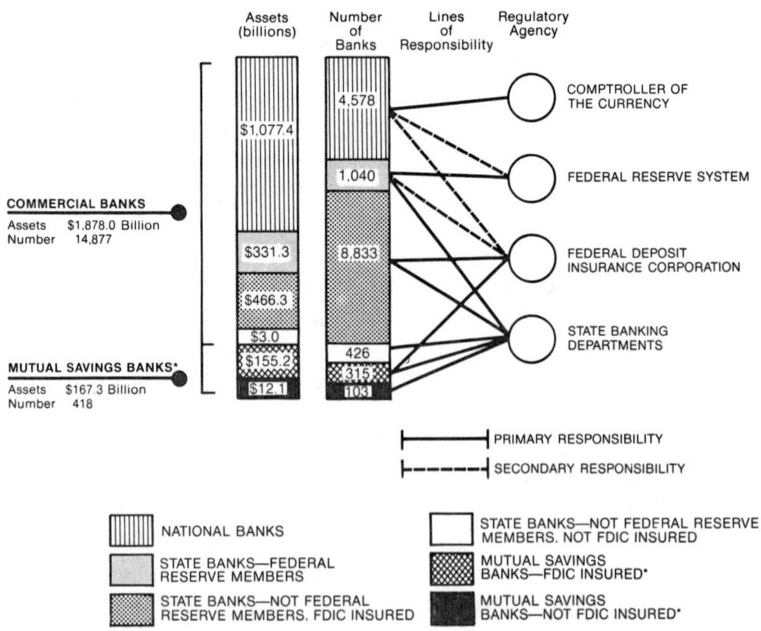

*Not included in the chart are six federally chartered mutual savings banks, which had assets at year-end 1982 of $6.9 billion. These institutions are chartered and supervised by the Federal Home Loan Bank Board and insured by the Federal Savings and Loan Insurance Corporation.

Source: FDIC *Annual Report*, 1982; National Association of Mutual Savings Banks.

when that System was established in 1913. Similarly, all bank members of the Federal Reserve System, both national and state, were required to become insured by the FDIC when that Corporation was established in 1933. The results of this evolutionary process are presented in Chart 1, which sets forth the distribution of regulatory authority for all commercial and mutual savings banks.

Chart 1 calls attention to the considerable overlapping of regulatory authority that has stemmed from the historical development of the structure. Bank regulatory chores, however, have been more or less apportioned among the three federal banking agencies in such a way as to minimize problems arising from overlapping authority. Much of this division of labor has been at the initiative of the agencies themselves, particularly in the examinations area. In addition, Congress has encouraged coordination of regulatory authority by establishing two formal interagency bodies—the Federal Financial Institutions Examination Council in 1978 and the Depository Institutions Deregulation Committee in 1980—to deal with specific problems in regulation. These bodies are discussed after the following description of the jurisdictions of the three federal banking agencies.

Almost all commercial banks in the nation have their deposits insured by the FDIC, as Chart 1 shows, but that Corporation regularly supervises only those insured state-chartered banks that are not members of the Federal Reserve System. This category includes the majority of the total number of banks in the country—more banks than are directly supervised by the other two federal agencies combined. However, because state nonmember insured banks are typically smaller institutions, their percentage of all commercial bank assets was only 24.8 percent at the end of 1982. In addition, the FDIC has regularly supervised the majority of the nation's mutual savings banks. Such institutions under FDIC supervision accounted for 92.8 percent of all mutual savings bank assets at the end of 1982. When the assets of mutual savings banks are taken into consideration, 30.4 percent of all bank assets were subject to the Corporation's supervision at the end of 1982.

While theoretically subject to supervision by the Federal Reserve and the FDIC, national banks in fact are regularly supervised only by the Office of the Comptroller of the Currency, except in unusual circumstances. Although national banks comprise under one-third of the nation's commercial banks, at the end of 1982 the assets of national banks constituted 57.4 percent of all commercial bank assets, and 52.7 percent of all bank assets.

For direct bank supervision, the Federal Reserve has the narrowest area of jurisdiction, measured in terms of number of banks.

That is, the Federal Reserve regularly supervises only those state-chartered banks that are members of the Federal Reserve System. At the end of 1982 there were 1,040 state member banks, as they are called, comprising only 7.0 percent of all commercial banks. However, because of their typically larger size when compared with other banks, at the end of 1982 state member banks held 17.6 percent of all commercial bank assets.

The Federal Reserve not only is responsible for the regular supervision of state member banks but also has sole regulatory authority over companies that own or control one or more banks. At the end of 1982 there were 4,557 such companies, called bank holding companies, having 6,659 bank subsidiaries in the United States with consolidated assets of $1,855 billion or 84.7 percent of all commercial bank consolidated assets. Consolidated assets are those held by both domestic and foreign offices.

One important aspect of the division of banks among regulatory agencies is that the banks themselves have some option as to the federal regulatory jurisdiction in which they may be placed. Banks are able to shift among the various agencies in certain ways, although not necessarily without difficulty. For example, a state member bank may withdraw from the Federal Reserve System but retain its insurance, in which case its supervisory agency becomes the FDIC. A national bank may convert to a state charter, or a state bank to a national charter, in either case changing the federal agency to which it is primarily subject. (See Chart 2.)

In 1978, existing mutual savings banks were given the option by statute of converting to federal charters. Prior to that time, there was no provision for federally chartered mutual savings banks. As of the end of 1982, there were six of these converted federally chartered mutual savings banks.

The Garn-St Germain Act of 1982 expanded the possibilities for the creation of federally chartered savings banks. Such banks can now be established on a *de novo* basis; that is, new ones may be chartered. They may also be established by the conversion of existing savings and loan associations. And very importantly, the act allows federal savings banks to exist in stock form. Mutual institutions have no stock, being owned by their depositors. During the first three months of 1983, 96 federal savings bank charters were granted by the Federal Home Loan Bank Board. Forty-six were granted as a result of the conversion of savings and loan associations, and fifty were granted as the result of the conversion of existing savings banks.

Federally chartered savings banks come under the supervision of the Federal Home Loan Bank Board (FHLBB), and their deposits are insured by its subsidiary agency, the Federal Savings and Loan Insurance Corporation (FSLIC). An exception involves state-chartered FDIC-insured savings banks that convert to federal charter. These institutions may remain insured by the FDIC until the insurance function is taken over by the FSLIC.

While bank conversions (either charter conversions or changes in Federal Reserve membership status by state banks) are seldom large in number in any single year, there have been occasions when both the number of conversions and the assets involved were of significance. Conversions may occur for a wide variety of reasons. Perhaps most common until recently was the desire by banks that were members of the Federal Reserve System to reduce the cost of carrying reserves as required by the Federal Reserve. This reason accounted for a number of conversions from national to state charter, and from state member to state nonmember status. The Depository Institutions Deregulation and Monetary Control Act of 1980, which imposed reserve requirements on practically all depos-

Chart 2: Charter Conversions of Commercial Banks, 1961–1982

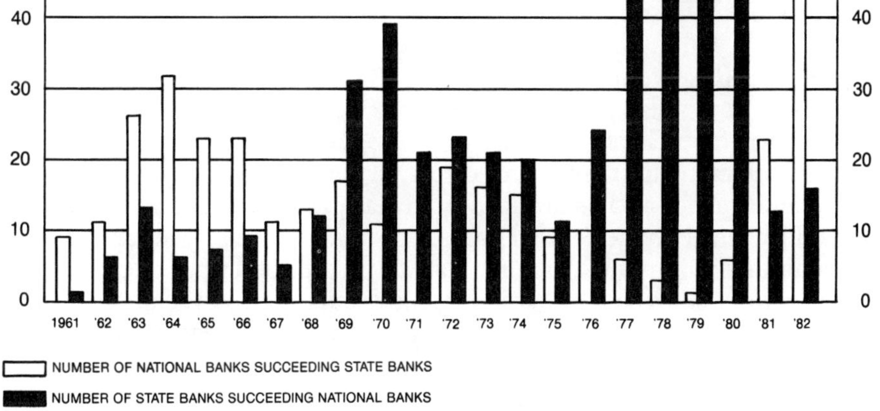

Source: FDIC, *Changes Among Operating Banks and Branches*, 1961–1982.

itory institutions offering transaction (checking) accounts or nonpersonal time deposits, eliminated this particular incentive to change regulatory status.

Early in the 1960s, a prominent reason for charter conversion was a belief on the part of many state banks—particularly some of the larger commercial banks—that greater operational freedom was to be found within the national bank system than within a particular state system. On the other hand, changes in state law occasionally make state charter status attractive to national banks. Chart 2 shows, for the years 1961 through 1982, conversion changes among banks.

COORDINATION EFFORTS

As discussed in the preceding section and as indicated by Chart 1, the banking regulatory structure is characterized by a considerable degree of overlapping authority. For example, questions can arise as to ultimate supervisory concern where the Federal Reserve supervises a holding company whose subsidiaries include national banks or state nonmember banks. To cite just one of many possible situations, the amount of capital in the lead bank of a holding company will be of supervisory significance to the bank's primary regulator and to the Federal Reserve, but the capital adequacy standards of the two agencies may differ.

Another such situation results from the ability of a bank holding company to choose between acquiring an additional bank directly or through merger into a subsidiary bank. In a direct acquisition the Federal Reserve is the agency responsible for passing on the transaction. In a merger, under the terms of the Bank Merger Act, the responsible agency depends upon the resulting bank: the OCC for a national bank, the FDIC for a state nonmember bank, and the Federal Reserve for a state member bank.

Overlap is also found with respect to federal and state authority. As shown on Chart 1, at the end of 1982, there was a total of 9,857 commercial banks subject to direct regulatory authority by both a federal agency and a state agency. In many instances, the federal and state agencies have devised procedures that minimize overlap problems inherent in the structure. For example, as described in Chapter 5, various shared examination methods cut down on the number of examinations that many state-chartered federally regulated banks have to undergo.

Indeed, cooperation among the regulatory agencies—both at the federal level and between the federal and state levels—has resulted in working relationships that have negated much of the potential for confusion and redundancy inherent in an overlapping authority situation. Until a few years ago, the cooperative efforts generally were initiated in the executive branch of the government, often by the banking regulators themselves. In 1938, the three federal banking agencies signed an agreement, amended in 1949, designed to bring uniformity to the classification of bank assets and the appraisal of bank-held securities. An interagency committee functioned from 1952 until about 1960, and the Interagency Coordinating Committee on Bank Regulation was formed in 1965. The Coordinating Committee was composed of the Chairman or a designated Governor of the Federal Reserve Board, the Comptroller of the Currency, the Chairman of the FDIC, and the Chairman of the Federal Home Loan Bank Board (FHLBB). The Committee attempted to bring a degree of uniformity to examinations and reporting procedures and provided a forum for the exchange of views on such topics as the various types of accounts the financial institutions were offering or should be allowed to offer.

Coordination reached a new level of importance and formality with the entry of Congress into the picture in 1978 and again in 1980. The Financial Institutions Regulatory and Interest Rate Control Act (FIRIRCA) of 1978 established the Federal Financial Institutions Examination Council (FFIEC), composed of the Comptroller of the Currency, the Chairman of the FDIC, a Governor of the Federal Reserve Board, the Chairman of the FHLBB, and the Chairman of the National Credit Union Administration Board. The FFIEC is empowered: (1) to establish uniform principles, standards, and report forms for the examination of federally regulated financial institutions; (2) to develop uniform reporting systems for such institutions, their holding companies, and nonfinancial subsidiaries of such institutions or holding companies; (3) to make recommendations for uniformity in other supervisory matters; and (4) to conduct schools for examiners employed by the federal financial institutions regulatory agencies, such schools to be open also to employees of state regulatory agencies. Financial institutions are defined to include commercial banks, savings banks, trust companies, savings and loan associations, and credit unions.

The law also requires the FFIEC to maintain a liaison committee composed of five representatives of state agencies. The purpose of the committee is to give the states a role in the efforts to achieve uniform examination principles and standards.

Administrative support for the FFIEC is provided by a small full-time staff composed of personnel detailed from the five agencies represented on the Council. Staff support in substantive areas is provided primarily by interagency task forces that utilize personnel in the agencies for research projects, investigative work, and preparation of reports. The FFIEC's administrative operations are funded through semiannual assessments on the five agencies. In 1982, these assessments totalled $875,000.

The second Congressional effort at mandating coordination was the creation of the Depository Institutions Deregulation Committee (DIDC) in 1980. The law that created the DIDC was the Depository Institutions Deregulation and Monetary Control Act. The members of the DIDC are the Secretary of the Treasury and the Chairmen of the Federal Reserve Board, the FDIC, the FHLBB, and the National Credit Union Administration Board. The Comptroller of the Currency is a nonvoting member. The DIDC's purpose is to oversee the orderly elimination of interest rate ceilings over a six-year period ending March 31, 1986. To accomplish this purpose, the DIDC has a considerable amount of discretion, including the power to gradually increase or eliminate ceilings and to create new categories of accounts without ceilings or with ceilings set at market rates.

The Garn-St Germain Act of 1982 speeded up the DIDC's work somewhat by instructing it to authorize an account for depository institutions that would be competitive with money market mutual funds. These accounts were authorized in December of 1982, and by March 31, 1983, had attracted $320.5 billion.

To summarize, any problems that have arisen over the years from the overlap of authority among federal and state banking regulators have been substantially eased by efforts at cooperation and coordination. Such efforts in a number of areas were raised to the level of legal requirements by Congressional actions in 1978 and 1980. Nevertheless, the three federal regulatory agencies—the OCC, the Federal Reserve, and the FDIC—are still of paramount importance, particularly from the standpoint of an individual bank, whose view of the regulatory structure is shaped by its constant contact with its primary regulator. In the next sections, the organization and financing of each of the three federal banking agencies are briefly described.

COMPTROLLER OF THE CURRENCY

The Office of the Comptroller of the Currency can be described as the most "pure" bank regulatory agency at the federal level. It is the only one of the three federal agencies that charters banks; it does not share authority for its banks with the states; and its bank supervisory and regulatory functions comprise virtually all of its responsibilities. The two other federal banking agencies are not chartering agencies; the banks they supervise are also supervised by state banking agencies; and they exercise their bank supervisory and regulatory powers as a result of, and in conjunction with, other responsibilities assigned to them.

Although the Office of the Comptroller is part of the Treasury Department, it occupies a semi-autonomous position within that department. The Comptroller is appointed by the President, with the advice and consent of the Senate, for a term of five years and may not be removed except for "cause."

As is the case with the other federal banking agencies, the Office of the Comptroller of the Currency is headquartered in Washington with regional offices located about the country. At the end of 1982, there were twelve such offices, each of which was headed by a Regional Administrator of National Banks. The OCC has since begun consolidating its operations into six district offices.

Most employees of the Comptroller's office are engaged in bank examinations or related activities. On December 27, 1982, there were 1,988 examiners. Some examiners specialize in such areas as trust and fiduciary activities, computer operations, and consumer affairs.

The Office is financed by assessments on national banks. Assessments are on a sliding scale based on consolidated domestic and foreign assets. Bank assessments accounted for 84.6 percent of the Comptroller's 1982 revenues of $128.7 million. Expenditures were $122.9 million, and the excess of revenues over expenditures resulted in an increase in the reserve fund known as "Comptroller's Equity." That fund stood at $40.7 million at year-end. The excess of revenues over expenditures had been expected to be approximately $10 million for the year. The OCC cut this to almost $6.0 million by declaring a "dividend" to national banks.

FEDERAL RESERVE

The Board of Governors of the Federal Reserve System has important bank and bank holding company regulatory responsibilities, in addition to its basic responsibility for the conduct of monetary policy. The Federal Reserve functions as an independent agency within government and is headed by a seven-member Board of Governors, each of whom is appointed by the President, with the advice and consent of the Senate, for a 14-year term. Two of the Board members are designated by the President, with Senate approval, as Chairman and Vice Chairman, respectively. The term of each of these offices is four years.

Although ultimate policy-making and decision-making authority resides with the Board of Governors in Washington, a major portion of the supervisory work of the Board of Governors is carried out by the twelve Federal Reserve Banks. Thus, for many purposes a bank holding company, or a state member bank, regards the Federal Reserve Bank of the district in which it is located as its primary federal regulatory authority. For example, bank examinations are handled directly by the Reserve Banks, each of which has a bank examination department. Despite the substantial authority possessed by the Reserve Banks, however, the Board in Washington has the final say and maintains a Division of Banking Supervision and Regulation to coordinate the various regulatory responsibilities of the System.

The primary source of income of the Federal Reserve is interest earned on its holdings of government obligations. The Federal Reserve does not receive appropriations from the Congress nor impose examination fees upon banks.

Federal Reserve income substantially exceeds expenses. Almost all of the overage is returned to the U.S. Treasury. For example, in 1982, earnings were $16.5 billion and expenses only $1.1 billion, which included current expenses of the Federal Reserve Banks and assessments on the Banks for expenditures by the Board of Governors. The System had a net loss of $69 million on sales of U.S. government securities and foreign exchange operations. After paying dividends of $79 million to member banks and transferring $78 million to surplus, the balance of $15.2 billion was turned over to the U.S. Treasury.

FEDERAL DEPOSIT INSURANCE CORPORATION

The FDIC is also an independent agency of the federal government. It is managed by a Board of Directors of three persons, one of whom is the Comptroller of the Currency who serves *ex officio*. The other two members are appointed by the President with the advice and consent of the Senate for six-year terms. Not more than two of the members can be from the same political party, and the three Directors elect one of their number as Chairman.

The Corporation maintains thirteen regional offices, each of which is headed by a regional director. Early in its history, when bank failures were more numerous, the majority of the Corporation's employees were in the Division of Liquidation. However, the largest proportion of employees is now engaged in examination and related activities; in 1982 the Division of Bank Supervision accounted for 60 percent of the Corporation's 2,845 permanent employees.

Operations of the FDIC are financed by assessments made on all insured banks. The basic annual assessment rate is one-twelfth of one percent of total deposits, adjusted for certain additions and exclusions. Since 1950, however, banks have received each year a net assessment income credit. For 1982, that credit was equal to 9 percent of the Corporation's gross assessments.

The Corporation's assessment income, even after provision for the net assessment income credit, customarily exceeds its operating expenses and its insurance losses during any given year. In 1982, for example, the net addition to the deposit insurance fund was approximately $1.5 billion. Accumulated surpluses since 1933 plus interest earned on the federal government securities held in the fund had given the Corporation a deposit insurance fund at the end of 1982 of $13.8 billion.

Originally, the Corporation issued capital stock that was subscribed in part by the Federal Reserve Banks and in part by the U.S. Treasury Department. However, all stock has been retired.

The bank regulatory powers of the FDIC arise mainly from the Banking Act of 1933, establishing the Corporation, and the Banking Act of 1935. The primary rationale for this grant of regulatory power was the need for the Corporation as an insurer of bank deposits to "inspect its risk." Such authority was believed necessary to keep the Corporation's risk within the bounds of its financial resources.

OTHER AGENCIES REGULATING BANKS

As banks expand geographically and diversify their operations, inevitably they come into regulatory contact with other federal agencies, most notably the Department of Justice and the Securities and Exchange Commission. This section briefly discusses these two agencies and mentions several others that banks will likely run across. The list is not meant to be exhaustive.

Department of Justice

The Department of Justice, through its Antitrust Division, has responsibility for enforcement of the nation's antitrust laws, which apply to bank mergers as a result of the Supreme Court's 1963 decision in *U.S.* v. *Philadelphia National Bank*, 374 U.S. 321, and Congressional action in the Bank Merger Act of 1966. The substantive provisions of the latter were added that same year to the Bank

Holding Company Act. In the case of bank mergers, Congress has directed that the banking agencies seek the opinion of the Department of Justice on the competitive aspects. The department also has the authority, which it uses on occasion, to seek to enjoin or dissolve bank mergers or bank holding company mergers and acquisitions, even if they have received the approval of the appropriate banking agency. Some of the most significant cases in the antitrust field have been Department of Justice attacks on mergers or acquisitions in the banking industry. Bank mergers and bank holding company mergers and acquisitions are discussed in further detail in Chapters 9 and 10.

Securities and Exchange Commission

Banking organizations come into contact with the Securities and Exchange Commission in a variety of contexts. The precise range of the contacts is complicated by two factors: first, the various securities laws provide a number of exemptions for banks; second, the bank regulatory agencies have been given the responsibility for enforcing certain provisions of the securities laws that the SEC enforces with respect to other business organizations.

In general, banking organizations come into contact with the SEC or with SEC rules enforced by the bank regulatory agencies in two areas: disclosure and permissible activities. Disclosure refers to the various disclosure and reporting requirements of, principally, the Securities Act of 1933, the Securities Exchange Act of 1934, and their amendments.

The Securities Act of 1933 requires disclosure, primarily through a registration statement and prospectus, of pertinent information regarding debt and equity securities that are to be sold in interstate commerce or through the mails, with exceptions. The exceptions include government securities, bank securities (but not those of bank holding companies), commercial paper, and certain intrastate or small offerings.

The Securities Exchange Act of 1934 extended the principle of disclosure to debt and equity securities already outstanding, if listed on national exchanges; it again specifically exempted banks but not bank holding companies. Disclosure requirements of the 1934 Act include registration statements, annual and other periodic reports, proxy statements, and reports of certain insider transactions.

In 1964, the 1934 Act was amended to cover essentially all companies, regardless of whether their securities are listed on exchanges, if they have total assets of $1 million and a class of equity securities held by 500 or more persons. The amendments also brought banks under the disclosure provisions of the act, but disclosure by banks was to be regulated by the three federal bank regulatory agencies rather than the SEC. The SEC was provided with greater authority over bank disclosure in 1974, however. As a result of an amendment to the Securities Exchange Act in that year, the banking agencies are now required to "issue substantially similar regulations" to those of the SEC, unless they find that such regulations "are not necessary or appropriate in the public interest or for the protection of investors. . . ."

In 1975, amendments to the 1934 Act gave the SEC the main responsibility for promulgating regulatory standards and record keeping requirements for the safeguarding of funds and securities by bank transfer agents and clearing agencies. Examination and enforcement powers, however, are lodged primarily with the bank regulatory agencies.

In the area of the permissibility of activities, bank-SEC contact primarily involves questions of whether in providing various depository and investment services a bank has stepped outside the exemptions afforded banks in the Securities Act of 1933 or the Investment Company Act of 1940. The latter law governs the creation and operation of investment funds that commingle the monies of fund purchasers. Bank trust departments often become entangled in Investment Company Act questions. The SEC may also become involved in disputes concerning the Glass-Steagall Act prohibitions on the underwriting or distribution of securities by commercial banks, although the enforcement of that act's provisions with respect to banks is primarily the responsibility of the banking agencies.

Some of the issues in the permissibility category have included dividend reinvestment services, commingled agency accounts, and the sale of third party commercial paper.

Other Agencies

Serving as trustees or administrators to pension and welfare plans brings banks into contact with the Department of Labor. Participating in the guaranteed student loan program triggers Department of Education jurisdiction. The Federal Trade Commission enters the picture through the requirement that the Federal Reserve Board prohibit certain unfair or deceptive practices by banks whenever, with certain exceptions, the FTC prohibits such practices on a general basis. Employee relations may arouse the concern of several federal bodies, including the National Labor Relations Board and the Equal Employment Opportunity Commission. Any financial planning is affected by the ubiquitous taxman, the Internal Revenue Service.

And finally, the limited authority they now possess to acquire failing thrift institutions may bring bank holding companies into contact with the Federal Home Loan Bank Board and its deposit insurance agency, the Federal Savings and Loan Insurance Corporation. This authority was set out in the Garn-St Germain Act of 1982. One FSLIC-insured thrift was acquired by a bank holding company—Citicorp of New York—immediately prior to that act's passage.

NOTES

The annual reports of the FDIC and the Federal Reserve and the *Quarterly Journal* of the OCC provide extensive data on the institutions each covers and on the agencies themselves. The Federal Financial Institutions Examination Council also issues a very helpful annual report, as does the Securities and Exchange Commission.

The division of authority over banks among the federal bank regulatory agencies is the result of a number of statutory provisions, which are located primarily in Title 12 of the U.S. Code. The powers of the Comptroller of the Currency originated in the National Currency Act of 1863 and the National Bank Act of 1864 and are set out generally in Chapters 1 (§§1–20) and 2 (§§21–216d) of Title 12. The powers of the Federal Reserve Board originated in the Federal Reserve Act of 1913 and are set out generally in Chapters 3 (§§221–530) and, concerning bank holding companies, 17 (§§1841–1850). The powers of the Federal Deposit Insurance Corporation originated in 1933 and 1935 amendments to the Federal Reserve Act, were given separate status in 1950 as the Federal Deposit Insurance Act, and are set out generally in Chapter 16 (§§1811–1832).

Specific provisions of Title 12 referred to in the text are as follows: §328 (withdrawal by state member banks from membership in Federal Reserve System); §§214–214c (conversion of national banks to state banks); §35 (conversion of state banks to national banks); §§1464(a) and (b) (establishment of federal thrift institutions, including savings banks, in both mutual and stock form); §1464(i) (conversion of state institutions, including savings banks, to federal charters); §1464(o) (provision for continued FDIC insurance for state-chartered savings banks converting to federal form); §1726(a) (insurance coverage of federal thrifts, including savings banks, provided by FSLIC); §461(b) (reserve requirements on depository institutions); §1842 (Federal Reserve Board authority over bank acquisitions by bank holding companies); §1828(c) (Bank Merger Act); §§3301–3308 (Federal Financial Institutions Examination Council); §§3501–3509 (Depository Institutions Deregulation Committee); §3503(c) (added by §327 of the Garn-St Germain Act; instructed the DIDC to authorize an investment vehicle competitive with money market mutual funds); §§1–2 (Office of the Comptroller part of the Treasury Department; appointment of Comptroller and term of office); §§481–482 (assessments on national banks and their affiliates); §241 (establishment of Board of Governors of the Federal Reserve System; appointments and terms of office); §§281–308, 341–364 (organization, powers, and duties of Federal Reserve Banks); §§1811–1812 (creation of FDIC; appointments and terms of office of Board of Directors); §1817(b) (FDIC assessments on insured banks); §1817(d) (net assessment income credit); §227, note (location of Banking Act of 1933); §228, note (location of Banking Act of 1935); §§1828(c)(4), (6) (requirement that Justice Department's opinion be sought on bank mergers); §1828(c)(7) and 1849(b) (Justice Department's power to attack bank mergers and bank holding company mergers and acquisitions on antitrust grounds); §§24 (Seventh), 377, 378, and 78 (principal provisions of the Glass-Steagall Act); and §1823(f) (added by §116 of the Garn-St Germain Act; allows bank holding companies to acquire failing thrifts).

Several statutory provisions in parts of the U.S. Code other than Title 12 were referred to in the Chapter. In Title 15, the Securities Act of 1933 is located generally at §§77a–77aa; the exemption of bank securities from the Securities Act is provided by §77c(a)(2). The Securities Exchange Act of 1934 is located generally at §§78a–78kk; §78l(i) requires the banking agencies to issue regulations substantially similar to those of the SEC. The locations of the provisions of the Securities Acts Amendments of 1975 are given in the note to §78a. The Investment Company Act of 1940 is located at §80a. And §57a(f) requires the Federal Reserve Board to follow the Federal Trade Commission's guidance in issuing regulations on unfair or deceptive practices.

In Title 29, Chapter 18 covers trustee responsibilities for employee benefit plans, and in Title 20, §§1071–1098 concern the guaranteed student loan program.

PART II

Entry and Exit

With the adoption of free banking, public policy with respect to banks implicitly added an important, though often unnoticed, element to bank supervision, namely, reliance on competition among banks to assure adequate performance in the public interest. Unlike public utility regulation, supervisors of banks were concerned primarily with the soundness and stability of the institutions rather than with prices charged or the convenience offered to the public. It was assumed that competition among banks would be adequate to provide the desired assurance against both monopoly pricing and inadequate service.

During the major portion of the nation's banking history, the extent of competition among banks was a problem only in the sense that it was viewed as excessive, i.e., that there were too many banks. Entry standards were relatively liberal. The extension of federal regulation to virtually all banks after 1933, however, coincided with, and was perhaps prompted by, the belief that these standards might have been too liberal. Accordingly, standards were raised, at both the federal and state levels, subjecting new entrants to much more thorough scrutiny. Thus, supervision of bank entry is a most important element in federal banking regulation and is the subject dealt with in Chapter 3.

Exit from the banking industry occurs typically in one of two fashions, either because of failure or because the bank is absorbed by another banking institution (voluntary liquidation is a very rare occurrence). Until recent years, government's only concern with exit had to do with bank failure. As noted in Chapter 1, as early as 1829 individual states were experimenting with insurance systems designed to protect the depositors of failed banks, and several states still had such insurance systems in operation as late as 1933. In that year, the federal government, with the establishment of the Federal Deposit Insurance Corporation, took a predominant role with respect to this method of bank exit. Chapter 4 describes this area of federal regulation.

With the tightening of entry standards after 1933, the focus of concern about maintaining the proper degree of competition in banking began to shift to regulation of exit from the industry through mergers. It should not be assumed, however, that there was, or is, agreement on what constitutes the proper degree of competition and what environmental and structural factors are conducive to achieving this degree. These questions are not unique to the banking industry but are part of the general debate over the scope and range of the antitrust laws. In any event, concern over bank mergers did grow in the years after 1933, slowly at first, and eventually resulted, in 1960, in significant federal bank merger legislation.

From the point of view of an acquiring bank, a merger represents an effort to grow in size and, in most cases, to expand the geographic area over which it operates. Accordingly, in this book federal regulation of bank mergers is discussed in Chapter 9, in connection with an analysis of other federal regulatory powers which act to control bank expansion. Chapter 9, however, could as easily have been placed in this section concerning entry and exit from the banking industry.

3

Bank Charters

With the triumph of "free banking" in the United States as a result of the passage of the National Currency Act in 1863, the country embarked on a bank-chartering policy without parallel elsewhere in the world. The ability to enter the banking industry was no longer dependent upon special legislative permission but was thrown open to all qualified persons who would conform to the standards established by statute or agency authority. In addition, since 1863 persons wishing to enter the banking industry have had the alternative of two chartering agencies: the Office of the Comptroller of the Currency if a national charter was desired, or a state bank regulatory agency if the new bank was to operate under state law.

It bears emphasis that permission of some sort to engage in the business of banking is required. Federal law prohibits any entity—a corporation, an unincorporated body, or an individual—from accepting deposits unless it is subject to examination, and in most cases regulation, by state or federal authorities. Thus "free banking" is only free to the extent that meeting the pertinent legislative and regulatory standards is all that is required to engage in the banking business.

BANK CHARTERING: AN OVERVIEW

For many decades chartering policies under this "dual" system were quite liberal, and the number of banks reached an all-time high of 31,076 in 1921. At that time the total number of offices that provided banking services to the public totaled only 32,531 because very few of the banks operated branches. The record for the period 1896–1982 is presented in Chart 3, showing the number of banks in operation in each year during this period. Mutual savings banks and "private banks," i.e., unincorporated firms engaged in the banking business, are included in the data. At one time there was a significant number of these private banks, and even today a few of them are still in operation.

During the 1920s the number of new charters granted by federal and state authorities continued to be large. However, bank failures and mergers outstripped new charters even during the prosperous years of that decade so that there was a gradual decline in the number of banks. By 1930 the number had fallen to 24,273. In the following three depression years, the shrinkage in the number of banks totaled 9,502, so that on June 30, 1933, only 14,771 banks were operating in the United States.

With the introduction of federal deposit insurance, the federal government for all practical purposes closed its ring of control

Chart 3: Number of Banks, 1896–1982, by Class of Bank

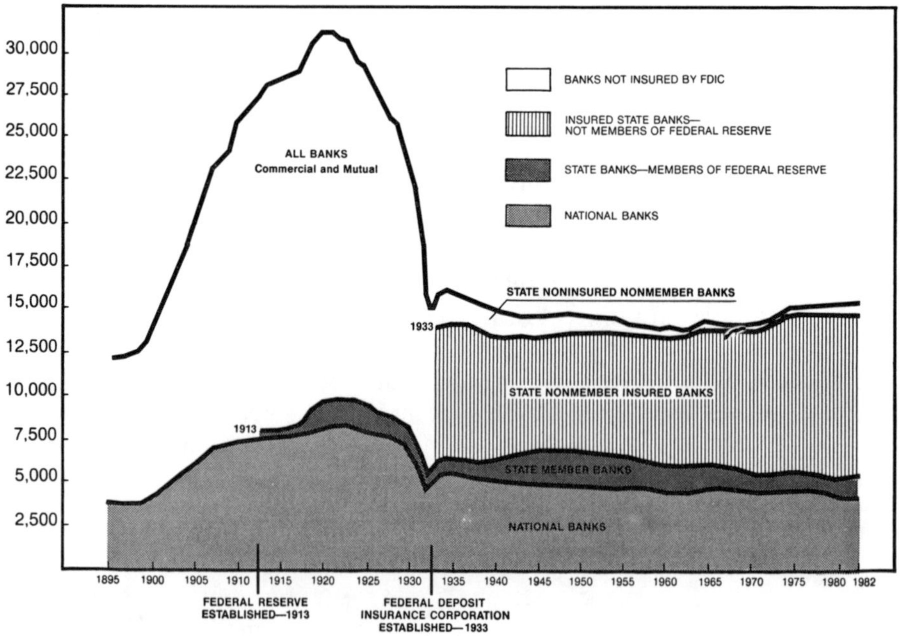

Source: Data for 1896–1970, *Historical Statistics of the United States, Colonial Times to 1970*, U.S. Department of Commerce, Bureau of the Census, 1975. Data for 1971–1982, FDIC, *Annual Report*.

around bank formations. Since 1933, insurance has been granted automatically to all new national banks and to all new state-chartered banks that are members of the Federal Reserve System. And because deposit insurance has been a necessity for virtually all banks if they are to operate successfully, new state-chartered banks outside the Federal Reserve System have been obliged to meet FDIC qualifications.

In years past, most state-chartered banks elected to have deposit insurance but not Federal Reserve membership. (See Chart 3.) The primary reason for this choice was the desire of such banks to enjoy the advantages of lower or more favorable reserve requirements to be found under state law if they remained outside of the System. It did not ordinarily reflect any difference in the application of regulatory standards. As noted in Chapter 2, the application of universal reserve requirements under the Depository Institutions Deregulation and Monetary Control Act of 1980 removed this particular disincentive to join the Federal Reserve System.

Thus, in the absence of a national charter, application for membership in the Federal Reserve System or directly to the FDIC for deposit insurance are the choices facing the proponents of a new bank. Over the years, statutory standards for admission to the Federal Reserve System or for deposit insurance without Federal Reserve membership have been supplemented by regulatory policy to the extent that the two federal agencies can veto any state charter unless the bank prefers to operate without the benefit of insurance—and few have done so.

Since the depression of the 1930s, the number of banks in the United States has remained fairly constant. Although many new banks have been established, they have been largely offset by those that ceased operations. There has been, however, a sharp increase in the number of banking offices over the past two decades, primarily because of the spread of branching. The total at the end of 1982 was 57,913 for all insured and uninsured commercial and mutual savings banks.

From the middle 1930s through the 1950s relatively few banks were chartered. (See Chart 4.) The war period accounted partly for this inactivity; bank chartering declined to a low of 18 new banks in 1942. In addition, the inactivity reflected the imposition of federal standards relative to deposit insurance as well as a general reluctance on the part of all chartering authorities—the Comptroller of the Currency and the state banking agencies—to grant new charters. Widely prevalent in the post-depression era was the belief among the bank supervisory authorities that many of the banking difficulties in the 1920s and the early 1930s stemmed from liberal chartering policies. Moreover, few individuals sought bank charters, particularly in the 1930s, because the opportunity for profit was relatively unattractive. As a matter of fact, except for the three years following the end of World War II (1946–48), the chartering of new banks during the years 1935–1959 was not sufficient to offset the shrinkage in the total number of operating banks caused by absorptions, suspensions owing to failure, or otherwise.

Bank chartering increased substantially in the 1960s. (See Chart 4.) For several years in the early sixties the increase in the chartering of national banks was especially noteworthy; thereafter the state authorities chartered substantially more banks than the Comptroller of the Currency. While, as indicated in the previous paragraph, for most years during the period 1935–1959 the number of banks declined from the total for the preceding year because the number of newly-chartered banks was insufficient to offset the number of banks leaving the industry, the reverse was true for the period 1960–1982. During the more recent period, the number of banks increased over the total for the preceding year in fifteen instances and declined from the total for the preceding year in eight instances.

Chart 4: New Banks,[1] 1935–1982

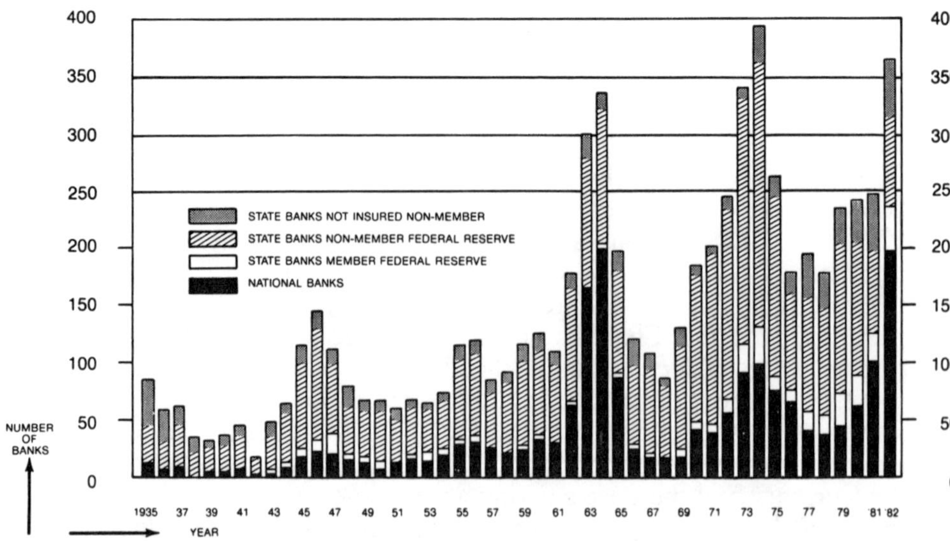

[1]Does not include mutuals. The formation of three or fewer banks in a category is generally not indicated.
Source: FDIC *Annual Report*, 1935–1982.

DIRECT CHARTERING BY FEDERAL AGENCIES

Stress has already been placed on the fact that the Office of the Comptroller of the Currency is the only federal agency empowered to charter a bank. As an indicator of bank chartering activity by that agency, Chart 4 shows the number of new national banks established each year for the period 1935–1982.

The steps necessary for the establishment of a national banking association, i.e., a national bank, are prescribed by the National Bank Act and by the Comptroller of the Currency's rules and regulations. Proponents of a new bank are required to file an "Application to Organize a National Bank." This document presents relevant information and furnishes a basis for an investigation of the proposal by the Comptroller's Office.

In investigating an application for a new bank, the Comptroller's Office evaluates the proposed bank's organizing group and the group's operating plan. The evaluation of the operating plan covers the proposed bank's earning prospects, the ability of the proposed management, the adequacy of initial capital, the reasonableness of anticipated community service, and the safety and soundness of intended operations.

The current focus on the organizing group and its operating plan is a result of a policy shift that was announced by the Comptroller in October of 1980. Prior to that time, the evaluation process for a proposed national bank appeared to place a substantial amount of emphasis on the economic and competitive characteristics of the community where the bank was to be located. In announcing the shift, the Comptroller stated:

This shift in emphasis reflects the OCC's experience that a strong organizing group with solid financial backing and a well-conceived and developed operating plan generally is able to establish and operate a successful bank even in the most economically distressed or most highly competitive markets.

The application process includes a requirement that notice of the application be published in a newspaper of general circulation in the community where the bank will do business. The application is made available for public inspection and copying, except for portions for which the applicants request, and are granted, confidential treatment. Timely written comments and data from interested parties are considered by the Comptroller's Office in reaching a decision on an application, and a hearing may be granted in unusual circumstances.

If the Comptroller of the Currency grants preliminary approval of an application to establish a national bank, the applicants may then complete the filing of the documents necessary for its corporate organization. Final approval of an application occurs when these documents are accepted for filing and the Comptroller certifies that the organization can commence the business of banking. The certificate so issued is the charter of the new national bank.

Successful applicants for a national bank charter qualify immediately for membership in the Federal Reserve System and for federal deposit insurance. Neither the Federal Reserve nor the FDIC acts upon the application or upon the decision.

National banks are required by statute to have the word "National" in their names. The phrase "N.A." for National Association is often encountered. The phrase is found in the official names of certain older banks. For new banks, however, the OCC does not consider the phrase to be an adequate substitution for "National."

INDIRECT CHARTERING BY FEDERAL AGENCIES

Chartering requirements for state banks vary considerably from state to state. As already noted, however, a new state bank lacking federal deposit insurance has dubious prospects for success. Indeed, most states, by statute, regulation, or policy, require that a charter will not be granted unless the bank qualifies for deposit insurance. This leaves the organizers of a bank chartered by a state authority with the choice of qualifying for membership in the Federal Reserve System (and thus becoming insured), or acquiring insured status by application directly to the FDIC.

An application for federal deposit insurance made by a state bank that chooses to remain outside the Federal Reserve System requires an investigation by the FDIC and approval of insured status by the Corporation's Board of Directors. Before an application is approved, the Board is required by law to consider six factors, namely:

1. The financial history and condition of the bank;
2. The adequacy of its capital structure;
3. Its future earnings prospects;
4. The general character of its management;
5. The convenience and needs of the community to be served; and
6. Whether or not its corporate powers are consistent with the purposes of the Federal Deposit Insurance Act.

In addition, the Board must determine that the bank's assets in excess of its capital requirements are adequate to meet all of its reported liabilities to depositors and other creditors.

By means of a certification process, the six factors listed above are applied to state banks that acquire insurance automatically as members of the Federal Reserve System and to national banks. Specifically, the Federal Deposit Insurance Act requires certification that the factors specified for consideration by the Board of Directors of the Corporation in approving the application of a state bank for insurance are likewise considered by the Board of Governors when it admits a state bank to membership in the Federal Reserve System and by the Comptroller of the Currency when a national bank is authorized to transact business. The FDIC, however, does not look beyond these certifications.

Banks obtaining state charters must, of course, meet the various requirements of their state banking codes with respect to such items as the number of organizers, location, and minimum capital. When the two federal agencies, the FDIC or the Federal Reserve, become involved, however, they are not limited by the provisions of state law. For example, irrespective of the applicable state law, a bank applying for membership in the Federal Reserve System is required typically to have sufficient capital to entitle it to become a national bank in the place where it is situated. And, when a state bank applies for federal deposit insurance, the Board of Directors of the Corporation passes upon the adequacy of its capital to meet the test of insurability. The capital adequacy standard applied by the FDIC may be stricter than that provided in state law or that required by the state chartering agency.

Investigations of new bank applications for admission to the Federal Reserve System or for deposit insurance are similar in nature to those made by the Comptroller of the Currency with respect to applications for national charters. More often than not these investigations by the Federal Reserve and the FDIC are made in conjunction or cooperation with the state chartering agency.

NOTES

The annual reports of the FDIC and Federal Reserve and the *Quarterly Journal* of the OCC provide data on increases and decreases in the number of banks and banking offices, with the FDIC's report being particularly useful. The FDIC's annual *Changes Among Operating Banks and Branches* provides even more detailed data, including the names of the banking organizations for which changes have occurred.

Relevant statutory provisions are located at the following sections of Title 12 of the U.S. Code: §378(a)(2) (requirement that anyone accepting deposits be subject to examination, and in most cases regulation, by state or federal authorities); §1814 (automatic FDIC insurance coverage for national and state member banks upon required certification by Comptroller or Federal Reserve, respectively); §461(b) (universal reserve requirements); §§21, 22, 23, 26, 27, and 28 (procedures for establishment of national bank; the requirement for the word "National" to be part of a national bank's name is given in §22); §282 (required membership in Federal Reserve System for national banks); and §§1814–1816 (factors considered in granting federal deposit insurance coverage).

4

Bank Failures and Depositor Protection

The possibility of bank failures is at the heart of government's concern for banks, and is a central reason for their regulation. For the most part, this concern has been directed at commercial banks because, alone among financial institutions, their liabilities for so many years served as circulating medium. Moreover, mutual savings banks had an almost unblemished safety record until the last several years, while problems faced in the past by savings and loan associations involved institutions that were not then of significant importance in the financial structure.

While there have been some commercial bank cases, the financial problems in recent years have been focused most noticeably among thrift institutions—savings banks and savings and loan associations. As in prior editions, this chapter retains as its central focus the examination of bank failures—commercial banks and mutual savings banks. However, because the problems of thrift institutions would be only partially covered if treatment were restricted to banks alone, a brief section on the savings and loan experience is included at the end of the chapter.

CAUSES OF BANK FAILURE

Banks by their very nature are vulnerable to failure. As institutions with a large proportion of their obligations to the public payable on demand—either contractually or by tradition—and with a large proportion of assets not readily convertible into cash, banks are obviously susceptible to a variety of forces that might necessitate their closing.

Indeed, banking would be entirely impossible were it not for the fact that depositors seldom act *en masse* in demanding their funds; quite the contrary, bank deposits tend to be rather stable year in and year out. Furthermore, banks have learned to manage assets so that they can be relied upon to produce funds as needed to satisfy the demands of depositors. Finally, the likelihood of a bank's failing merely because of a lack of liquid assets at a particular point in time is not much of a danger. The ability of banks to obtain credit against sound assets has increased over the decades since 1913 as the Federal Reserve System's role as the "lender of last resort" has expanded. Today, as a result of the Depository Institutions Deregulation and Monetary Control Act of 1980, any bank, and any other depository institution, in which transaction accounts or nonpersonal time deposits are held has the same Federal Reserve discount and borrowing privileges as do member banks.

Interest rate risk has become an important problem in recent years, particularly for mutual savings banks and other thrift institutions. High and volatile interest rates payable on liabilities, combined with heavy concentrations of long-term fixed rate assets, have resulted in earnings problems for some institutions, often of such severity as to erode or eventually extinguish capital or net worth margins.

Among the factors that contribute importantly to the danger of bank failure, poor asset condition is one that stands high on the list. Poor management is usually the explanation. However, deterioration in the quality of assets can be caused by developments beyond the control of the bank—a crop failure in the area served by the bank or the collapse of industry in the locality. In such instances, even quite competent managements may be trapped by failure.

Failures may also occur because of grossly incompetent or fraudulent management—a factor which in the totality of bank managements is fortunately quite rare, but which nevertheless has accounted in some years for most of the few failures that have occurred.

A recent review by the FDIC of the causes of 135 bank failures (124 commercial banks and 11 mutual savings banks) between 1971 and 1982 offers additional insights. All of the savings bank failures were attributed to interest rate risk. For commercial banks, a combination of factors were responsible for failures, and chief among them was losses on assets. Such losses were the primary cause of failure in over three-fourths of the commercial bank cases, whereas poor funds management (including interest rate risk) accounted for only about seven percent of the failures, and fraud and embezzlement for the remainder (17 percent).

Finally, it should not be forgotten that failures have resulted from abrupt changes in the public's confidence in banks as a group or in an individual bank. Such changes may have much or nothing to do with the condition of bank assets or the quality of bank management. In periods of extreme crisis, such as 1929–33, banks that would be quite sound under ordinary conditions may be compelled to close.

BANK FAILURES AND BANK STRUCTURE

A banking system comprised of thousands of independent units, many of them quite small in size, is more vulnerable to bank failures than one consisting of a handful of giant institutions. Various reasons account for this. For example, if economic misfortune strikes a particular service area, what would amount to a partial loss of business for a large multi-office bank becomes a total loss for the small unit bank situated in the troubled area. A substantial fraud worked on a large bank may be absorbed with some difficulty; in a small bank it may wipe out the entire capital. In the endeavor to recruit superior management, the large bank can afford to pay a premium because the cost can be spread over a relatively large base of banking resources, whereas a small unit bank may not be able to afford the cost or, for that matter, to use high quality management with equal effectiveness.

Bank failures are not, it should be emphasized, solely an attribute of small banks; difficulties can and do occur in large institutions as well. But it would be unrealistic to overlook the special problems of bank failure inherent in the existing banking structure.

Of the 620 closed or failed insured banks handled by the FDIC since 1933, over half had deposits of less than $1 million, and 95 percent had deposits of less than $50 million. During the past five years, larger banks have become more prominent in the list of failed banks, due in part to the problems faced by some of the large mutual savings banks. Of the 79 insured banks that failed or closed during this period (1978–82), 63 were still in the less-than-$100 million deposit size category (61 had deposits of less than $50 million). However, 16 had deposits in excess of $100 million; and four of these had deposits in excess of $1 billion.

Notwithstanding the relationships between structure and failures, public policy considerations have long held that the present banking structure—or something much like it—is desirable. Long ago the nation decided that the business of banking should not be concentrated in a few institutions. In its approach toward bank failures, therefore, the role of the federal government has been directed as much toward preserving the structure as it has been toward protecting the public against the consequences of bank failure. This is seen most clearly in the establishment of federal deposit insurance.

In 1933 many supporters of federal deposit insurance legislation made it quite clear that even more important than reimbursing the depositors of failed banks, they hoped to establish protection against bank failures which would make the existing structures workable. Particularly strong support for deposit insurance came from those who viewed it as a safeguard against the spread of branch banking and the concentration of banking in giant institutions. The legislator most responsible for ultimate passage of the measure, Congressman Steagall of Alabama, was both blunt and succinct on this point when, in the course of debate, he stated: "This bill will preserve independent, dual banking in the United States. . . . This is what this bill is intended to do."

THE HISTORICAL RECORD

The bank failure problem plagued the nation for well over a century prior to 1933. Failures were numerous even in prosperous times. During the boom years of the 1920s an average of about 600 banks annually suspended operations; then in the four years 1930–1933, more than 9,000 commercial banks were closed. (See Chart 5.) A few of these were rehabilitated financially and opened again, but for all practical purposes the restored bank was a new institution.

Since 1933 the record of bank failure has been remarkably good. From 1934 through 1982 a total of 764 banks have been closed—a number not very much greater for this entire 49 year period than average annual failures during the 1920s. The largest number of failures occurred in 1937 (84 banks). Most years after 1933 had less than 10 failures. During the last decade, the number of bank failures averaged about 13 per year. The 42 failures in 1982, however, were the most since 1940.

Most important among the reasons for the sharply improved record since 1933 has been the absence of any major recessions and

Chart 5: Commercial Bank Suspensions, 1892–1933

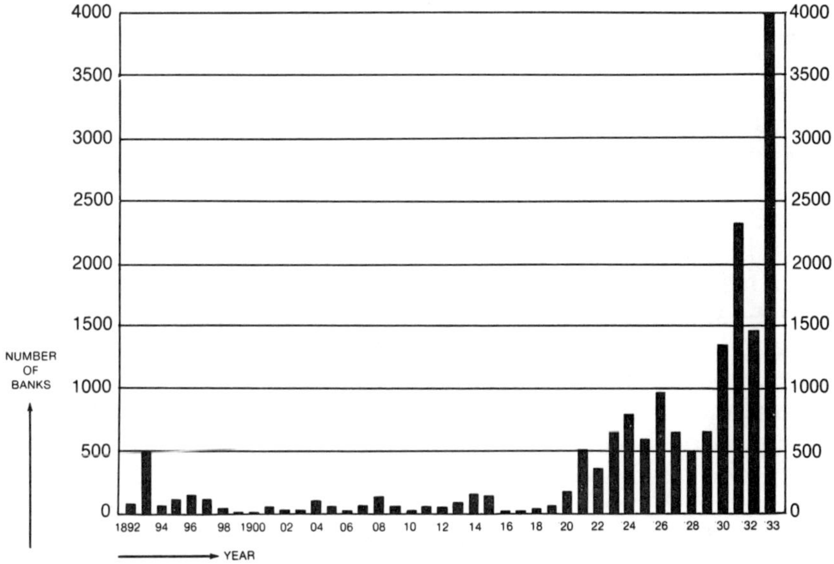

Source: *Historical Statistics of the United States, Colonial Times to 1970*, U.S. Department of Commerce, Bureau of the Census, 1975.

the long sustained economic upswing in the economy. But also important have been: (1) the establishment of the Federal Deposit Insurance Corporation, which removed one major cause of bank failure, namely, abrupt changes in public confidence in the banking system or in a particular bank; (2) the tightening of standards for obtaining the right to open a new bank; and (3) the extension of federal regulation to virtually all commercial banks, coincident with a general upgrading of supervisory standards at both the state and federal levels.

Before examining the recent record more closely, it will be helpful to review what is meant by "bank failure." Beyond question a bank has failed when it does not open on a business day because of its inability to meet the demands of its depositors. This ultimate condition of failure, however, is the result of a process that commences whenever a bank experiences financial difficulties. In the course of the process, failure in the ultimate sense may be averted in many different ways. Some of the methods will spare the bank the ignominy of failure in any sense, technical or otherwise. Inevitably in circumstances such as these, the tests applied to a bank case before it is recorded as a failure are complicated.

If a bank is in financial difficulties serious enough to raise concern on the part of the chartering authority as to its ability to meet the demands of depositors, various actions can be taken to restore the bank to a sound condition. For example, the chartering agency—whether it be a state authority or the Comptroller of the Currency—may demand and obtain the immediate replacement of lost capital. Or a merger may be arranged with a sound bank without any recourse to the Federal Deposit Insurance Corporation for assistance. Actions of these kinds are usually not publicized—at least until after the event.

Whether a bank in financial difficulties finally becomes identified as a failed institution depends upon the applicable law—federal or state—and the facts of the particular case. For example, if a chartering authority arranges a "distress" merger between a failing bank and a sound bank, with financial assistance from the FDIC (i.e., the Corporation disburses funds to facilitate the merger), the bank being merged is deemed to have failed or closed due to financial difficulties. Not so classified is a bank that has been rehabilitated without FDIC assistance. Similarly, but perhaps with less justification, a failing bank rehabilitated as a result of FDIC aid and continuing in operation is not counted as failed, even though the FDIC's disbursement may have been substantial.

The Comptroller of the Currency may close a national bank whenever he becomes satisfied that it is insolvent, and such a bank is counted as "failed." The procedure calls for an examination to ascertain the condition of the bank and the appointment of a receiver to liquidate assets and pay creditors. Pursuant to statute, the Federal Deposit Insurance Corporation must be designated as receiver for an insolvent national bank. State chartering authorities have similar powers and follow largely the same procedure. The FDIC may accept appointment as receiver of an insolvent state bank, and frequently is so requested.

Against this background, it will be helpful to look more closely at the record of bank failures since 1933. (See Table 1.) Of the 764 banks that closed in this period, 628 were insured and 136 were non-insured. The closed insured banks with deposits aggregating $19,999 million were on the average larger than the non-insured banks with deposits totaling $144 million.

A few of the insured banks that have closed since 1933 did not require disbursements from the FDIC for the protection of depositors. However, some 620 banks did require such disbursements, either in the form of payments to depositors of the insured portions of their deposits after the bank was placed in receivership, or as disbursements to failing banks in order to facilitate the assumption of their deposit liabilities by sound insured banks. In addition, five

Table 1: Number and Deposits of Banks Closed Because of Financial Difficulties, 1934–1982

	Number			*Deposits (thousands)*		
Year	*Total*	*Insured*	*Non-Insured*	*Total*	*Insured*	*Non-Insured*
Total	764	628	136	$20,143,213	$19,999,713	$143,500
1934	61	9	52	37,332	1,968	35,365
1935	32	26	6	13,988	13,405	583
1936	72	69	3	28,100	27,508	592
1937	84	77	7	34,205	33,677	528
1938	81	74	7	60,722	59,684	1,038
1939	72	60	12	160,211	157,772	2,439
1940	48	43	5	142,788	142,430	358
1941	17	15	2	29,796	29,717	79
1942	23	20	3	19,540	19,185	355
1943	5	5	. . .	12,525	12,525	. . .
1944	2	2	. . .	1,915	1,915	. . .
1945	1	1	. . .	5,695	5,695	. . .
1946	2	1	1	494	347	147
1947	6	5	1	7,207	7,040	167
1948	3	3	. . .	10,674	10,674	. . .
1949	9	5	4	9,217	6,665	2,552
1950	5	4	1	5,555	5,513	42
1951	5	2	3	6,464	3,408	3,056
1952	4	3	1	3,313	3,170	143
1953	5	4	1	45,101	44,711	390
1954	4	2	2	2,948	998	1,950
1955	5	5	. . .	11,953	11,953	. . .
1956	3	2	1	11,690	11,330	360
1957	3	2	1	12,502	11,247	1,255
1958	9	4	5	10,413	8,240	2,173
1959	3	3	. . .	2,593	2,593	. . .
1960	2	1	1	7,965	6,930	1,035
1961	9	5	4	10,611	8,936	1,675
1962	3	1	2	4,231	3,011	1,220
1963	2	2	. . .	23,444	23,444	. . .
1964	8	7	1	23,867	23,438	429
1965	9	5	4	45,256	43,861	1,395
1966	8	7	1	106,171	103,523	2,648
1967	4	4	. . .	10,878	10,878	. . .
1968	3	3	. . .	22,524	22,524	. . .
1969	9	9	. . .	40,134	40,134	. . .
1970	8	7	1	55,229	54,806	423
1971	6	6	. . .	132,058	132,058	. . .
1972	3	1	2	99,784	20,480	79,304
1973	6	6	. . .	971,296	971,296	. . .
1974	4	4	. . .	1,575,832	1,575,832	. . .
1975	14	13	1	340,574	339,574	1,000
1976	17	16	1	865,659	864,859	800
1977	6	6	. . .	205,208	205,208	. . .
1978	7	7	. . .	854,154	854,154	. . .
1979	10	10	. . .	110,696	110,696	. . .
1980	10	10	. . .	216,300	216,300	. . .
1981	10	10	. . .	3,826,022	3,826,022	. . .
1982	42	42	. . .	9,908,379	9,908,379	. . .

Source: FDIC, *Annual Report*, 1982, Table 122.

insured banks received FDIC financial assistance so as to be able to continue in operation; these five are not included in Table 1 but are discussed later in the chapter.

The 620 insured banks that required FDIC disbursements to protect depositors through payoffs or assumptions constitute the group of banks most frequently identified in financial histories as "failed banks." Obviously it is the group for which the most data are available with respect to FDIC disbursement, and depositor and FDIC losses. Nevertheless, it should be obvious that data on "failed banks" must be handled warily by serious students of banking, since classifications in this area can be arbitrary and not entirely logical.

DEPOSITOR PROTECTION, INCLUDING MERGERS

Federal deposit insurance protects each depositor up to $100,000 in each insured bank. The covered limit is established by statute and has been increased over the years by the Congress, from an initial $2,500 for each depositor in early 1934 to the present level, which took effect in 1980. From periodic surveys of insurance coverage, the FDIC estimates that approximately 95 percent of all deposit accounts in insured banks have account balances of less than $100,000 and are therefore fully protected. Depositors with account balances in excess of $100,000 are also protected up to the statutory maximum. However, such accounts, though relatively few in number, typically have very large balances. As a consequence, the total amount of deposits covered by insurance is estimated to be approximately 73 percent of all deposits held by the insured banks.

Worthy of note perhaps is that deposit insurance coverage can only be estimated for operating banks because it is depositors rather than accounts that are protected. For example, three $50,000 accounts held by a depositor in the same bank and in the same capacity and the same right would be combined for purposes of determining insurance coverage; in this example (and assuming that the depositor had no debts due and payable to the bank) $100,000 would be insured and $50,000 uninsured. The phrase "in the same capacity and in the same right," however, is a legalism describing a feature of the deposit insurance system which provides the depositor in certain circumstances with separate coverage for more than one account: for example, a depositor's account in his own name and a second account standing in his name as a trustee for another person would each be insured to the maximum of $100,000. The actual level of insurance coverage in a bank is only determined after the bank has failed; then all accounts held in the same right and capacity by each depositor are combined and adjusted for each depositor's debts that are due and payable to the bank.

Federal deposit insurance law provides several ways to protect depositors when an insured bank fails or gets into serious financial straits. After consideration of the facts in each case, the FDIC adopts that one that seems most appropriate. The method first provided by statute, and up to now the one used most often, is to arrange for the payment of the insured portion of the depositors' balances after the bank is closed and placed in receivership by the chartering authority. Through 1982, depositors in 319 failed insured banks were paid in this fashion.

In 1935, the deposit insurance law was amended to enable the FDIC to facilitate mergers of sound banks with weak or distressed banks, thereby providing a second way to protect depositors. The FDIC could arrange for the assumption of the distressed bank's liabilities by another insured bank, whenever, in the judgment of the Board of Directors, it would have averted a risk to the Corporation or reduced a threatened loss.

The Garn-St Germain Act of 1982 altered somewhat the criteria for the FDIC's use of the power to facilitate mergers. First, the FDIC can now resort to this power whenever a bank: (1) is closed; (2) is in danger of closing; or (3) requires, when severe financial conditions exist which threaten the stability of a significant number of insured banks or of insured banks possessing significant financial resources, assistance in order to lessen the risk to the FDIC. Second, unless it determines that the continued operation of the bank is essential to provide adequate banking services to the community, the FDIC's assistance under the power to facilitate mergers cannot exceed the cost of liquidating, including paying the insured accounts of, the bank.

The FDIC most frequently makes use of its merger power by purchasing the bad assets of the failing bank, replacing these assets with sufficient cash so that an on-going bank may then acquire a volume of sound assets equal to the deposit liabilities it has assumed. The Corporation has used the deposit assumption, often referred to as "purchase and assumption," method of protecting depositors in 301 cases (1935–1982).

In addition to making alterations in the criteria for the FDIC's use of the purchase and assumption power, the Garn-St Germain Act gave the agency, but only for a three-year period, the authority to permit certain interstate mergers. In the case of a commercial bank, the institution must have assets of $500 million or more and be closed, and in the case of a mutual savings bank, the institution must have assets of $500 million or more and be in danger of closing. The merger partner of the failed bank or failing savings bank must be located in the same state, but it can be owned by an out-of-state bank or bank holding company. The law calls for a fairly detailed procedure to be followed, and appropriate in-state merger partners must be uninterested. As of June 1983, no transactions had taken place under this provision.

A basic difference between the deposit payoff procedure and the purchase and assumption procedure is the extent of protection provided individual depositors. When a bank is placed in receivership and deposits are paid by the FDIC up to the insurance maximum, depositors with balances in excess of this prescribed limit must depend upon receiver's dividends from the liquidation of assets to achieve full repayment. Recoveries by the receiver may not be sufficient to accomplish this. On the other hand, when a deposit assumption transaction is arranged, all depositors receive full protection, regardless of the amounts of their deposits. This is because the sound insured bank assumes all depositors' liabilities so that the matter of the insurance ceiling never comes into play.

From 1934 through 1982 the FDIC protected depositors in 620 closed insured banks by the two procedures already described. Table 2 shows the results achieved: depositors with approximately 6.5 million accounts containing deposits of almost $20 billion recovered virtually all (98.9 percent) of their deposits. The bulk of the accounts and deposits were in the 301 closed banks handled by the deposit assumption procedure. This method of providing depositor protection in failing bank situations is generally used where larger banks are involved and, as already noted, automatically results in 100 percent insurance protection. However, even in the 319 deposit payoff cases, where depositors were paid only the amounts of their insured deposits, the combination of FDIC payments plus recoveries from other sources (primarily receivers' dividends to depositors with balances in excess of the insurance ceiling) returned 80 percent of all deposits, resulting in complete protection for 98.4 percent of the number of depositors. Moreover, most of the $221 million not received by depositors is involved in cases where the receiverships are still active, and it is estimated by the FDIC that $170 million will become available to depositors through offsets or receivers' dividends.

Until 1982 it was often pointed out that the purchase and assumption procedure was becoming the favored type of FDIC action to protect depositors, with deposit payoffs relegated only to fairly small institutions for which it was difficult or impractical to arrange for a deposit assumption, and for whose depositors protection was likely to be virtually complete under the $100,000 coverage limit. However, in 1982 the FDIC used the deposit payoff device for depositors of Penn Square Bank, N.A., in Oklahoma City, a bank with deposits of $465 million, and the largest deposit payoff case in the FDIC's history. Uninsured deposits in that case were more than half the bank's total deposits of $465 million, and account for much

Table 2: Protection of Depositors of Failed Banks Requiring Disbursements by the Federal Deposit Insurance Corporation 1934–1982

Item	*All cases (620 banks)*		*Deposit payoff cases (319 banks)*		*Deposit assumption cases (301 banks)*	
	Number or amount	*Percent*	*Number or amount*	*Percent*	*Number or amount*	*Percent*
Number of depositors or accounts—total[1]	**6,542,841**	**100.0**	**689,206**	**100.0**	**5,853,635**	**100.0**
Full recovery received or available	**6,531,478**	**99.8**	**677,843**	**98.4**	**5,853,635**	**100.0**
From FDIC[2]	6,483,007	99.1	629,372[3]	91.3	5,853,635	100.0
From offset[4]	41,703	.6	41,703	6.1	....	....
From security or preference[5]	3,361	.1	3,361	.5	....	....
From asset liquidation[6]	3,407	.1	3,407	.5	....	....
Full recovery not received as of December 31, 1982	**11,363**	**.2**	**11,363**	**1.6**	....	....
Terminated cases	3,842	.1	3,842	.6	....	....
Active cases	7,521	.1	7,521	1.1	....	....
Amount of deposits (in thousands)—total	**$19,958,566**	**100.0**	**$1,084,924**	**100.0**	**$18,873,642**	**100.0**
Paid or made available	**19,737,546**	**98.9**	**863,904**	**79.6**	**18,873,642**	**100.0**
By FDIC[7]	19,527,219	97.8	653,577	60.2	18,873,642	100.0
By offset[8]	69,437	.3	69,437	6.4	....	....
By security or preference[9]	86,989	.4	86,989	8.0	....	....
By asset liquidation[10]	53,901	.3	53,901	5.0	....	....
Not paid as of December 31, 1982	**221,020**	**1.1**	**221,020**	**20.4**	....	....
Terminated cases	3,245	.0	3,245	.3	....	....
Active cases[11]	217,775	1.1	217,775	20.1	....	....

[1]Number of depositors in deposit payoff cases; number of accounts in deposit assumption cases.
[2]Through direct payments to depositors in deposit payoff cases; through assumption of deposits by other insured banks facilitated by FDIC disbursements of $6,010,412 thousand in mergers and deposit assumption cases.
[3]Includes 64,672 depositors, in terminated cases, who failed to claim their insured deposits (see note 7).
[4]Includes only depositors with claims offset in full; most of these would have been fully protected by insurance in the absence of offsets.
[5]Excludes depositors, paid in part by the FDIC, whose deposit balances were less than the insurance maximum.
[6]The insured portions of these depositor claims were paid by the Corporation.
[7]Includes $583 thousand unclaimed insured deposits in terminated cases (see note 3).
[8]Includes all amounts paid by offset.
[9]Includes all secured and preferred claims paid from asset liquidation; excludes secured and preferred claims paid by the corporation.
[10]Includes unclaimed deposits paid to authorized public custodians.
[11]Includes $169,766 thousand representing deposits available expected through offset, or expected from proceeds of liquidation.

Source: FDIC, *Annual Report*, 1982, Table 128.

of the $221 million in deposits, mentioned earlier, that have not yet been recovered by depositors in all deposit payoff cases.

ASSISTANCE TO OPERATING BANKS

An important form of depositor protection in recent years has been accomplished by the FDIC through financial aid to distressed insured banks in order to make possible their continued operation. As already noted, such banks do not appear on the lists of failed or closed banks, so that protection accorded depositors because of such FDIC disbursements is not shown in Table 2. Nonetheless, the resulting depositor protection is as real as that accomplished through disbursements in payoff and assumption cases, and to that extent the amounts disbursed for the protection of depositors in distressed insured banks is understated in several of the official FDIC tabulations.

Authority for the FDIC to assist operating banks in serious financial condition was added to the Federal Deposit Insurance Act in 1950. The Corporation was empowered to assist an insured bank when in danger of closing—or to open a bank if closed—if the Board of Directors determined that the continued operation of the endangered bank was essential to provide adequate banking services to the community.

The Garn-St Germain Act made alterations in the FDIC's power to provide assistance to banks similar to the alterations made in the agency's purchase and assumption power. The FDIC can now provide assistance: (1) to prevent a bank from closing; (2) to reopen a closed bank; or (3) to lessen the risk posed to itself by a bank threatened by instability due to severe financial conditions which threaten the stability of a significant number of banks or of banks possessing significant financial resources. Unless it determines that the continued operation of the bank is essential to provide adequate banking services to the community, the FDIC's assistance cannot exceed the cost of liquidating, including paying off the insured accounts of, the bank.

The FDIC has used its power to provide assistance to banks only infrequently. One reason might be that some view the power to aid banks as more of a central bank function than an insurance agency function. Indeed, no use was made of this authority for more than two decades after its granting by the Congress.

Assistance to an operating bank was first provided by the FDIC in 1971, taking the form of an unsecured subordinated $1.5 million loan to a small bank that had been established to serve a minority group. Since then, through 1982, the FDIC has disbursed funds to prevent the failures of four other distressed insured banks, each of which was of substantial size in its respective community and state. Of the total of five banks so assisted, only one was subsequently closed—American Bank and Trust, Orangeburg, South Carolina—and merged into a sound insured bank with further FDIC assistance.

Probably the most significant use of the assistance to operating banks power occurred in 1980 when, with the cooperation of some 20 commercial and mutual savings banks, the FDIC fashioned an assistance package to prevent the failure of the First Pennsylvania Bank (Philadelphia, Pennsylvania). The package consisted essentially of a $500 million loan, of which $325 million was provided by the FDIC, subordinated to other indebtedness of the distressed institution and with interest arrangements favorable to the bank. The FDIC was given in return certain protections relating to the bank's operations.

Assistance to distressed operating banks has involved substantial FDIC disbursements—well in excess of $400 million by the end of 1982. This amount is approximately equal to all principal disbursements by the FDIC since 1934 to depositors in deposit payoff cases, excluding the recent large disbursements in the Penn Square Case. On the other hand, the volume of deposits protected (in the sense that failure was averted and deposit payoff made unnecessary) was also substantial. Depending on the selection of reporting dates, the five banks receiving assistance had total deposits of about $6 billion, or roughly six times the total of deposits in all 319 deposit payoff cases.

To sum up, at the beginning of federal deposit insurance, in 1933, the Corporation's procedure was to pay each depositor in a failed insured bank the amount of his deposit up to the maximum provided by law. This procedure is followed at present in deposit payoff cases. In 1935, the protection of depositors was extended so that the FDIC could arrange for the deposits of an insured bank to be assumed by another insured bank when this would facilitate a merger. In such cases, all of the deposits held by the insured bank experiencing financial difficulties are protected. Fifteen years later, in 1950, the FDIC was given the authority to protect depositors in an insured bank that is in danger of closing. This power was first used in 1971 to preserve a small bank, and since then has been used in four other instances. The criteria for the use of both the power to facilitate mergers and the power to provide assistance to operating banks were altered by the Garn-St Germain Act of 1982.

Before leaving the topic of the FDIC's powers to protect depositors—directly, by facilitating mergers, or by providing assistance to operating banks—mention should be made of the net worth certificate program. Authorized by the Garn-St Germain Act of 1982, this program permits the FDIC to purchase from banks it insures—and the FSLIC to purchase from organizations it insures—capital certificates. Institutions can issue the certificates if their capital ratios are below certain levels. Payment for the certificates is by promissory notes of the FDIC, or the FSLIC as the case may be. These notes bolster the capital of the institutions issuing the certificates. As of the end of 1982, the FDIC had rendered assistance to fifteen institutions under the net worth certificate program. The total assistance provided was $174.5 million. Authority for the net worth certificate program is only temporary, expiring in 1985.

IMPACT OF INSURANCE PROTECTION ON THE FDIC

Protection afforded depositors of failing insured banks has been exceptionally good, in that only a negligible amount of deposits in those banks has not been recovered in the more than 49 years that the FDIC has been in existence. However, the question remains as to what the experience of the FDIC has been as an insurer in providing this extent of depositor protection.

Here too the results have been exceptionally good. Of the $8,612 million disbursed through 1982 (including assistance to operating banks), the FDIC has recoverd $6,668 million and sustained losses of $1,944 million. (See Chart 6.) On an average annual basis since the Corporation came into being, this would amount to a loss of about $40 million a year.

Chart 6: Losses in Failed Insured Banks, 1934–1982

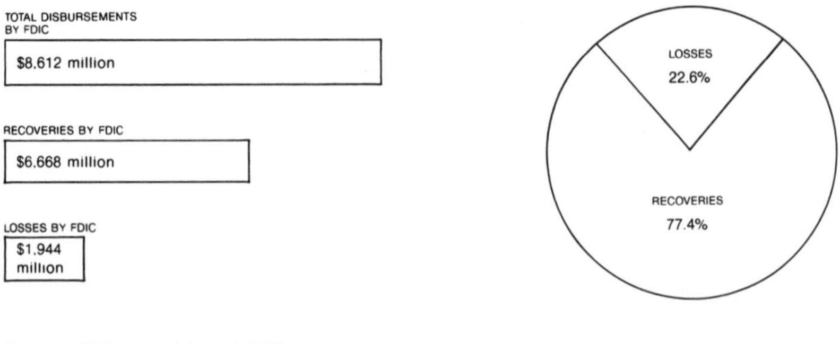

Source: FDIC, *Annual Report*, 1982.

Losses sustained by the FDIC in providing insurance protection have been well within the Corporation's financial capabilities. Indeed, the total losses since 1934 of $1,944 million are less than FDIC income in each of the last several years, and not much larger than interest income alone ($1,512 million in 1982).

At the end of 1982 the insurance fund was $13,771 million, an amount equal to 0.89 percent of all deposits in insured banks and higher, relatively, than at any time in the FDIC's history.

SAVINGS AND LOAN ASSOCIATIONS

In sharp contrast to the data on banking, available information on savings and loan failures is sketchy, particularly for earlier years in this century. Even today, material provided to the public by the Federal Home Loan Bank Board and its insurance agency, the Federal Savings and Loan Insurance Corporation (FSLIC), does not approach the meticulous and detailed reporting by the FDIC of bank failures. Probably the explanation lies in part in the fact that, from the outset, banking's monetary function accorded to analyses of bank failures a much higher priority than analyses of the failures of other depository institutions.

Depression Experience

Savings and loan associations suffered severely during the depression years of the early 1930s and indeed, as was the case with commercial banks, during most of the decade. Savings and loan assets declined from almost $9 billion in 1930 to less than $6 billion in 1935. From 1930 through 1939, more than 1,700 associations failed, and the total number of associations declined from 11,777 in 1930 to 7,521 by 1940.

The causes of failure (and of other problems resulting in a fall in the number of associations) are well known. The sharp decline in real estate values was the primary culprit, resulting in a loss of liquidity and lower earnings, among other consequences.

Federal government assistance was an important factor in helping sustain the industry. Reconstruction Finance Corporation loans were made even prior to the establishment of the FHLBB. The Home Owners Loan Corporation, established in 1933 and placed under the direction of the Home Loan Bank Board, had about one-sixth of the urban mortgage debt held by private lenders, including savings and loan associations, transferred to it between 1933 and 1936. And the FSLIC was created in 1934 to help restore confidence in the savings and loan business.

FSLIC Powers and Procedures

Although there are numerous differences between the FDIC and FSLIC, in major outline the two insuring agencies are quite similar. Indeed, the general public probably does not perceive any significant differences.

Both agencies insure deposit accounts to $100,000 for each depositor. Both obtain their funds from assessments based on their members' "domestic deposits," and in each case the basic annual rate is one-twelfth of one percent of deposits, albeit with differences as to rebates and supplemental charges. Both have essentially the same options available in the handling of failing institutions, with probably some greater flexibility available to the FSLIC (even after passage of the Garn-St Germain legislation in 1982, intended in part to give the FDIC additional flexibility in dealing with distressed banks).

The regulatory and supervisory powers of the FDIC and FSLIC are similar, although the structures within which they operate are quite different. The FSLIC, for example, is a subagency of the FHLBB. It is not, as is the FDIC, an independent agency. Many types of functions performed by the FDIC are in the case of the FSLIC performed by its parent, the FHLBB.

The FHLBB is also the federal chartering authority for savings and loan associations and savings banks, and as is the case with federally chartered commercial banks, all federally chartered associations and savings banks must have deposit insurance; state-chartered associations may volunteer for insurance. All FSLIC-insured institutions must be members of the Federal Home Loan Bank System.

Both the FDIC and FSLIC maintain insurance funds. Their respective sizes at the end of 1982 were $13,771 million and $6,418 million. Relative to insured deposits, however, the two funds were quite similar on that date: 1.21 percent for the FDIC and 1.16 percent for the FSLIC. Each agency has an assured borrowing power from the U.S. Treasury. The amounts are $3 billion for the FDIC and $750 million for the FSLIC.

Recent Failure Experience

High and volatile interest rates, particularly during the years 1980–82, led to serious problems for thrift institutions and, indeed, for all depository institutions whose portfolios were heavily weighted with long-term, fixed rate assets, such as residential mortgage loans. Very broadly, the failure problem of thrift institutions was not the result of loan losses but, rather, of rising interest costs that seriously depleted reserves. For example, in 1981 interest paid by savings and loan associations was equal to 97 percent of operating revenues, compared with about 75 percent during the mid-1970s and 85 percent in 1980. By mid-year 1982, there were about 500 associations whose ratios of net worth to assets were under two percent—the minimum required by the FHLBB.

Unlike the FDIC, the FSLIC rarely resorts to its authority to pay depositors of distressed associations only the amount of their insured deposits. The FSLIC relies almost entirely on formulating transactions that, in one fashion or another, result in mergers of distressed institutions into those that are financially and managerially strong. In 1982, for example, the FSLIC took action in 78 cases, all but one of which were resolved by merger. These included 47 assisted mergers, some of which involved the merger of several associations into one institution. In the one instance in 1982 where a merger partner could not be found, a transfer of insured deposits to another association was arranged, avoiding a deposit payout by the FSLIC.

The number of FSLIC-assisted mergers has increased sharply in recent years. The 1982 total of 47 can be contrasted with 23 in 1981 and 11 in 1980. As in 1982, the number of associations disappearing in each of these earlier years was presumably greater than the number of mergers because of cases involving more than two institutions.

As described earlier, the FDIC, in effect, treats as "failed" banks (at least for statistical purposes) any bank that disappears—whether by liquidation, purchase, or merger—where a disbursement by the FDIC was required, or was needed to facilitate the transaction. The FSLIC, on the other hand, does not follow the same practice in its reports. Thus data are not readily available on the total number of accounts or amount of assets of all distressed associations handled by the FSLIC in any single year or collection of years. Only partial figures are available. For example, in 1982, of the 78 cases handled by the FSLIC, 14 went into receivership before assisted mergers could be arranged (mergers were subsequently arranged for 13 of these cases). The 14 associations placed in receivership had 751,000 accounts and assets of $3.7 billion.

An indication of the magnitude of the task faced by the FSLIC in recent years is provided by the record of the present value of the total cost of FSLIC-assisted cases. This figure, very roughly, is comparable to the FDIC's "insurance disbursement" figure. In 1980, the present value cost to the FSLIC of handling distressed associations was $167 million; in 1981, it increased almost six-fold to $988 million; while for 1982 the total was $1,131 million.

Depositor and FSLIC Losses

One must assume from the manner in which the FSLIC handles distressed associations that any depositor losses have been negligible. In 1982, for example, it would appear that no association depositor suffered a loss. In 1981, when at least one receivership and payout occurred, there was presumably some depositor loss, but probably of an amount that was insignificant when compared with deposits in all distressed associations. In any event, the FHLBB annual report does not include, in the section devoted to the FSLIC, annual or cumulative data on depositor losses.

FSLIC losses will depend in part on the manner in which various transactions work out over the years ahead. Again, the annual reports do not provide data on cumulated losses. However, the 1982 annual report does reflect the Corporation's confidence that it has weathered successfully the problems of 1981 and 1982: FSLIC assets were reported at an all-time high; income in 1982 exceeded expenses by $102 million; and the reserve fund has been restructured to provide for increased liquidity.

NOTES

The annual reports of the Federal Deposit Insurance Corporation, the federal banking agency responsible for deposit insurance, provide the most complete yearly and cumulative data on bank failures and depositor protection. The annual reports of the Federal Home Loan Bank Board, in the sections dealing with the Federal Savings and Loan Insurance Corporation, provide data for savings and loan association failures.

In 1983, the federal insurance agencies were directed by Congress to prepare analyses of their insurance operations. The report prepared by the FDIC contains particularly useful information on bank failures. The report is entitled "Deposit Insurance in a Changing Environment," April 15, 1983.

Relevant statutory provisions are located at the following sections of Title 12 of the U.S. Code: §461(b)(7) (access by depository institutions to Federal Reserve's discount and borrowing facilities); §1821(b) (definition of closed bank); §191 (power of Comptroller to close national bank when he becomes satisfied of its insolvency); §1821(c) (requirement that FDIC be receiver for closed national bank); §1821(e) (requirement that FDIC accept receivership of state bank when offered by state authorities); §1821(a) and §1728(a) ($100,000 limit on insured deposits); §1813(m) (requirement that deposits held in the same capacity and right in a bank by same depositor be aggregated for insurance coverage purposes); §1821(f) (payment of deposits method of handling failed banks); §1823(c) (purchase and assumption method of handling failed banks, and assistance to operating banks); §1823(f) (temporary authority to permit interstate and interindustry acquisitions of large failed banks or failing savings banks); §1823(i) and §1729(f)(5) (the temporary net worth certificate program); §1728(b) (payment of deposits method of handling failed S&Ls); §1729 (the FSLIC's powers to handle closed or distressed S&Ls); §1730a(m) (the FSLIC's temporary authority to permit interstate and interindustry acquisitions of distressed institutions). The Federal Deposit Insurance Act in general is codified at 12 U.S.C. §§1811–1832.

PART III

The Regulatory Process

The regulatory process as it affects banking is still shaped to a considerable extent by the concern that government must have over the condition of institutions which furnish the bulk of the nation's money supply and which hold all or a very large portion of the cash resources of millions of individuals. Yet at the same time regulators must deal with a system comprised of thousands of individual banks—a situation not found in any other advanced nation.

Heavy reliance must be placed on regular and timely information on the condition of each bank subject to regulation. Over the years a reporting and examination framework has been developed and refined so that today each bank regulatory agency, whether federal or state, possesses a remarkable amount of information about each of the banks subject to its supervision. Chapter 5 discusses in broad outline the tools used by the federal bank regulatory agencies to obtain this information.

Another feature of bank regulation is the imposition by statutory authority of certain limits on the business that banks conduct. These limitations can be in furtherance of any one or several of a number of objectives, the most important of which is probably bank soundness. The prohibition on commercial banks engaging in certain investment banking activities is probably the most far-reaching limitation, but there are numerous others. Chapter 6 gives an overview of these limitations.

Any system of bank regulation depends ultimately upon the

ability of the regulators to enforce applicable laws, regulations, and policies. Bank chartering agencies have the authority to revoke the charter of any institution that operates in a manner deemed to be inconsistent with banking law or sound banking practice. This is an extreme sanction, however, and in any event, two of the three federal banking agencies are not chartering agencies and thus do not possess this specific authority. Devising appropriate enforcement powers is particularly difficult for a system that relies in part upon competition among a large number of banks to achieve its objectives. Achieving objectives through competition in the marketplace and achieving objectives through the imposition of decisions by the regulators are approaches that often conflict. The enforcement powers of the federal banking agencies are discussed in Chapter 7.

5

Reports and Examinations

Banks are subect to a pervasive system of supervision. The primary goal of the system is to maintain the soundness of banks and the banking industry, although such secondary goals as assuring compliance with consumer protection laws have become increasingly important in recent years. The basic tools used by the bank regulators to carry out their supervisory functions are reports and examinations: banks make reports to the regulators and are subject to examinations by the regulators.

By reviewing reports, the regulators are able to inspect banks without actually visiting them. Such inspections are called remote inspections. Reports also assist the regulators in preparing for and conducting on-site examinations. The widespread use of computers has increased the usefulness of reports. Data provided by banks to the regulators and stored in computers can be analyzed and evaluated much more readily and thoroughly than in the past. Thus, computers have enhanced the ability of the regulators to make remote inspections and have alleviated some of the reliance previously placed upon on-site examinations. Today, the bank supervisory process is often described as consisting of remote and on-site inspections rather than reports and examinations. This changing terminology reflects the alterations computers have brought to the supervisory process.

This chapter gives an overview of the supervisory system. First, the division of supervisory responsibilities among the three bank regulatory agencies—the Office of the Comptroller of the Currency, the FDIC, and the Federal Reserve Board—is reviewed. This division was initially presented in Chapters 1 and 2. Then the reporting and examination components of the supervisory system are described. These descriptions are followed by discussions of the "CAMEL" system for rating bank condition and soundness, of the monitoring systems that the agencies have developed for the early ascertainment of financial weaknesses in banks, and of efforts that have been made to keep supervisory capabilities abreast of the growth of multinational banking.

SUPERVISORY RESPONSIBILITIES

The existence of three federal and fifty state bank regulatory agencies suggests the possibility of a bureaucratic thicket of overlapping authority that could lead to contradictory actions. Through statutes, regulations, interagency agreements, and coordination efforts, however, much, though certainly not all, of the duplication and redundancy that could result from the overlapping authority has been avoided. Among the federal agencies, the primary responsibility for examining and supervising the different types of banking organizations has come to reside as follows: national banks, the OCC; bank holding companies and state member banks, the Federal Reserve; and state nonmember insured banks, the FDIC. State banks are also examined and supervised by state banking authorities. Concerning those banks for which the Federal Reserve and the FDIC have some supervisory authority but not primary responsibility, those agencies rely in large part upon receiving reports and examination results from the regulator that does have the primary responsibility.

A major attempt by Congress to ensure that the bank supervisory system is subject to a degree of coordination was the establishment in 1978 of the Federal Financial Institutions Examination Council. The Council's functions were summarized in Chapter 2 but bear repeating here: (1) to establish uniform principles, standards, and report forms for the examination of financial institutions; (2) to make recommendations for uniformity in other supervisory matters; (3) to develop uniform reporting systems for federally supervised financial institutions; and (4) to conduct examiner schools for federal examiners and to make such schools available to employees of state supervisory agencies. The Council also maintains a liaison committee, composed of five representatives of state agencies, whose purpose is to encourage the application of uniform examination principles and standards by state and federal supervisory agencies.

One coordination problem that has attracted considerable attention concerns bank holding companies. The fact that the Federal Reserve examines and supervises all bank holding companies but only banks that are state member banks means that a holding company and its bank subsidiaries are often examined and supervised by different regulators. The Federal Reserve has primary jurisdiction over the holding company while the OCC or the FDIC is likely to have primary jurisdiction over the bank subsidiaries. The danger from the standpoint of the soundness of the bank subsidiaries is that affiliate transactions and relationships might not receive the proper scrutiny. In 1979, the Federal Financial Institutions Examination Council recommended, and the bank regulatory agencies adopted, a series of steps designed to achieve more coordination in the supervision of bank holding companies. For example, coordinated inspections and examinations of a holding company and its lead bank were mandated for all holding companies with consolidated assets of $10 billion. The three banking agencies have since reduced this threshold level to $1 billion.

Another coordination problem involves state banks that are subject to both state regulators and the jurisdiction of either the Federal Reserve, because they are state member banks, or the FDIC, because they are insured banks. To ease the examination burdens on such state banks, federal and state authorities have devised various cooperative efforts. In some instances the examination report is a joint product. This requires the adoption of a standard report form, and the work of assembling the information is divided on some mutually satisfactory basis. Examiners for both the federal and state authorities may sign identical reports.

Often the federal and state examining authorities are not in sufficient agreement on procedures to make a joint examination. Substantial economies are still derived, however, by scheduling examinations so that federal and state examiners can work in the bank at the same time. Such concurrent examinations embody much of the same information, though the federal and state examiners prepare and sign separate reports covering their work.

The newest wrinkle in federal-state examination cooperation is the divided examination program. The FDIC has had a divided program for several years, and as of March, 1983, 27 states were participating. Since 1981, the Federal Reserve Board has also had a divided examination program, called the Alternate Year Examination Program. As of December, 1982, 18 states were participating. The general concept of a divided examination program is that a bank will be examined by the state and the federal agencies in alternate years, and examination reports exchanged. The divided program avoids the problem, inherent in the joint or concurrent programs, of coordinating the examination schedules.

REPORTS

Banks must file a wide variety of reports with the regulators. For example, the reports that national banks must file include: reports of condition; reports of income and dividends; trust department reports; reports of international operations and foreign exchange activities; reports on ownership of the reporting bank and on indebtedness of executive officers and principal shareholders to the reporting bank and its correspondent banks; past due loan reports; reports filed under the federal securities laws; and foreign country lending exposure reports.

The basic and most important report is the report of condition, the balance sheet of a bank. The report of condition quantifies the assets, the liabilities, the reserves, and the capital accounts of a bank at a point in time. Related to the report of condition is the report of income, which furnishes information about the results of operations—income, expenses, and changes in capital accounts—for a fiscal period. Both of these reports can have supporting schedules that furnish information in greater detail for certain items. For example, figures on different types of loans are called for in a supporting schedule to the report of condition.

The three federal banking agencies have collaborated in designing reports of condition and income. The amount of detail and precise format of the reports depend upon the size category into which a bank falls, with the smaller banks having to provide a lesser amount of data. The four categories that the regulators have established for reporting purposes are small banks—total consolidated assets of less than $100 million; medium size banks—total consolidated assets of more than $100 million but less than $300 million; large banks—total consolidated assets of more than $300 million; and banks with foreign offices, regardless of size.

Reports of condition and income are filed quarterly with the appropriate regulatory agency.

A report of condition is often referred to as a "Call Report." The term originated from the banking agencies' practice of "calling" for condition reports as of a date prior to the time of the call and not at regular intervals. The purpose of the practice was to prevent banks from engaging in "window dressing," or temporary alterations to improve the appearance of the asset and liability structures. Currently, reports of condition are ordinarily filed as of the last day of the calendar quarter. Memorandum items such as daily averages or total loans and total deposits for a specified period ending with the report date have eliminated many of the dangers of "window dressing." Furthermore, the statistical usefulness of "bench mark" data—data compiled at regular intervals—largely offsets the desire to guard against reporting aberrations by the use of surprise reporting dates.

Reports of condition and income are public records, and copies can be obtained from the regulatory agencies. In addition, data obtained from the reports are made available to the public in a variety of forms. One of the most commonly used is the volume entitled *Bank Operating Statistics,* published annually by the FDIC. The contents consist of selected aggregates and ratios, and the presentation is designed to permit comparisons of bank operations for various size groups of banks by state and within smaller geographical subdivisions in states without statewide branching. A second useful compilation of data is found in the statistical tables in the FDIC's annual reports.

A third way data is made available is the Uniform Bank Performance Report (UBPR). The UBPR is an analytical tool created for bank supervisory, examination, and management purposes. First made available to the public in 1982, it is produced each quarter for each insured commercial bank in the United States. Several years of data are presented in the form of ratios, percentages, percentile rankings, and dollar amounts. Each UBPR also contains data for a bank's peer group and state, along with peer group percentile rankings for most ratios. The three basic groups of data in the UBPR are: (1) the individual bank's data, (2) data for both the peer group and the state, and (3) percentile rankings.

And a fourth way that call report data is available is on tape. Called the Interagency Call Report Tape, this item is generally available 90 days after the reporting date for the quarter.

Although it is not compiled directly from report of condition data, another publication that is extremely helpful to those concerned with the structure of the banking industry deserves mention. This publication, the latest edition of which is entitled *Banks & Branches Data Book,* is based on special reports obtained by the FDIC. A survey is usually conducted yearly as of June 30. Deposits for each banking office are obtained for various deposit categories—such as demand deposits of individuals, partnerships, and corporations—and aggregated for states, counties, and standard metropolitan areas. The survey gives the FDIC data on potential liability to depositors and provides all the regulatory agencies and the public with data on the deposit structure of local banking markets.

As indicated at the beginning of the section, the reports that banks have to file are many and varied. Some, like the reports of condition and income, are primarily for the purpose of ascertaining the financial condition of individual institutions. A number of them, however, are designed to provide information on the monetary affairs and the general economic condition of the nation. Because of its broad responsibilities in these areas, the Federal Reserve Board is the prime designer and recipient of these latter types of reports.

EXAMINATIONS

Bank examinations are the second basic tool available to bank regulators in the exercise of their supervisory functions. Examinations arose out of the need to ascertain the financial condition of banks. The growing complexity of the banking business, however, and the increase in social welfare and consumer protection legislation have enlarged the scope of bank examinations beyond the purely financial area and have led to the existence of several types of bank examinations. Today, separate examinations can be made of commercial departments, consumer protection laws compliance, electronic data processing systems, trust departments, international branch operations, and bank holding companies.

Despite the expanded scope and the different types of examinations, the primary concern of the regulators remains the financial condition of institutions. Thus, the most important examination is focused on bank soundness. In its *Comptroller's Handbook for National Bank Examiners,* the OCC states that the essential objectives of an examination are:

(1) to provide an objective evaluation of a bank's soundness; (2) to permit the OCC *to appraise the quality of management and directors; and (3) to identify those areas where corrective action is required to strengthen the bank, to improve the quality of its performance, and to enable it to comply with applicable laws, rulings and regulations.*

In conducting an examination, examiners use a variety of techniques and focus on a variety of subjects. Questionnaires are used to test the adequacy of a bank's internal controls in providing institutional protection and in assuring adherence to management's policies. Bank employees are interviewed and observed as they carry out their duties. Sampling techniques are applied to a variety of bank records to accomplish such goals as ascertaining the effectiveness of audit systems, assessing the quality of various types of assets, and checking compliance with laws and regulations. More complete review may be made of such items as past due loans, loans previously classified in a subpar category, and investment securities.

Over the last two decades or so, as both volume and types of activities engaged in by banks have increased, the emphasis in examinations has shifted from detailed audit and verification procedures by examiners to review of the adequacy of a bank's planning and control measures. The objective of this shift is to have a bank police itself. Problems such as excessive bad loans, inadequate capital, and concentration of credits still receive considerable attention, but substantial attention is now also given to the competence of a bank's board of directors and management and their involvement in the affairs of the institution. Accordingly, examinations include a thorough analysis of a bank's policies, practices, procedures, and controls with the view towards identifying managerial weaknesses that could lead to the kinds of problems that were the focus of attention in the past.

A milestone in the shift of examination emphasis was a 1974–75 study of OCC operations by an outside accounting firm. The study, commissioned by the then Comptroller, James E. Smith, was the first major outside review of the OCC since its establishment in 1863.

An examination results in a comprehensive report that is reviewed at higher levels in the regulatory agency and that serves as a basis for discussions between examiners on one hand and bank management and the board of directors on the other. An examination also results in ratings under the Uniform Interagency Bank Rating System, discussed in the following section. Problems that cannot be resolved to the satisfaction of the regulators by informal meetings and discussions may result in formal enforcement actions, which are dealt with in Chapter 7.

The OCC's current examination policy for sound banks is an examination every 12 months for banks with assets of $300 million or more and every 18 months for banks with assets under $300 million. The maximum interval that the FDIC will allow between examinations of sound banks is 36 months. More frequent examinations are the norm, however. In addition, when an examination is not conducted, at least one visitation or off-site review must be performed in each 12-month period. The Federal Reserve Board's policy is for an examination every 18 months provided that there has been no material deterioration in financial conditions since the last examination and no change in ownership or control at the policy making level during the time. For banks that do not meet criteria for sound financial conditions, each of the agencies conducts more frequent examinations.

CAMEL SYSTEM

The mention in the preceding section of criteria for measuring the soundness of banks may give the impression that the determination of financial condition is an exact science. Obviously, this is not the case. In a theoretical sense, the only perfectly "sound" bank is one whose assets consist entirely of cash, in which case it would not be a bank for very long. Banks in fact take in funds from a variety of sources and place them in a variety of investments, or assets. The funds being taken in, liabilities, a good portion of which are deposits, are merely on loan to the banks. If all or a substantial number of those who made such loans to a bank decided to ask for the return of their funds at the same time, the bank would be unable to comply. The bank could not liquidate, or call in, its investments fast enough.

This theoretical problem poses the difficulty of deciding in a practical sense what constitutes soundness. There being a great many possible opinions on the topic, it was natural that each of the federal banking agencies developed its own view. Partly as a result of a General Accounting Office study criticizing the existence of divergent approaches, the three federal banking agencies, and the National Credit Union Administration and the Federal Home Loan Bank Board, adopted the CAMEL System in 1978–79. This system provides a general framework for a uniform approach to rating financial institutions. Given the substantial degree of subjectivity inherent in judging the components of soundness, however, the CAMEL System has not brought, and most likely will not bring, complete uniformity to the approaches of the regulatory agencies. The CAMEL System is also more formally known as the Uniform Interagency Bank Rating System (UIBRS) or the Uniform Financial Institutions Rating System (UFIRS).

The CAMEL System has two principal elements. First, an assessment is made of five critical aspects of a bank's operations and condition. These factors are: (1) adequacy of capital; (2) quality of assets; (3) ability of management and effectiveness of administration; (4) quantity and quality of earnings; and (5) liquidity, or the capacity to meet the demand for payment of obligations. The five factors produce the acronym CAMEL—Capital adequacy, Asset quality, Management, Earnings, and Liquidity. Each of the factors is rated on a scale of 1 through 5 with 1 being being the most favorable.

A detailed description of the rating guidelines for each of the factors would be quite lengthy. Several general observations can be made, however. First, peer group comparisons in such matters as capital ratios and earnings are of some importance. Second, access to capital markets and other sources of funds can offset to an extent certain negative elements; thus larger banking organizations having ready access to capital markets generally are permitted by the regulators to have lower capital ratios than are smaller banks. (Capital ratios are discussed in Chapter 6.) Finally, the management factor can significantly influence the other factors. For example, demonstrated ability to manage lower quality assets can result in a higher asset quality rating than would normally be the case.

The second element of the CAMEL system is the combination of the five factor ratings into a composite rating, although an agency is not precluded from considering additional factors in arriving at a composite rating. Again, the range of ratings is 1 through 5 with 1 being the most favorable. Composite rating 1 indicates a sound bank in almost every respect, and composite rating 2 indicates a fundamentally sound institution that may have modest weaknesses correctable in the normal course of business. Composite rating 3 indicates a combination of weaknesses ranging from moderately severe to unsatisfactory. Banks with this rating are considered to be only nominally resistant to the onset of adverse business conditions. Composite rating 4 indicates an immoderate volume of asset weaknesses, or a less than satisfactory combination of other conditions. A potential for failure of the bank is present but not pronounced. Composite rating 5 indicates that immediate corrective action and constant supervisory attention are necessary. There is an extremely high immediate or near-term probability of failure.

The three banking agencies usually do not begin to give banks extra attention until composite rating 3 is reached. Thus, composite ratings 1 and 2 indicate financially sound institutions in the sense that these institutions do not receive any extra regulatory attention.

MONITORING SYSTEMS

Each of the banking agencies has developed monitoring systems or programs that go beyond the traditional supervisory task of bank reports and examinations. In part, these systems are designed to provide early warning of impending financial weaknesses and in part they are attempts to cope with the growing complexity of individual institutions and the financial system in general. The systems depend to a large extent on computer-aided analyses of banks' call reports of condition and income.

The National Credit Union Administration for federally supervised credit unions and the Federal Home Loan Bank Board for thrifts under its supervision have also devised computer-aided surveillance programs. A 1981 report prepared for the Federal Financial Institutions Examination Council placed the computer screening programs of the five agencies into two distinct categories. The FDIC and the NCUA identify institutions warranting further investigation by comparing an institution's actual financial ratio values with predetermined critical values. The Federal Reserve Board and the OCC, on the other hand, rely more on peer groups. Institutions falling in the bottom of their peer groups become candidates for further investigation. The Federal Home Loan Bank Board uses both methods.

Another major difference among the agencies is that three of them—the FHLBB, the OCC, and the Federal Reserve Board—use a composite score technique. Under such an approach, various financial ratios, which differ from agency to agency, are aggregated to produce a composite score. The NCUA and the FDIC do not base their monitoring programs on composite scores.

The computer is not the only component of monitoring systems that go beyond the traditional supervisory tools of reports and examinations. Some monitoring systems make use of organizational arrangements, such as special purpose divisions. The Comptroller of the Currency has probably gone the farthest in devising such organizational arrangements.

The remainder of this section discusses in greater detail the monitoring systems of the OCC, the FDIC, and the Federal Reserve Board.

Comptroller of the Currency

There are three principal monitoring systems or programs in the OCC. These are the National Bank Surveillance System, the Special Projects Division, and the Multinational Banking Division. The National Bank Surveillance System (NBSS) is a computer-based system whose primary purpose is the early detection of adverse conditions in individual banks and the banking industry in general. The system currently consists of five elements. First, in the Bank Performance Report (BPR), data covering several years are taken from reports of condition and income and from other sources and displayed in a variety of ratios, percentages, and dollar figures. For comparative purposes, each report contains certain information for the bank's peer group. Second, the Anomaly Severity Ranking System (ASRS) is a computerized scoring system that assigns the highest scores to banks with the most abnormal positions, changes, and trends in performance or composition. Third, specially trained examiners review the BPRs and other available information on banks with high ASRS scores. The reviews may result in further investigation, discussions with bank management, or special examinations. Fourth, an Action Control System provides periodic reports to OCC officials on those banks selected for special attention. And fifth, a bank holding company performance report displays data and information similar to that displayed in the BPR but on an integrated holding company basis.

The Special Projects Division covers all banks with assets up to $10 billion and any other bank experiencing certain difficulties. The Division plans and directs a comprehensive program involving intelligence gathering, independent analysis, and implementation and coordination of action. It makes use of a wide range of source materials, such as bank examination reports, securities laws filings, and NBSS analyses.

The Multinational Banking Division was created in 1978 to centralize the examination, analysis, and supervision of multinational banks, currently defined as those with assets in excess of $14 billion. The Division also covers the international activities of all national banks with overseas branches. The Division was created because of the recognition that (1) multinational banks have little in common with most of the banking organizations that are supervised by the regional offices of the OCC and (2) overseas activities pose special regulatory problems calling for centralized coordination with foreign banking authorities.

Federal Deposit Insurance Corporation

The FDIC's principal monitoring program is the Integrated Monitoring System whose main component is JAWS, or Just A Warning System. JAWS uses data submitted by banks in their reports of income and condition to make tests concerning capital adequacy, asset quality, liquidity, asset and liability mix and growth, and profitability. The tests consist of comparisons of ratios derived from a bank's data with predetermined critical values. Through the use of CRT terminals in the FDIC's Washington and regional offices, testing can begin as soon as reports of income and condition are received by the regulator. This initial testing phase allows the regional offices to get an early start on potential problems. After the data base created by a quarter's reports of income and condition has been screened for errors, the FDIC's Washington office runs more formal JAWS tests. The regional offices are then furnished with a listing of all banks failing the JAWS criteria. The FDIC also makes use of the Uniform Bank Performance Report, which was discussed earlier in this chapter.

Federal Reserve Board

The Federal Reserve System has a computer screening program that calculates key financial ratios and a composite score. The ratios and score for a bank or bank holding company are compared to the institution's peer group. Those banking organizations falling into the bottom percentiles of their peer groups are subject to attention by the Federal Reserve District Banks. The Board also does some monitoring of the large banks in its weekly bank reporting program.

SUPERVISION IN THE INTERNATIONAL ARENA

The growth of international banking and the expansion of banks outside their home countries have posed difficulties for banking regulators. The crux of the difficulties is that national borders restrain regulators to a much greater extent than they restrain banks. A 1980 study by the OCC estimated that 520 banking institutions around the world had a banking presence outside their home countries. These foreign offices took the following forms: 440 subsidiaries, 1,232 affiliate relationships, and 4,375 branches or agencies.

Of the three U.S. banking agencies, the Comptroller of the Currency and the Federal Reserve Board have been more directly confronted with the difficulties arising from the internationalization of the banking industry. Both agencies have responded. The OCC's Multinational Banking Division has already been discussed. The creation of this Division was an attempt by the OCC to keep track of the worldwide activities of large U.S. banking organizations. The Federal Reserve Board has undertaken a number of initiatives concerning foreign bank holding companies—foreign banking organizations that control a U.S. bank. The Board requires a substantial amount of financial information at the time a foreign organization seeks to acquire a U.S. bank and solicits the views of regulators in the foreign organization's home country. Once the foreign organization is permitted to enter the U.S., the Board follows a continuing pervasive program of reports and examinations. Areas of particular interest are intercompany transactions and common customer credits.

Each of the federal banking agencies conducts on-site examinations of overseas offices of U.S. banks for which it has primary responsibility. The OCC's overseas program is probably the most extensive; that agency even maintains a permanent office in London.

In addition to such unilateral actions by regulators in the U.S. and other countries, there has been an increasing amount of cooperation among national banking authorities. The most important cooperative effort is the Committee on Banking Regulations and Supervisory Practices, known informally as the Cooke Committee or the Basle Committee. The Committee was established in 1974 and consists of representatives from the supervisory authorities and central banks of the countries of the Group of Ten (the United States, Canada, Japan, Belgium, France, West Germany, Italy, the Netherlands, the United Kingdom, and Sweden) plus Switzerland and Luxembourg. The Committee serves as a clearing house for information and as a discussion forum where supervisory practices can be compared. It also attempts to establish broad principles upon which all members can agree. Its most significant actions to date have been the Concordats of 1975 and 1983, which parcelled out in a general way responsibility for the foreign activities of banking organizations.

International loans by banks became a hot topic in 1982–83 as a number of foreign countries sought to reschedule debt payments—of principal, interest, or both—to some degree. In 1979, the three bank regulators adopted a program to monitor certain aspects of the international lending activities of U.S. banks. The program is administered by an Interagency Country Exposure Review Committee. Among other tasks, this committee evaluates foreign countries as to their ability to meet debt obligations. These evaluations form part of the basis for making judgments about the overseas exposures of U.S. banks during the bank examination process. Other elements that enter into the judgments are a bank's procedures and controls for managing its overseas risks.

As a result of the events of 1982–83, many members of Congress and officials in the regulatory agencies came to the conclusion that the program to monitor the international lending activities of U.S. banks was inadequate. Accordingly, a number of legislative and regulatory proposals appeared during the early part of 1983. The likelihood that one or more of these proposals will find their way into statute or regulation seems high. Generally, the proposals call for more control over the international lending activities of U.S. banks by the U.S. bank regulators.

NOTES

The OCC, the FDIC, and the Federal Reserve have publicly available examination manuals that cover the examination process in depth. The FDIC's is entitled *Manual of Examination Policies.* The OCC's is entitled *Comptroller's Handbook for National Bank Examiners.* Section 408.1 of the latter contains a convenient summary of the reports national banks must file. And the Federal Reserve's is entitled *Bank Holding Company Supervision Manual.* A description of computer screening methods used by the financial regulators is contained in "Computer Screening Methods Employed by The Five Financial Regulatory Institutions To Identify Banks Having Actual Or Potential Financial Problems." The report was prepared by Barron H. Putnam for the FFIEC and is dated November 13, 1981.

In recent years, the General Accounting Office has made several reports to Congress on financial institution supervision. These include: *Federal Supervision of State and National Banks* (January 1977); *Banks Having Problems Need Better Identification and Disclosure* (January 24, 1979); *Federal Supervision of Bank Holding Companies Needs Better, More Formalized Coordination* (February 12, 1980); *Federal Examinations of Financial Institutions: Issues That Need to be Resolved* (January 6, 1981); *An Economic Overview of Bank Solvency Regulation* (February 13, 1981); *The Federal Structure for Examining Financial Institutions Can Be Improved* (April 24, 1981); *Federal Reserve Could Improve The Efficiency of Bank Holding Company Inspections* (August 18, 1981); *Formal Supervisory Process For Savings and Loan Associations Should Be Strengthened* (September 17, 1981); *Despite Recent Improvements, Bank Supervision Could Be More Effective and Less Burdensome* (February 26, 1982); and *Stronger Supervision of Credit Unions Needed* (October 6, 1982).

Statutory provisions concerning the general division of responsibilities among the federal banking agencies were listed in the notes to Chapter 2. Specific provisions referred to in Chapter 5 are located at the following sections of Title 12 of the U.S. Code: §§3301–3308 (Federal Financial Institutions Examination Council); §§161, 324, and 1817(a) (reports of condition); and §§325, 326, 330, 481, and 1820(b)–(d) (bank examinations).

6

Federal Limitations on Banking Operations

The business of banking can be defined broadly as the acceptance of deposits from the general public and the lending at interest of the funds obtained. This is not, however, a particularly useful definition. There are many related activities that traditionally have been part of the banking business—for example, the provision of safekeeping services—and there is a wide variety of limitations on just what a bank may do. This chapter is concerned with certain important types of limitations. Chapter 10 treats limitations on the activities of bank holding companies—an organizational form through which many bank-related activities are conducted.

A discussion of the limitations on the activities of banking organizations should begin by mentioning the basic statutory provisions that attempt to restrict such organizations to the general field of banking. There are two basic provisions at the federal level. Section 24(Seventh) of the National Bank Act gives national banks the power to exercise "all such incidental powers as shall be necessary to carry on the business of banking." And Section 4(c)(8) of the Bank Holding Company Act permits bank holding companies to engage in activities that the Federal Reserve Board finds "to be so closely related to banking or managing or controlling banks as to be a proper incident thereto." As can be imagined, and as is discussed further in Chapter 10 regarding bank holding companies, deriving precise limitations from such broad language has not proved to be an easy task for the regulators or the courts, where many of the regulators' attempts are judged.

At the state level, state banking codes contain similar broad language attempting to limit the activities of state-chartered banks to the field of banking.

Once past these broad definitional limitations, one encounters numerous specific statutory provisions delineating the range of activities in which banking organizations may engage and prescribing the manner in which permissible activities may be conducted. At the federal level, these provisions may apply to any one type or all of the banking organizations subject to some degree of federal control: bank holding companies, national banks, state member banks, state nonmember insured banks, and even in some instances, state noninsured banks.

This chapter discusses a number of the more important federal limitations on banks and the business of banking. The discussion begins with one of the most significant federal attempts to establish limits for the banking business: the 1933 Glass-Steagall Act's separation of commercial banking from certain types of investment banking activities. The discussion then proceeds to a variety of topics: the regulation of interest rates; lending limits; insider lending; truth-in-lending; electronic banking; investor information about securities issues by banks; fair credit reporting and privacy; changes in bank ownership; extending credit to meet local community needs; and bank protection. Also, mention is made of certain indirect limitations that result from the regulators' concern for such measures of bank soundness as capital adequacy and asset quality.

The limitations imposed by the federal government on banking fall roughly into two categories: those intended to assure the safety and soundness of banks and the banking system, such as prohibitions against certain types of lending thought to involve an unusual degree of risk, and those designed to accomplish other public policy objectives, such as ensuring adequate flow of credit to residential housing. The existence of these underlying themes, however, does not necessarily mean that the federal statutory structure encompassing the banking business reflects a systematic approach to bank regulation. Indeed, each of the limitations described in this chapter typically came about as a result of legislative reaction to a particular financial problem or crisis. The passage of time can bring into question the continued need for such legislative solutions. For example, federal interest rate ceilings had come to seem so inappropriate by the end of the 1970s that a law to phase them out was passed. And the extensive separation between investment and commercial banking has received considerable scholarly reevaluation in recent years.

The group of limitations treated in this chapter is not exhaustive. Others are discussed in chapters dealing with branching, mergers and acquisitions, international banking, and as has been noted, bank holding companies. Taken as a whole, all of the federal limitations on banking have resulted in a system of limitations on the business of banking, on the products banks may offer, and on the areas in which they may offer them, that is probably more pervasive and constraining than that applied to any other industry, financial or non-financial.

BANKS AND INVESTMENT BANKING

Prior to the enactment by Congress of the Banking Act of 1933, there was no federal control over the underwriting and distribution of securities by banks. Commercial banks had been actively engaged in the investment banking business for more than a century. Indeed, during the early decades of the 19th century it is likely that commercial banks did the great bulk of the investment banking business.

The involvement of commercial banks in investment banking became somewhat less significant during the latter decades of the 19th century, but by the 1920s the banks were again prominent in the business. This was particularly the case with larger metropolitan banks, some of which established affiliates for this purpose.

Collapse of the financial boom in 1929 and the onset of the Great Depression disclosed evidence of market manipulation and self-dealing in the securities industry, resulting in sweeping reform legislation, most notably the Securities Act of 1933 and the Securities Exchange Act of 1934. Evidence was also disclosed pointing to the dangers of combining banking with securities underwriting and distribution activities. In several instances, for example, a bank had attempted to free itself of bad loans by unloading them on the investing public in the form of shares or bonds.

To correct the latter types of situations, the Banking Act of 1933, a landmark of omnibus legislation dealing with many banking reforms, contained several sections, frequently referred to as the "Glass-Steagall Act," that were intended to separate the investment banking business from commercial banking. The most important of these sections are 16 and 21. Section 16 prohibits national banks from underwriting securities. The prohibition also applies to state member banks. Section 21 prohibits investment banking firms from accepting deposits; the section provides that it is unlawful:

(1) For any person, firm, corporation, association, business trust, or other similar organization, engaged in the business of issuing, underwriting, selling, or distributing, at wholesale or retail, or through syndicate participation, stocks, bonds, debentures, notes, or other securities, to engage at the same time to any extent whatever in the business of receiving deposits subject to check or to repayment upon presentation of a passbook, certificate of deposit, or other evidence of debt, or upon request of the depositor. . . .

Two other sections, 20 and 32, of the Glass-Steagall Act prohibit, respectively, affiliations between Federal Reserve member banks and securities firms, and an officer, director, or employee of a member bank from serving as an officer, director, or employee of a securities firm.

The Glass-Steagall Act did not completely divorce commercial banking from the securities business. For example, banks are specifically permitted to underwrite and deal in obligations of the United States and its instrumentalities, along with obligations of states and their sub-divisions—for example, cities, counties, and school districts—provided the debt is supported by a pledge of the full faith and credit of the issuer. In addition, banks are permitted to provide securities brokerage services for customers.

There have been efforts to extend bank underwriting activities by permitting banks to deal more fully in so-called "revenue bonds" issued by public authorities. Such issues were virtually unknown in 1933 but today constitute a major portion of state and municipal obligations. Revenue bonds are not supported by a pledge of the taxing power; rather, the debt service as regards principal and interest represents a claim on the revenues of the public authority that created the obligation. At the present time, banks can underwrite a few types of such bonds.

Another Glass-Steagall issue that has received considerable attention concerns the offering of investment vehicles similar to mutual funds by commercial banks. These bank-offered investment vehicles, called commingled agency accounts, were held by the U.S. Supreme Court in 1971 to be in violation of Glass-Steagall. (*Investment Company Institute v. Camp*, 401 U.S. 617.) On the other hand, in 1981 the Supreme Court upheld a tightly-drawn Federal Reserve Board regulation that permits a bank holding company or a subsidiary to serve as an investment adviser to a closed-end investment company. In this capacity, the bank holding company or subsidiary may sponsor, organize, and control such a company, but not participate in the sale or distribution of the company's securities. (*Board of Governors v. Investment Company Institute,*

450 U.S. 46.) The Board's regulation also permits purely advisory activities with respect to a mutual fund, or open-end investment company. The permissibility of such a relationship between a bank holding company and a mutual fund was not an issue in the case, but the Court noted this aspect of the regulation in a seemingly approving manner.

The difference between a closed-end investment company and a mutual fund, or open-end investment company, is primarily the amount of securities selling and distribution activities that each does. A closed-end fund typically sells its shares only once, when it is initially organized. Thereafter, a shareholder wishing to dispose of his shares, or a person wishing to purchase shares of the fund, must do so in the open market. A mutual fund, on the other hand, stands ready to redeem shares from shareholders. To prevent the shrinkage of its assets as it redeems shares, the fund must constantly sell shares. Thus a mutual fund engages in securities selling and distribution activities on a regular basis.

For at least the last decade, Congress has grappled with whether to give banks revenue bond underwriting and mutual fund powers. As of mid-1983, these questions were still in the legislative arena. Nevertheless, the Glass-Steagall Act is not the barrier between the banking and securities businesses that it was once considered to be. Erosion of the perceived barrier has taken place on several fronts.

For many years after the passage of the act, the authority of banks to buy and sell securities for customers was narrowly construed. This restrictive view has changed, however, and banks have begun to enter the field with alacrity. The activity of buying and selling securities for others is also referred to as brokering securities and is distinguished from underwriting or distributing new issues of securities. Brokering securities is not one of the activities proscribed in the act.

In 1982, the Comptroller of the Currency allowed several national banks to acquire or establish operating subsidiaries that engage in the brokerage business. In early 1983, the Federal Reserve Board allowed BankAmerica Corporation, a bank holding company, to acquire the nation's largest discount broker, The Charles Schwab Corporation. And a number of banking organizations have begun to offer brokerage services directly, without setting up or acquiring separate subsidiaries for the purpose. In some cases, the banks are providing the services themselves, and in other cases they are working with securities firms. The latter type of alliances often involve "sweep" arrangements in which excess funds in a bank account are transferred to a money market fund run by or associated with the securities firm. The Glass-Steagall Act has been asserted to be a barrier to many of these involvements by banking organizations in the brokerage business, but has resulted in few, if any, of the transactions being denied or the arrangements being declared illegal.

Another situation permitted by a literal reading of Glass-Steagall that has also seen an increase in activity concerns Section 21 of the act. Although this provision prohibits organizations that accept deposits from also engaging in many investment banking activities, it does not extend to subsidiaries or affiliates of such organizations. The sections of Glass-Steagall—Sections 20 and 32—that largely prohibit affiliate and subsidiary relationships between banks and investment banking firms do not apply to state-chartered banks that are not members of the Federal Reserve System. Thus, the Glass-Steagall Act does not prevent an investment banking or securities firm from owning a state-chartered nonmember bank, or such a bank from having a securities firm or an investment banking firm as a subsidiary or an affiliate. The principal exploiters of this situation in recent years have been mutual fund organizations that have set up bank or trust company subsidiaries. Through these subsidiaries, the mutual fund organizations are able to perform many custodial and fund transfer activities that previously had to be performed by outside banks or trust companies. In May of 1983, the FDIC proposed rules that, if adopted, could result in many more securities firms and state-chartered nonmember banks being under the same corporate umbrellas.

Perhaps more controversially, the Comptroller of the Currency has held that Sections 20 and 32 also do not prevent certain mutual fund organizations from owning *national* banks, which unlike state-chartered nonmember banks are members of the Federal Reserve System. The OCC's reasoning is based in part on the premise that the mutual fund organizations do not own or control the actual funds themselves. Thus, national banks owned by the mutual fund organizations are not affiliated with the funds that are advised or run, but not owned or controlled, by the mutual fund organizations. In decisions in early 1983, the OCC gave two mutual fund organizations, The Dreyfus Corporation and J. & W. Seligman & Co., permission to set up national banks.

It should be noted that the ownership of banks by firms in the securities industry gives rise to Bank Holding Company Act as well as Glass-Steagall Act questions. For example, a mutual fund organization that seeks to acquire a bank risks the possibility of being a bank holding company and thus subject to Federal Reserve Board jurisdiction and the constraints of the Bank Holding Company Act. A way to try to avoid this result is to keep the bank from meeting the definition of a bank in the Bank Holding Company Act. This definition is an organization that both accepts demand deposits and makes commercial loans. A bank that is not a bank for the purpose of the Bank Holding Company Act has come to be called a "nonbank bank." This phenomenon is discussed in greater detail in Chapter 13. Asserting both the Glass-Steagall Act and the Bank Holding Company Act, the Federal Reserve Board has contested actions by the FDIC and the OCC to allow securities firms to acquire "nonbank banks."

In summary, there has been a considerable reduction in the barriers the Glass-Steagall Act was long viewed as imposing between the securities and commercial banking businesses. This reduction has taken place with little action on the part of Congress, which for many years was the focus of efforts to change the act. The recent events in the marketplace and the recent actions of the regulators may have made some long-sought legislative changes unnecessary. As for other changes, the marketplace events and regulatory actions may eventually bring statutory revisions. Somewhat similar prods resulted in Congressional action to end interest rate ceilings, the topic of the following section.

REGULATION OF INTEREST ON DEPOSITS

Regulation of interest payments on deposits has come almost full circle over the last half century. Interest rates were not controlled before the 1930s, when controls were introduced as part of the financial reform legislation of that time. Controls developed and became more complex in the ensuing decades, until the Depository Institutions Deregulation and Monetary Control Act of 1980. This act provides for the phasing out of limitations on interest rates on all but demand deposits.

Interest rate controls came into being because the payment of excessive interest on deposits was one widely accepted explanation of the banking troubles characterizing the 1920s and the crisis and financial panic that followed. Proponents of this explanation maintained that unhealthy competition among banks developed in many parts of the country as these institutions sought to attract funds by bidding up the rate of interest paid to depositors. To cover the cost of these funds, it was argued, the banks in turn had to invest their resources on terms which sacrificed asset quality for yield. In addition, by being able to offer high rates of interest on deposits, the large banks in the financial centers were thought to have drained funds from much of the rest of the country.

In the years since 1933, the accuracy of this explanation has been seriously questioned. Indeed, there now seems little reason to believe that the banking difficulties prior to 1933 were in fact the result of excessive competition for interest-bearing funds. Rather, it is now argued, banking problems were symptomatic of far more fundamental adverse economic conditions. For whatever reason, however, interest rate controls were introduced by the federal government in the Banking Acts of 1933 and 1935.

Two different steps were taken at the federal level. First, the payment of interest on demand deposits was completely prohibited, in 1933 for Federal Reserve member banks and in 1935 for all insured banks. Second, the Federal Reserve and the Federal Deposit Insurance Corporation were given the power to establish maximum interest rates payable to depositors on their time and savings accounts. These powers were implemented by the Federal Reserve Board's Regulation Q applicable to member banks, and by FDIC Regulation 329 applicable to insured nonmember banks. The Office of the Comptroller of the Currency was not given a role to play in this area.

Although the prohibition of payment of interest on demand deposits had an immediate effect on banks and their customers, interest rate ceilings on savings and time deposits at first were of little significance since market rates (or at least the rates that banks were willing to pay) were all well below the ceilings. By the late 1950s, however, interest rate levels were rising and competition between commercial banks and thrift institutions for savings and time deposits intensified. Ceilings were moved upward in successive steps. Then, in 1966, as it appeared that competition would threaten both the stability of the thrift institutions and the flow of funds to finance housing, interest rate controls were extended to savings and loan associations, such controls to be administered by the Federal Home Loan Bank Board. The 1966 legislation also required the various agencies establishing ceilings to consult with each other before exercising this authority.

Interest rate regulation in the years following 1966 was difficult. Notwithstanding the establishment of a "differential" letting thrift institutions pay higher rates on certain types of savings and time deposits, it proved impossible to assure a steady flow of funds to residential housing markets. The primary problem was rising and volatile market rates of interest, which tempted savers to seek higher rates of return in the unregulated sectors of the financial system as, for example, in U.S. Treasury securities.

One significant deregulatory action occurred in 1970, relating to large certificates of deposit. Up to that time, ceilings on rates had covered time deposits of all sizes. The Penn Central railroad failure in 1970 caused concern among investors about many companies' commercial paper. Unable to sell their commercial paper, large corporations had to rely to a greater extent on bank lending. Partly to insure that banks had funds available to loan, the Federal Reserve exempted certificates of deposit of $100,000 or more from the rate ceilings.

But the problem of smaller savers still remained, and this was exacerbated during the late 1970s and in 1980 when market rates, driven by inflation, reached unusually high levels. Notwithstanding continued efforts by the agencies to devise flexible regulations for various types of deposits (resulting in a proliferation of interest ceilings), new and unregulated competitors for funds appeared on the scene, the most important of which were the money market funds. At the same time, interest rate controls came under attack from consumer groups, complaining of the lower-than-market rates available to small savers and of the complete prohibition on the payment of interest on demand deposits.

An early response to the latter complaint was the development of the so-called NOW (negotiable order of withdrawal) account, initially by mutual savings banks in Massachusetts. Such accounts permit interest or dividends to be paid on funds that may be withdrawn by negotiable instrument for the purpose of making a transfer to a third party. In effect, consumers were offered an interest-bearing checking account. Federal legislation authorized NOW accounts for all of the principal depository institutions in the New England states by 1976, and then in New York and New Jersey in 1978 and 1979, respectively. However, it was clear by 1980 that the question of interest regulation had to be addressed in broader terms.

The Depository Institutions Deregulation and Monetary Control Act (DIDMCA) of 1980 was the result. That act extended nationwide the authority of depository institutions to issue NOW accounts or their equivalent. Such accounts, however, can only be made available to individuals or to certain non-profit organizations. Thus the prohibition of interest on demand deposits held by individuals has been effectively removed, although any interest paid on such deposits may be subject to interest rate ceilings.

More significant was Title II of DIDMCA, providing for the phase-out and eventual elimination of the limitations on the maximum rates of interest and dividends that may be paid on time and savings deposits and accounts by depository institutions. While the act calls for this elimination to occur "as rapidly as economic conditions warrant," it also provides for the gradual phase-out over a six year period, with all authority to impose interest rate ceilings ending by March 31, 1986.

The vehicle for accomplishing this objective is the Depository Institutions Deregulation Committee, whose members are the Secretary of the Treasury and the Chairmen of the Federal Reserve Board, the FDIC, the FHLBB, and the National Credit Union Administration Board. The Comptroller of the Currency is a nonvoting member. Except for credit unions, all authority to establish rules regarding the payment of interest and dividends on deposits and accounts is now vested in the DIDC. This authority includes the power to establish new classes of deposits or accounts that might not be subject to interest rate controls.

After a few false starts, largely due to a reluctance on the part of elements of the thrift industry to actually remove interest rate ceilings, the DIDC began making substantive changes. Congress gave a major impetus to the DIDC's work in the Garn-St Germain Act of October, 1982. A provision of that act instructed the DIDC to develop an account substantially equivalent as an investment vehicle to money market mutual funds. Accordingly, in December of 1982 the DIDC authorized depository institutions to offer the money market deposit account (MMDA). The minimum investment for the MMDA is $2,500, but an institution can set whatever interest rate it wants. Depositors can make up to six withdrawals or transfers from the account by check or in a similar manner per month. The DIDC followed the MMDA in January of 1983 with a Super NOW account. This account also has a minimum deposit of $2,500 and no interest rate ceilings, but the number of transfers per month are not restricted.

The MMDA was an immediate success, attracting deposits of $183.6 billion as of January 31, 1983. Approximately 16 percent of this was estimated to have come from money market funds. From a peak of $241.0 billion in November of 1982, the amount in money market funds had fallen to $187.7 billion as of the end of April, 1983. The amount in MMDA's as of the end of March, 1983, was $320.5 billion.

Thus, federally imposed interest rate ceilings seem to be well on their way out. A few areas of control remain. For example, demand deposit accounts, in contrast to NOW accounts, cannot have interest paid on them. And businesses cannot have NOW accounts. But for the most part, interest rate ceilings for depository institutions may soon be a thing of the past.

LENDING LIMITS

Banks are subject to a variety of statutory and regulatory limits on the loans they may make. Such limits on national banks are imposed by federal law. State-chartered member and insured nonmember banks are subject to both federal and state law, although not all of the federal limitations on national banks apply to state banks, and state limitations are generally less stringent than are federal limitations.

Table 3 is a summary listing of federal laws pertaining to lending limits. A general limitation is contained in Section 84 of Title 12 of the U.S. Code and provides that the total unsecured loans by a national bank to any one borrower shall not exceed 15 percent of the bank's unimpaired capital and surplus. Additional loans amounting to 10 percent of unimpaired capital and surplus can be made if they are fully secured by readily marketable collateral. The general limit is subject to a number of exceptions, which are based on the quality, security, or liquidity of the obligations involved. The purpose of a general limit is to prevent overconcentration of loans to any one borrower and the resulting excessive loss to the bank if the borrower proves unable to pay. Prior to the Garn-St Germain Act of 1982, the general limit of Section 84 was 10 percent of unimpaired capital and surplus.

Another change that the Garn-St Germain Act made was to remove the upper limit on real estate-related loans. Prior to the act, the basic limitation was that national bank real estate loans secured by first liens could not exceed the greater of capital stock and surplus or time and savings deposits. The terms, conditions, and limitations concerning real estate-related loans by national banks are now subject to the OCC's orders, rules, or regulations. The upper limit on real estate loans that existed prior to the Garn-St Germain Act was in contrast to the lack of such a limit on commercial, industrial, agricultural, and consumer loans.

Loans to affiliates of a member bank, including the bank's parent bank holding company and its subsidiaries, are in general limited by Section 371c of Title 12 to 10 percent of the bank's capital and surplus to any one affiliate and 20 percent to all affiliates. Loans to bank insiders are covered in the following section.

INSIDER LENDING

The use of a position of responsibility in any organization—not just in banks—to obtain preferential treatment has long been a

Table 3: Reference List (Partial) of Federal Laws and Regulations On Lending Limits

	*Laws**	*Regulations†*	*Rulings†*
General Power to Make Loans	§ 24		
Lending Limits—General	§ 84		§§ 7.1100 through 7.1630
Loans Secured by Real Estate	§ 371		§§ 7.2000 through 7.2600
Debts Previously Contracted	§ 29		§ 7.2000(c)
Loans to Affiliates	§ 371c		§§ 7.7360, 7.7370, and 7.7390
Loans to Executive Officers, Directors, and Principal Shareholders and Their Interests	§§ 375a and 375b	Part 215	
Collateral			
Loans Secured by Bank Stock-Reporting Requirements	§§ 1730(*l*)(2)-(3) and 1817(j)		
Loans Secured by Own Stock	§ 83		§ 7.6030
Loans Collateralized by U.S. Notes	§ 582		
Regulation U (Margin Regs)		Part 221	
Regulation X (Margin Regs)		Part 224	
Loans Secured by U.S. Government Obligations		Part 6	
Loans Secured by Time Deposits		Part 217	
Trust Accounts		Part 9	
Criminal			
Commission or Gift for Procuring Loans	18 U.S.C. § 215		
Loans to Examiners	18 U.S.C. § 212		
Political Contributions	18 U.S.C. § 591 and 2 U.S.C. § 441b		
Extortion	18 U.S.C. § 894		
False Representations by Borrowers	18 U.S.C. § 1014		
Other			
Tie-in Provisions	§ 1972		

***12 U.S.C., unless specifically stated otherwise.**
†12 C.F.R.

Source: *Comptroller's Handbook for National Bank Examiners.*

concern of society. In the banking industry, many of the serious problem situations in recent decades have resulted from insider transactions. Thus, as might be expected, insider loans in banking are subject to federal limitations, which were significantly strengthened by the Financial Institutions Regulatory and Interest Rate Control Act of 1978, but relaxed a bit in the Garn-St Germain Act of 1982.

For extensions of credit by a bank to its executive officers, the Garn-St Germain Act removed dollar limitations on mortgage loans, which had been $60,000, and educational loans, which had been $20,000. It replaced a $10,000 limit on other loans to executive officers by a grant of authority to the bank supervisory agencies to set appropriate limits. All executive officer loans must be on terms not more favorable than loans to other borrowers.

Concerning loans to insiders—executive officers, directors, or persons owning or controlling more than 10 percent of any class of voting stock, and to companies controlled by and to political committees that will benefit these individuals—the Garn-St Germain Act removed a requirement that amounts over $25,000 be approved by the bank's board of directors. Approval for insider loans over a certain amount must still be obtained, but the threshold figure is left to the discretion of the appropriate bank supervisory agency to establish by regulation. Insider loans must be on substantially the same terms, including interest rate and collateral, as those prevailing at the time for comparable transactions with other persons. In addition, such loans must not involve more than the normal risk of repayment.

Loans by a bank to insiders in a correspondent bank are also the object of federal scrutiny. Such loans must be on substantially the same terms as comparable transactions with other persons and involve no more than normal risk. Both loans by a bank to its own insiders and loans received by insiders from correspondent banks are subject to reporting and disclosure requirements. The Garn-St Germain Act eliminated certain statutory requirements and instructed the supervisory agencies to develop their own.

TRUTH-IN-LENDING

A contention of the consumer groups that began to achieve recognition in the 1960s was the sentiment that small borrowers—for example, individuals who use credit to finance the purchase of automobiles, durable household goods, and other non-business expenditures—had been unfairly treated by creditors. Mostly, the characterization of "unfairness" was supported by reference to high interest rates and other charges not fully and clearly disclosed to the borrower at the time of a transaction. Noteworthy also was the belief that borrowers would be more circumspect in the use of their credit if they knew what it cost.

Banks were caught up by the movement, even though typically they are the lower (and often lowest) cost lenders. The Truth-in-Lending Act of 1968 applies to all consumer lenders. With respect to banks, one agency, the Federal Reserve, is responsible for establishing the disclosure guidelines, and all three federal banking agencies use their examination and investigative processes to make certain that the requirements are met by the banks subject to their supervision.

The basic purpose of the act is to assure consumers that they are given "meaningful information" with respect to the cost of credit. In this way a consumer can compare the various credit terms available and make an informed choice. However, implementing the objective has not proved easy, and a widespread opinion that truth-in-lending regulations were unduly complex led in 1980 to Title VI of DIDMCA which attempted to simplify and reform much of the original law and its amendments.

ELECTRONIC BANKING

A major development in the delivery of banking products and services in the 1970s was the growth of electronic banking. Plastic cards and electronic terminals, including automated teller machines (ATMs) and point-of-sale (POS) devices, have given the consumer more convenient access to the institutions serving his banking needs. The range of products and services that will likely be provided through electronic means in the 1980s will have a profound effect on the banking industry and its relationships with its customers.

In the Electronic Fund Transfer Act of 1978, which was Title XX of the Financial Institutions Regulatory and Interest Rate Control Act, Congress attempted to deal with one type of problem resulting from electronic banking. The act provides a framework for establishing the rights, liabilities, and responsibilities of participants in electronic fund transfer systems, with the emphasis being the protection of individual consumers. The act includes provisions concerning disclosure of terms and conditions of electronic fund transfers, requirements for written documentation of transfers, limitations on consumer liability for unauthorized transfers (the basic limitation is $50), and conditions under which financial institutions are liable for damages caused by failures to make transfers or to stop pre-authorized transfers.

A second type of problem, from the regulatory standpoint, created by the growth of electronic banking involves the geographic restraints to which banking organizations have long been subject. In threatening to eliminate the need for brick and mortar facilities, electronic banking threatens to bypass those restraints. Congress has not yet acted either to prevent electronic banking from overriding the geographic restraints on the banking industry or to facilitate such an outcome. This topic is treated in greater detail in Chapter 8.

BANK INVESTOR INFORMATION

By statutory amendments in 1964 and 1974, certain registration and reporting requirements of the Securities Exchange Act of 1934 were made specifically applicable to banks. A basic thrust of the securities laws is to provide holders of securities as well as the investing public in general with a continuing flow of information about the firms subject to the reporting requirements. Banks with assets in excess of $1 million and 500 or more shareholders are obliged to register with the appropriate federal banking agency in lieu of the Securities and Exchange Commission. Registered banks are required to file periodic financial reports which are available to the public. Proxy statements are subject to regulation to insure proper financial disclosure. "Insider trading" rules apply to a bank's officers, directors, and beneficial owners of more than 10 percent of the bank's outstanding stock.

The banking agency regulations in this area must, as a result of the 1974 amendments, follow the regulatory outlines established by the SEC. Among other matters, the regulations prescribe uniformity in accounting concepts and procedures so that bank-to-bank comparisons of data are not misleading. The responsibility for administering securities laws registration and reporting requirements as they apply to national banks is assigned to the Comptroller of the Currency; for state-chartered member banks, the designated authority is the Federal Reserve; state-chartered nonmember insured banks are controlled by the Federal Deposit Insurance Corporation; and holding companies and non-FDIC-insured banks are controlled by the SEC itself.

FAIR CREDIT REPORTING AND PRIVACY

Banks have long been recognized as a primary and dependable source of credit data owing to their strategic position in the payments mechanism—the banks know about their customers' sources of income as well as their bill-paying habits. In addition, as lenders, banks build up their own files of credit experience. As a consequence, members of the business community have looked to their banks for help when they were in need of credit data about actual or prospective customers. If the information were not available directly, it could often be obtained via the network of interbank relationships.

Federal law now imposes substantial obligations upon the providing of information concerning the credit worthiness of individuals and firms by banks and others. In general, the objective is to make certain that the subject of a credit report is apprised of the facts contained therein so that errors may be corrected and misapprehensions dispelled. The federal bank supervisory agencies administer the provisions of the Fair Credit Reporting Law for the banks they supervise.

The Right to Financial Privacy Act of 1978 also protects individuals when their financial status is being reported. This act, however, deals with the situation where a federal agency requests bank records. It basically prohibits access to an individual's financial records by the government unless that person gives permission or the records are requested pursuant to legal process, such as a subpoena or search warrant.

Banks are entitled to reimbursement from the government for the cost of producing records under this act. There are, however, a number of exceptions to this reimbursement provision. Among those exceptions are instances when the records requested pertain to federal loans, loan insurance, and loan guarantee programs or when they are required to be disclosed by law. Examples of the latter are disclosures under the Internal Revenue Code and under the Federal Rules of Civil or Criminal Procedure. As with the Fair Credit Reporting Act, the federal banking agencies administer the provisions of the Privacy Act for the banks they supervise.

CHANGES IN BANK OWNERSHIP

Prior to the Financial Institutions Regulatory and Interest Rate Control Act (FIRIRCA) of 1978, there was little control by the federal banking agencies over changes in bank ownership between or among individuals. Officials of any insured bank were merely required to report to the appropriate federal supervisory agency any change in the ownership of the outstanding voting stock which would establish control, or would represent a change in control, of the bank. This absence of federal control over the buying and selling of banks by individuals was in sharp contrast to federal control over changes in ownership as a result of bank mergers, discussed in Chapter 9, or bank holding company mergers and acquisitions, discussed in Chapter 10.

FIRIRCA, however, contained a provision called the Change in Bank Control Act that imposes more stringent control over changes in bank ownership between or among individuals. The act basically requires approval by the appropriate federal agency before any individual or group takes control of an insured bank. The acquirer must file written notice of the proposed acquisition with the appropriate agency. If the agency does not disapprove of the acquisition within 60 days, the transaction is considered approved.

An agency may deny a change in control if the acquisition would result in a monopoly or restrain trade or if the anticompetitive effects would not be clearly outweighed by the probable public benefits in meeting the convenience and needs of the community. Other statutory reasons for denying a change in control are that the acquiring person might jeopardize the financial stability of the bank or that the acquiring person or one of the proposed management personnel might not have the competence, experience, or integrity necessary to protect the interest of the depositors.

Within ten days of a notice of disapproval the acquiring person may request an agency hearing on the acquisition. Review of the results of the agency hearing may be obtained in federal court. The agency finding can be set aside if it is considered to be arbitrary or capricious or if it is found to violate one of the procedures for disapproving the acquisition.

From the passage of the Change in Bank Control Act in 1978 to the end of 1982, the three federal banking agencies received 1,462 change in bank control notifications and disapproved 24.

LOCAL CREDIT NEEDS

The Community Reinvestment Act of 1977 was the culmination of a long-standing debate between consumer groups and the banking industry. Consumer groups claimed that banks have a duty to help finance inner-city housing and other similar needs in their local communities, a duty which they contended was not being fulfilled in many instances. Banks, on the other hand, argued that they served their communities best, and in conformity with their duty to depositors, by investing depositors' funds in sound assets.

The passage of the Community Reinvestment Act reflected a Congressional intent to heighten awareness on the part of depository institutions of the credit needs of their communities. In effect, the act imposes a continuing and affirmative obligation to meet the local credit needs. The three federal banking agencies and the Federal Home Loan Bank Board are required to supervise compliance with the act. This is done in two ways. When a supervisory agency conducts its examination of an institution, it must assess the institution's record in meeting the credit needs of the local community. In addition, such an evaluation is made when an institution applies for a depository facility such as a new branch or an acquisition of an existing bank.

BANK PROTECTION

Yet another aspect of banking subject to regulation by the federal supervisory agencies is the protection of banks against robbery. Because of an increase in violent crimes against banks, the Bank Protection Act was signed into law in 1968. Pursuant to this legislation the federal banking agencies promulgate standards for the installation, maintenance, and operation of security devices and procedures designed to discourage robberies and to assist in the apprehension of robbers. Implementation of the standards is checked by reports and examinations.

INDIRECT LIMITATIONS ON BANK OPERATIONS

Equally as important as the controls over banking activities specifically assigned by law to the federal supervisory agencies are the indirect limitations that result from their exercise of general supervisory powers. A primary objective of the supervisory system is to ensure the soundness of banks. In Chapter 5, the factors that the banking agencies consider in making assessments concerning bank soundness were listed. These factors are covered by the acronym CAMEL: Capital adequacy, Asset quality, Management, Earnings, and Liquidity. None of these factors is susceptible to precise quantification. Nevertheless, in making a soundness evaluation, a supervisory agency rates a bank on each of the five factors, and the agency can turn to various enforcement powers to induce improvement in deficient areas. The mere possession by a supervisory agency of these enforcement powers, which are discussed in Chapter 7, makes their use necessary only on infrequent occasions.

Thus, significant limitations on bank operations result from the necessity of meeting regulatory standards on the factors that are considered in soundness evaluations. The following discussion briefly reviews two of the factors: capital adequacy and asset quality, the latter more specifically in terms of the asset categories of loans and investments.

Limitation of the discussion to these two factors is not meant to denigrate the others: management, earnings, and liquidity. Only in recent years, however, have these latter factors received strong and specific supervisory attention, and therefore fewer working rules have been developed concerning them. For many years, on the other hand, capital adequacy and asset quality received most of the attention of the regulators. Although imprecise, the standards that have developed with respect to them continue to play an extremely important role in the soundness evaluation process.

Capital Adequacy

Historically, the "free banking" acts, both state and federal, have prescribed minimum capital requirements for chartered banks. With the passage of time, the dollar amounts specified in these laws have become unrealistic. and there has been little or no disposition to bring the figures up-to-date. The present federal statute states that the minimum capital for obtaining a national charter shall not be less than $100,000 unless the bank is located in a place with a population of 6,000 or less. If the population is at that figure or below, the minimum capital is $50,000. If the population is greater than 50,000, $200,000 is required except in certain instances when state law permits a bank in the locality to have capital of $100,000 or less.

As a practical matter, however, the OCC requires at least $1 million for a national bank charter, as does the Federal Reserve for membership in the System. There is no statutory capital requirement for deposit insurance, but FDIC policy is not to grant insurance coverage unless capital is at least $750,000. The actual amount of capital which each agency seeks to obtain in a newly organized bank is related to the estimated volume of deposits to be acquired within a three to five year period.

The more important issue concerning bank capital is not the absolute amount but the proportionate amount. How does capital appear in relation to other balance sheet categories, and how does one institution's capital margin compare to that of other institutions? Over the years, the supervisory authorities have experimented with many different methods for analyzing pertinent data in efforts to measure capital adequacy. These methods range from simple ratio calculations (e.g., capital accounts expressed as a percentage of total deposits or assets) to exceedingly complicated exercises.

Despite these efforts, a generally accepted definition of adequate capital continues to elude the regulatory agencies, as well as other searchers for such a standard. One reason is the number of subjective factors that can enter into a capital adequacy determination. These factors include management competence, asset quality, growth prospects, earnings retention ability, and deposit trends. How much weight to assign to peer group comparisons of various types has become an important issue in recent years.

Perhaps a more fundamental reason for the inability to achieve agreement on capital adequacy standards, however, is uncertainty as to the function capital is supposed to serve. One school of thought—probably the most common—views capital as a cushion to absorb losses and shrinkages in asset values and as a means to meet unanticipated adversity. A second school, however, points out that the deposit insurance system has come to perform many of the loss-protection functions capital is supposed to fulfill, and that in theory a bank could survive with no, or even negative, capital.

Two issues have long dominated the capital adequacy debate. The first is whether there should be some form of mandatory capital ratio. In 1981, the three federal banking agencies, against the background of rising Congressional clamor, moved to establish capital ratio standards. The results are set out in Table 4.

The second issue concerns the lower capital ratios that have come to be accepted by many large banks. For example, at midyear 1982 the ratio of total capital to total assets for all insured banks was 6.0 percent, while the same ratio for banks with over $5 billion in assets was 4.3 percent. The arguments used to justify lower ratios for larger banks are that the diversified product and geographical bases of such banks reduce the risks they face, they have better access to capital markets, and their managements are more capable of handling the difficulties presented by a dynamic economy. As might be expected, such arguments carry little credence with smaller banks that are urged to maintain higher capital ratios, and indeed they are not accepted by all the regulators. As can be seen from Table 4, the FDIC, whose constituency consists mostly of smaller banks, does not recognize different capital standards based on bank size.

Table 4: Capital Adequacy Standards as of July, 1983

Federal Reserve Board and Comptroller of the Currency

The Federal Reserve Board and the OCC consider two ratio measures of capital. These are (1) primary capital to total assets and (2) total capital to total assets. Primary capital consists of common stock, perpetual preferred stock, capital surplus, undivided profits, reserves for contingencies and other capital reserves, mandatory convertible instruments, the allowance for possible loan and lease losses, and any minority interest in the equity accounts of consolidated subsidiaries. Total capital includes the primary capital components plus limited life preferred stock and qualifying notes and debentures.

Institutions affected by the standards are categorized as multinational organizations, regional organizations, or community organizations. Multinational organizations are designated by their respective supervisory agency. Regional organizations are all other institutions with assets in excess of $1 billion. Community organizations are institutions that have less than $1 billion in total assets. The standards generally are applied on a consolidated basis. For those bank holding companies with consolidated assets under $150 million, however, the guidelines apply only if: (1) the company does not engage directly or indirectly in any nonbanking activity involving significant leverage; and (2) no significant debt of the parent company is held by the general public.

Primary Capital to Total Assets

The minimum levels of primary capital to total assets are as follows:

Multinational and Regional	*Community*
5%	6%

Total Capital to Total Assets

The standards for total capital to total assets are as follows:

	Multinational and Regional	*Community*
Zone 1	Above 6.5%	Above 7.0%
Zone 2	5.5% to 6.5%	6.0% to 7.0%
Zone 3	Below 5.5%	Below 6.0%

For banking institutions operating in Zone 1, the regulator will presume that capital is adequate if the primary capital ratio is acceptable and is above the minimum level. For institutions in Zone 2, the regulator will presume that the institution may be under-capitalized, particularly if the primary and total capital ratios are at or near the minimum guidelines. And for institutions in Zone 3, the regulator will strongly presume that there is under-capitalization.

Federal Deposit Insurance Corporation

The FDIC looks at one capital ratio. This is adjusted equity capital to adjusted total assets. Adjusted equity capital is equity capital minus assets classified loss and one half of assets classified doubtful. Adjusted total assets are total assets minus assets classified loss and one half of assets classified doubtful. Equity capital includes common stock, perpetual preferred stock, capital surplus, undivided profits, contingency reserves, other capital reserves, mandatory convertible instruments, and reserves for loan losses. Limited life preferred stock and subordinated notes and debentures are *not* considered in evaluating capital adequacy.

Adjusted Equity Capital to Adjusted Total Assets

The FDIC has established the following adjusted equity capital to adjusted total assets ratios:

Threshold Level	6%
Minimum Acceptable Level	5%

The ratios apply to *all* banks, regardless of size. The threshold level triggers a requirement for the submission by the bank of a comprehensive capital plan acceptable to the FDIC and the state banking department. The minimum acceptable level means that the FDIC will insist on a specific program for promptly remedying the equity capital deficiency.

Asset Quality

Asset appraisal is a time-consuming but important part of the bank examination process. The quality of assets has an obvious bearing on the soundness of a bank and the adequacy of its loan loss reserve and its capital. Moreover, asset quality is evidence of the capabilities and competence of management and of the sufficiency of lending policies and procedures. The principal assets that present both regulators and bankers with appraisal difficulties are loans and investments.

Bank examiners normally do not evaluate all the loans held by a bank. Sampling techniques are used for most of the portfolio, with total review being made only of past due and previously classified loans. The federal banking agencies use essentially the same three classifications for lower quality loans, called classified loans. Substandard loans are those inadequately protected by the current sound worth and paying capacity of the obligor. Doubtful loans have the added ingredient that collection or liquidation in full is highly questionable and improbable. And loss loans are considered uncollectable. A fourth category, Other Loans Especially Mentioned (OLEM), precedes the first three and includes loans currently protected but potentially weak.

The other asset category that presents appraisal difficulties, the investment portfolio, is reviewed by bank examiners to ascertain quality, liquidity, and pricing information. The securities that a bank may hold for investment purposes are defined by statute as "marketable obligations . . . in the form of bonds, notes and/or debentures." Data published by rating services, such as Standard & Poor's and Moody's, may be used by examiners to aid in the evaluation of securities quality.

An effect of the asset appraisal standards employed by the supervisory agencies is that banks are discouraged from making loans and purchasing securities likely to be classified as unsuited for the asset portfolio. Thus, in seeking to ensure bank soundness, federal authorities not only limit the scope of investments that banks may make but also help determine which elements of the economy are recipients of bank credit.

CONCLUSION

This chapter has covered a myriad of federal limitations on banking institutions and operations. The limitations range from Glass-Steagall's attempt to maintain a separation between commercial banking and investment banking, to the Bank Protection Act's requirements for the establishment of physical security measures, to the indirect limitations that arise out of supervisory concern for such items as capital adequacy and asset quality. The purpose of the chapter has been to acquaint the reader with the pervasiveness of federal limitations on the business of banking and with the content of the more important limitations. As mentioned at the beginning of the chapter, other limitations are to be found in the chapters on branching, mergers, bank holding companies, and international banking.

NOTES

The wide ranging nature of this chapter precludes reference to one or two items that would cover the entire subject more fully, although current information on many topics can be found in the annual reports of the FDIC and the Federal Reserve and the *Quarterly Journal* of the OCC. These publications also often contain brief descriptions of pending and recently enacted legislation. For those who wish to acquire an in-depth knowledge of a particular type of limitation on banking, the legislative history of the law or laws imposing the limitation can be quite helpful, but legislative history research can be time-consuming. The separation of commercial banking and the securities business has been the subject of many books and articles. Two useful works in this area are "Commercial Banks and Investment Banking" and "Commercial

Banking and the Glass-Steagall Act," research papers prepared in 1976 and 1982, respectively, by Golembe Associates for the American Bankers Association.

Statutory provisions concerning lending limits are given in Table 3. Other relevant statutory provisions are located at the following sections or chapters of Title 12 of the U.S. Code: §24(Seventh) (incidental powers clause of the National Bank Act); §1843(c)(8) (nonbanking provision, §4(c)(8), of the Bank Holding Company Act); Chapters 2, 3, and 6 generally (Banking Act of 1933; for more detailed information on the codification of the 1933 Act, see the note to §227); §§24(Seventh), 377, 378, and 78 (respectively, §§16, 20, 21, and 32 of the Glass-Steagall Act); §335 (application to state member banks of the prohibition in §16 of the Glass-Steagall Act on the underwriting of securities by national banks); §1841(c) (Bank Holding Company Act's definition of a bank); §§3501–3509 (Title II of DIDMCA providing for the phasing out of interest rate ceilings for time and savings deposits); §§371a and 1828(g)(1) (prohibition of payment of interest on demand deposits for member and insured nonmember banks); §1832 (authorization for NOW accounts); §3503(c) (§327 of the Garn-St Germain Act; this section instructed the DIDC to develop an investment vehicle competitive with money market mutual funds); §§3401–3422 (Right to Financial Privacy Act); §1817(j) (Change in Bank Control Act); §§2901–2905 (Community Reinvestment Act); §§1881–1884 (Bank Protection Act); §§51 and 329 (initial capital required for national and state member banks); and §24(Seventh) (definition of permissible investment securities).

The following laws are codified in Title 15 of the U.S. Code: the Securities Act of 1933 at §§77a–77aa; the Securities Exchange Act of 1934 at §§78a–78kk; the Truth-in-Lending Act at §§1601–1667; the Electronic Fund Transfer Act at §§1693–1693r; and the Fair Credit Reporting Act at §§1681–1681t. The provision of the Securities Exchange Act making certain registration and reporting requirements specifically applicable to banks is §78l(i).

7

Enforcement Powers of Federal Supervisory Authorities

An understanding of the nature and extent of enforcement powers available to the federal banking agencies must begin with a review of what the agencies are seeking to achieve. Two of the major objectives of supervision are, first, to ensure that banks conform to the applicable laws and regulations, and second, to maintain standards in the business activities of banks that are deemed by the authorities to constitute safe and sound banking.

Federal banking agencies share the first objective with other governmental bodies, both state and federal. For example, violations of federal criminal statutes are prosecuted by the Justice Department. Crimes in the banking field covered by these statutes include embezzlement or misapplication of funds and the making of false entries or statements by an individual associated with a bank. As another example, trust and investment activities by banks may bring the Securities and Exchange Commission into the picture. In part, the SEC is concerned that investment vehicles offered by banks do not exceed the registration exemptions afforded these institutions in the various securities laws.

The role of the federal banking agencies in ensuring that banks conform to laws may consist of nothing more than referring violations to the appropriate federal or state officials. On the other hand, the banking agencies have been given certain enforcement powers that enable them to handle many violations themselves. The powers may be roughly classified as general or specific. As an example of specific powers, which are concerned with specific statutory provisions, the Comptroller of the Currency may impose a fine of $100 per day for failure by a national bank to make a timely report of condition. The general powers are the more important and pertain to more than one statutory provision. The Financial Institutions Regulatory and Interest Rate Control Act of 1978 (FIRIRCA) significantly expanded the general enforcement powers.

The general enforcement powers are especially applicable to the second supervisory objective, ensuring the safety and soundness of banks. Unlike the first objective, ensuring the safety and soundness of banks is almost wholly within the province of the banking agencies. It is an objective that cannot be easily defined. Much supervisory work comes down to pitting the judgment of the supervisors against that of the bankers over a broad range of matters, such as quality of loans or investments, expansion plans, or the adequacy of capital. In the event of disagreement over these matters, few if any statutes can be relied upon to resolve the differences. For example, if a bank has a larger volume of municipal securities than the supervisors deem wise, or if its capital falls below some standard thought to be appropriate, the supervisors cannot enforce their view by reference to specific statutory criteria. There is no statutory provision stating that a certain volume of municipal securities is too high or that a certain capital ratio is too low.

For many years, the federal banking agencies' enforcement powers were limited to drastic measures, principally charter revocation, FDIC insurance termination, or removal from Federal Reserve membership. Thus, if persuasion could not obtain the result desired by a banking agency, it had to accept the unpalatable situation—at least until an appropriate lever presented itself, such as a branch application by the offending institution—or it had to put the bank out of business. Two laws, the Financial Institutions Supervisory Act of 1966 and FIRIRCA of 1978, have given the banking agencies some intermediate alternatives. These alternatives—the issuance of cease-and-desist orders, the imposition of civil money penalties, and the suspension and removal of directors, officers, and others connected with a banking organization—will be discussed after the powers that enable the agencies to put banks out of business are reviewed.

REVOCATION OF CHARTER

The fundamental power of a bank regulatory agency that is also a chartering agency is to close the bank and revoke its charter when the agency believes that the public's funds are in danger. Even though the power is only used in extreme cases, its mere existence gives immense weight to the findings and recommendations made by the regulatory agency with respect to bank operations.

As the chartering authority pursuant to the National Bank Act, the Comptroller of the Currency almost literally has the power of life and death over individual national banks. A national bank must have the Comptroller's permission before it can be established. If after establishment the examination process reveals shortcomings or weaknesses in a national bank, the Comptroller can order corrections; and if they are not forthcoming, he can institute proceedings to close the institution. Specifically, he may bring suit to dissolve a national bank for violations of the National Bank Act that the bank's directors knowingly commit or permit bank officers or employees to commit. More importantly, he may, upon becoming "satisfied of the insolvency" of a national bank, and without the necessity of court proceedings, appoint a receiver to dissolve the bank. Similar charter revocation powers are found in state banking codes.

TERMINATION OF DEPOSIT INSURANCE

The Federal Reserve and the FDIC are not empowered to revoke charters and close banks. Technically, these two federal agencies must depend upon the chartering agencies—the Comptroller or a state agency—to close banks that persistently violate the canons of sound banking. As a practical matter, however, both the Federal Reserve and the FDIC have powers of a different form that are fully as effective as those of the chartering agencies.

The Federal Reserve has the authority, after a hearing, to remove erring banks from membership in the System. Failure to comply with the applicable provisions of the Federal Reserve Act provides grounds for loss of membership. Loss of deposit insurance protection automatically follows loss of Federal Reserve membership. Admittedly, the bank deprived of membership could apply to the FDIC for insurance as a state nonmember bank, but in such circumstances its prospects for obtaining coverage would appear to be quite dim. Thus the key element of control is the power to terminate deposit insurance with the resultant threat to the bank's survival.

The FDIC may take steps which lead to the termination of

deposit insurance coverage for any insured bank, pursuant to Section 8(a) of the Federal Deposit Insurance Act. This action calls for a finding by the Corporation's Board of Directors that the insured bank: (1) is engaged in unsafe and unsound practices; (2) is in an unsafe and unsound condition; or (3) has violated applicable law—including rules, regulations, and orders, as well as formal agreements and conditions. The power to institute termination-of-deposit-insurance proceedings is applicable to all insured banks—state-chartered or national—and it has been so used by the Corporation. As might be expected, however, the power has been employed most frequently in the supervision of insured state banks that are not members of the Federal Reserve System.

Deposit insurance termination procedure is complicated and likely to be time consuming in most cases. The FDIC is required to give the federal or state chartering authority (and also the Federal Reserve in the case of a state member bank) and the bank a statement designed to obtain correction of the wrongdoing. The statute prescribes a maximum correction time of 120 days. The appropriate agency may set a lesser time limit, but not less than twenty days, in aggravated situations. If the specified corrections are not forthcoming, further proceedings call for a 30-day notice of intention to terminate the insurance status of the bank and the fixing of a time and place for a hearing on the merits of the case. Should the evidence developed at the hearing support appropriate findings regarding violations or unsafe and unsound practices or conditions, the FDIC Board of Directors may order termination of the bank's insured status. In such cases, however, the bank has a statutory right to obtain judicial review of the termination order.

To sum up, since involuntary termination of a bank's insured status will almost certainly result in the closing of the bank, it is tantamount to the power of a chartering agency to revoke a bank's charter. As is the case with charter revocation authority, the mere existence of the FDIC's power—or that of the Federal Reserve to expel a bank from membership with the almost certain loss of deposit insurance—is a significant element in the enforcement of supervisory judgments. On the other hand, because of the consequences the full use of this power is limited to extreme cases.

From the beginning of deposit insurance in 1934 through 1982, one estimate is that 281 actions were instituted by the FDIC to terminate the insurance of an erring bank. In only fifteen cases were orders for the termination of insurance actually issued. Most of the remaining proceedings ended with the banks agreeing to make the corrections demanded by the FDIC, the banks being absorbed by other banks, or the banks ceasing operations prior to the establishment of a date for insurance termination.

DIRECT ENFORCEMENT POWERS

Most supervisory problems—even most of the serious cases—do not justify closing the bank with the attendant deprivation of banking services to the affected community, losses to stockholders, and possible losses to depositors. Nevertheless, up to the middle of the 1960s the only enforcement powers available to the federal bank supervisory authorities contemplated the revocation of the bank charter or the involuntary termination of federal deposit insurance. To provide these supervisors with powers somewhat less drastic than charter revocation or the loss of insured status and yet strong enough to be effective, the Congress enacted the Financial Institutions Supervisory Act of 1966, which gave the banking agencies the power to issue cease-and-desist orders against banks and to suspend and remove officers, directors, and certain other bank-related individuals.

These less drastic enforcement powers were significantly expanded in 1978 in FIRIRCA. Bank holding companies, their nonbank subsidiaries, and Edge and Agreement corporations were added to banks as organizations subject to enforcement powers. The coverage of cease-and-desist orders was extended to include individuals as well as organizations. The imposition of civil money penalties was added as an enforcement weapon. And the removal powers were expanded.

As a result of the 1966 and 1978 acts, the enforcement powers that the banking agencies possess are the issuance of cease-and-desist orders, the imposition of civil money penalties, and the suspension and removal of officers, directors, and other bank-related individuals. In the following discussion of these powers, the term "organization" is used to refer to all the institutions subject to the enforcement powers of a federal banking agency. Depending on the particular statutory provision being considered, the term can refer to insured banks, bank holding companies and their nonbank subsidiaries, Edge and Agreement corporations, and certain foreign banks and companies. The appendix to this chapter depicts in table form the enforcement powers of the federal banking agencies. It should be noted that the Federal Home Loan Bank Board and the National Credit Union Administration have enforcement powers similar to those of the banking agencies.

Cease-and-Desist Powers

The appropriate supervisory agency may issue cease-and-desist orders against actual or threatened violations of laws, rules, regulations, or written conditions or agreements, and against unsafe or unsound practices. The orders may be issued against an organization itself or against a director, officer, employee, agent, or any other person participating in the affairs of the organization. The proceedings start with a notice of charges issued by the supervisory agency and served on the organization or individual. The notice states the nature of the wrongdoing and specifies the time and place for an administrative hearing to determine whether a cease-and-desist order should be issued. The hearing is required to be scheduled for a date not less than 30 nor more than 60 days after service of the notice. If the factual basis for the action is established at the hearing, or if the organization or individual consents to the issuance of a corrective order, the agency may order the organization or individual to stop the wrongdoing and, in appropriate instances, to remedy objectionable conditions. Judicial review of the agency action may be obtained in a federal court of appeals.

A temporary cease-and-desist order, effective from the time of service, may be issued to stop activities determined by a bank supervisory agency as likely to cause insolvency, to cause a substantial dissipation of assets or earnings, to seriously weaken the condition of the organization, or to seriously prejudice the interests of the depositors. Unless set aside by a federal district court, a temporary order remains effective during the proceedings on the permanent order.

Civil Money Penalties

The power of the supervisory agencies to impose civil money penalties was added by FIRIRCA in 1978. The penalties may be imposed on an organization or on officers, directors, employees, agents, or others participating in the affairs of the organization for violations of various banking statutes, or regulations or orders, including cease-and-desist orders, issued pursuant to the statutes. The maximum amount of a penalty in most instances is $1,000 per day for each day a violation continues. Infractions of certain lesser important statutory provisions carry a penalty of only $100 per day. On the other hand, violations of the Change in Bank Control Act can bring a penalty of up to $10,000 per day.

The penalty is assessed by the appropriate banking agency by written notice. In determining the size of the penalty, the agency is supposed to take into account the financial resources and good faith of the organization or individual involved, the gravity of the violation, the history of previous violations, and "such other matters as justice may require." Except for a Change in Bank Control Act violation, an organization or an individual subject to a civil money penalty may obtain a hearing if a request is made within ten days of the assessment of the penalty. An unfavorable hearing decision may be appealed, within ten days of the issuance of the decision, to the appropriate federal court of appeals.

Suspension and Removal Powers

The suspension and removal powers of the supervisory agencies cover directors, officers, and other individuals participating in the affairs of an organization. The powers of a particular agency over persons connected with the organizations it supervises cover not only conduct regarding such organizations but also conduct regarding any other insured bank or any business institution. There are minor variations in the criteria for suspension or removal, depending on whether an individual's relationship with an organization is as a director or an officer or is in some other capacity, and depending on whether the wrongful conduct is in regard to that organization or to some other insured bank or business institution. Suspension and removal powers over directors and officers for conduct regarding organizations in which they hold these positions will serve as a sample of the criteria.

Directors and officers of an organization may be suspended or removed for conduct concerning that organization that is a violation of law, a violation of a cease-and-desist order, an unsafe or unsound practice, or a breach of fiduciary duty. The agency must determine that the organization has suffered or will suffer substantial financial loss, that the interests of the depositors will be seriously prejudiced, or that the director or officer has benefited financially from the wrongdoing. Further, the agency must determine that the wrongdoing involved personal dishonesty or disregard for the safety or soundness of the organization. A hearing is required, and judicial review can be obtained.

A director, officer, or other person participating in the affairs of a bank—but only of a bank and not, unlike in the preceding discussion, of a bank holding company or one of its nonbank subsidiaries or an Edge or Agreement corporation—may also be suspended from office or prohibited from participating in the affairs of the bank if he or she is charged with a felony involving dishonesty or breach of trust. If the charge results in conviction, the banking agency may remove the individual from office or make permanent the prohibition from participating in the bank's affairs. A hearing is not required under this provision, but may be requested by the party concerned. Judicial review is not specifically permitted by statute but probably can be obtained.

Enforcement statistics for the last several years for the three federal banking agencies are given in Table 5.

Other

Mention should also be made of the power of the Federal Reserve Board to require a bank holding company or a nonbank subsidiary to terminate activities. The power can be exercised when the Board determines that continuation of an activity or control of a nonbank subsidiary constitutes a serious risk to the financial safety, soundness, or stability of an affiliated bank and is inconsistent with sound banking principles or the purposes of certain specified statutes.

A bank holding company has the right to notice and opportunity

Table 5: Enforcement Statistics

Final Cease and Desist Orders

	FDIC	FRB	OCC
1982	61	15	16
1981	29	12	21
1980	28	10	28
1979	43	7	9
1978	31	5	14

Civil Money Penalties

	FDIC	FRB	OCC
1982	11	10	24
1981	3	12	21
1980	4	2	8
1979	0	0	3
1978	0	0	0

Removal of Officers

	FDIC	FRB	OCC
1982	2	0	2
1981	0	1	2
1980	3	0	0
1979	2	0	0
1978	0	0	0

Source: Annual reports of the FDIC, the Federal Reserve Board, and the OCC, and the OCC's *Quarterly Journal*.

for hearing before the Board issues a termination order. And judicial review of a final order may be obtained in a federal court of appeals.

SUBTLE ENFORCEMENT POWERS

To remedy the overwhelming majority of the problems revealed by the bank examination process, it is quite unnecessary for the supervisory authorities to use cease-and-desist powers, to impose civil money penalties, to suspend or remove officers or directors, or to take such drastic steps as charter revocation or suspension of insured status. Of course, these measures are available in aggravated cases, but for less serious departures from sound banking practices, other enforcement powers are available to the federal banking agencies to bring about corrections that they consider desirable.

In general, most banking problems revealed through the examination process or in some other fashion are solved simply because reasonable men want solutions. That is, both the banker and the regulator recognize the existence of the problem and generally agree upon its solution. In many instances, such agreed upon solutions are put in writing. Failure of an organization to abide by a written agreement can lead to such an enforcement action as a cease-and-desist order.

If a regulator perceives a problem but the banker and the regulator cannot agree upon a solution and the problem does not warrant formal enforcement action, the regulator may have to rely upon a more subtle method to achieve a desired end. For example, the regulator might "enforce" its judgment as to the amount of capital a bank should have by attaching a requirement for increased capital to the next application that the bank makes to it for, say, the establishment of a branch or the receipt of trust powers. Or a bank that ignores increasingly strong recommendations by the regulator for correction of certain practices might find that it is placed on one of the so-called problem lists. This generally results in more frequent examination and closer surveillance of operations than would ordinarily be the case.

Illustrations of the ways in which the federal agencies can achieve conformity with their recommendations could be multiplied. At the same time, it must be recognized that many bankers resist instituting changes in response to supervisory recommendations over long periods, and occasionally such resistance prevails.

NOTES

The Federal Reserve Board and the FDIC publish enforcement information and data in their annual reports, and the OCC publishes such information in its *Quarterly Journal.*

Relevant statutory provisions are located at the following sections of Title 12 of the U.S. Code: §164 (Comptroller's power to impose fine for failure by national bank to file timely report of condition); §93 (Comptroller's power to bring suit to close national bank because of violation knowingly committed); §191 (Comptroller's power to close national bank because of insolvency); §327 (Federal Reserve's power to remove bank from membership); §1818(o) (loss of Federal Reserve membership automatically results in loss of deposit insurance); §1818(a) (FDIC's power to terminate deposit insurance); §1818(b)(3) (expansion of certain enforcement powers to cover bank holding companies, their nonbank subsidiaries, and Edge and Agreement corporations); §§1818(b)–(c) (cease-and-desist orders); §§93(b), 504, 505, 1817(j)(15), 1818(i)(2), 1847(b), and 1972(2)(F) (civil money penalties); §§1818(e)–(g) (suspension and removal powers); §1818(h) (hearings and judicial review); §1844 (power to terminate activities of bank holding companies and nonbank subsidiaries); §§1464(d), 1730, and 1730a(j) (enforcement powers of the FHLBB and FSLIC); and §1786 (enforcement powers of the NCUA).

In addition, two provisions of Title 18 of the U.S. Code are mentioned in the chapter: §656 (embezzlement or misapplication of funds); and §1005 (false entries).

APPENDIX—CHAPTER 7

This appendix depicts in table form the enforcement powers of the banking agencies. The table originally appeared in the *Legal Times of Washington,* October 25, 1982, and was prepared by John D. Hawke, Jr. The table accompanied an article by Mr. Hawke entitled "Banking Regulators' Clout Increases Dramatically," and is reprinted with the permission of *LTW.*

	Cease-and-desist order (12 U.S.C. §1818(b))	Temporary cease-and-desist order (12 U.S.C. §1818(e))	Removal from office (12 U.S.C. §§1818(e) and (g))	Temporary suspension from office (12 U.S.C. §§1818(e) and (g))	Civil money penalties (12 U.S.C. §§93, 504, 505, 1817(j), 1818(i), 1847, 1972(2)(F))	Termination of activity (12 U.S.C. §1844)
Persons and entities subject to sanctions	insured banks, bank holding companies and nonbank subsidiaries, Edge Act and agreement corporations, foreign banks and companies subject to §8 of the International Banking Act, and directors, officers, employees, and agents, and persons participating in the affairs, of such institutions	same	directors and officers of insured banks, bank holding companies and nonbank subsidiaries, Edge Act and agreement corporations, and persons participating in the affairs of such institutions	same	insured banks, bank holding companies, officers, directors, employees, and agents of, or other persons participating in the affairs of, such institutions, and individuals and companies otherwise subject to various laws noted	bank holding companies and nonbank subsidiaries
Grounds for issuance of order	1. unsafe or unsound practice, *or* 2. violation of law, rule, or regulation, *or* 3. violation of written condition imposed in grant of application, *or* 4. violation of written agreement with agency	where violation or practice that is ground for permanent cease-and-desist order is likely, before completion of proceeding thereon, 1. to cause a. insolvency, *or* b. substantial dissipation of assets or earnings, *or* 2. to seriously weaken condition of institution, *or* 3. to seriously prejudice interests of depositors	A. 1 a. violation of law, rule, regulation, *or* cease-and-desist order, *or* b. participation in unsafe or unsound practice, *or* c. breach of fiduciary duty *and* 2. agency determines that a. institution has suffered or may suffer financial loss or other damage, *or* b. interests of depositors could be seriously prejudiced, *or* c. individual has received financial gain by such conduct *and* 3. violation, practice or breach of duty a. involves personal dishonesty, *or* b. demonstrates willful or continuing disregard for safety or soundness of institution *or*	A. where agency determines suspension to be necessary to protect institution or interests of depositors pending completion of removal proceeding, *or* B[2] 1. where individual is charged with crime involving dishonesty or breach of trust, *and* 2. agency determines that continued service or participation may a. pose threat to interests of depositors, *or* b. threaten to impair public confidence in bank	A. violation of following statutes and regulations thereunder 1. National Bank Act 2. sections 22 and 23A of Federal Reserve Act (insider and affiliate loans) 3. Change in Bank Control Act of 1978 4. section 19 of Federal Reserve Act (reserve requirements and interest rate limits) 5. Bank Holding Company Act of 1956 B. 1. Violation of a temporary or permanent cease-and-desist order	where Federal Reserve Board determines that continuation of activity or control of nonbank subsidiary 1. constitutes a serious risk to financial safety, soundness, or stability of an affiliated bank, *and* 2. is inconsistent with sound backing principles or purposes of FISA or FIRIRCA

	Cease-and-desist order (12 U.S.C. §1818(b))	Temporary cease-and-desist order (12 U.S.C. §1818(c))	Removal from office (12 U.S.C. §§1818(e) and (g))	Temporary suspension from office (12 U.S.C. §§1818(e) and (g))	Civil money penalties (12 U.S.C. §§93, 504, 505, 1817(j), 1818(i), 1847, 1972(2)(F))	Termination of activity (12 U.S.C. §1844)
Grounds for issuance of order (cont.)			B 1 where individual has engaged in conduct with respect to another bank or business a that resulted in substantial financial loss or damage *and* b has evidenced (i) personal dishonesty *or* (ii) willful and continuing disregard for safety and soundness of other firm *and* c has evidenced unfitness to continue in office with or participating in affairs of institution *or* C[1] 1 individual is finally convicted of crime involving dishonesty or breach of trust *and* 2 agency determines that continued service or participation may a pose threat to interests of depositors *or* b threaten to impair public confidence in bank			
Sanction	order requiring respondent 1. to cease and desist from such violation or practice. *and* 2. to take affirmative action to correct conditions resulting from violation or practice	order requiring respondent 1 to cease and desist from such violation or practice. *and* 2. to take affirmative action to prevent such insolvency. dissipation. condition. or prejudice	1 removal from office 2 prohibition from further participation in affairs of the institution	1 suspension from office 2 prohibition from further participation in affairs of the institution	A 1. 2 and 5. and B $1.000 per day A 3 $10.000 per day A 4 $100 per day	order directing termination of activity or termination of control of subsidiary

	Cease-and-desist order (12 U.S.C. §1818(b))	Temporary cease-and-desist order (12 U.S.C. §1818(c))	Removal from office (12 U.S.C. §§1818(e) and (g))	Temporary suspension from office (12 U.S.C. §§1818(e) and (g))	Civil money penalties (12 U.S.C. §§93, 504, 505, 1817(j), 1818(i), 1847, 1972(2)(F))	Termination of activity (12 U.S.C. §1844)
Procedural rights of respondent before agency	right to evidentiary hearing before independent administrative law judge before entry of order	none	A. & B. right to evidentiary hearing before independent administrative law judge before entry of order C. within 30 days after removal. individual convicted of crime may request informal hearing before agency to demonstrate that continued service or participation does not pose threat to depositors or public confidence in bank	A. none B. within 30 days after suspension. individual charged with crime may request informal hearing before agency to demonstrate that continued service or participation does not pose threat to depositors or public confidence in bank	A. 1. 2. 4 and 5. and B right to evidentiary hearing before independent administrative law judge after assessment of penalty A. 3 right to submit data. views and argument informally before assessment of penalty	right to notice and opportunity for hearing before entry of order
Judicial review	direct review of final order in United States court of appeals by petition within 30 days after service of order	action to enjoin order may be brought in United States district court within 10 days after service of order	A. & B. direct review of final order in United States court of appeals by petition within 30 days after service of order C. none specified 1applies only to officers and directors. and persons participating in the affairs. of an insured bank	A. action for stay of suspension or prohibition may be brought in United States district court within 10 days after service of order B. none specified 2applies only to officers and directors. and persons participating in the affairs. of an insured bank	A. 1. 2. 4 and 5. and B direct appeal to United States court of appeals by notice of appeal within 10 days after date of final penalty order A. 3 none specified	direct review of final order in United States court of appeals by petition within 30 days after entry of order

PART IV

The Regulation of Bank Expansion

A public policy objective underlying much of the federal government's interest in the structure of banking is that of guarding against the concentration of banking power in a handful of institutions. This concern was perhaps the major reason for the adoption of a "free banking" system and has since been a factor in such federal moves to shape the structure of the banking industry as federal branching laws, the regulation of bank mergers, and the control of the formation and activities of bank holding companies.

On the other hand, banks are subject to the pressures that are found in any business enterprises to increase in size and profits and to offer a wider range of products and services. A variety of reasons may account for these pressures, including anticipated gains in efficiency, demands from customers, concern over increased competition, or perhaps just entrepreneurial pride. In responding to such pressures, banks must take into account the limitations imposed by the federal government on expansion.

Branching—the opening of additional offices offering a full or partial range of banking services—is discussed in Chapter 8. Historically, the subject has been the source of serious divisiveness within the banking industry, often overlaid with considerable emotion. The result is a bewildering variety of branching laws as the 50 states have opted for widely different banking structures.

Closely related to branching is the subject of bank mergers, discussed in Chapter 9. In expanding through branching, banks usually have the option of opening a new office or acquiring an existing institution. Indeed, in some jurisdictions the only means of establishing a branch is through the acquisition of an already-operating bank. In any event, the large majority of bank mergers result in continuation of the merged institutions as branch offices of the acquiring banks.

Bank mergers have long served as one of the principal exit routes from the banking industry. Thus, as was pointed out in the Introduction to Part II, the discussion of mergers could have been included with the chapters dealing with entry into and exit from the banking industry. It is included here, however, because of the close relationship between mergers and bank expansion.

Chapter 10 deals with the regulation by federal authorities of another vehicle for bank expansion: bank holding companies. In one sense, a bank holding company with two or more bank subsidiaries can be viewed as an alternative to branch banking. To that extent, a holding company's expansion through the opening or acquisition of additional offices (i.e., bank subsidiaries) is subject to many of the same federal rules and standards as discussed in Chapters 3 and 9. Bank holding companies, however, are also a particularly important vehicle for expansion through product diversification. This aspect of bank holding companies, together with some other special features of holding company regulation, justify separate treatment of these banking organizations.

The years since World War II have seen an enormous growth in the international operations of both U.S. and foreign banks. This growth has been facilitated by the establishment by banking organizations of multinational offices, or physical presences outside their home countries. Banking organizations have established foreign branches and agencies, and have established or acquired foreign subsidiary banks. Multinational offices of banking organizations and certain other aspects of international banking are discussed in Chapter 11.

8

Branching

The traditional and still most common form of geographic expansion by banks is branching. It is one of several forms of multi-office banking. Other forms include holding company banking, discussed in Chapter 10, and chain banking. The latter term describes the situation in which two or more banks are owned by an individual or individuals in a personal capacity. This chapter's primary focus is on branching in the United States by U.S. banks. Foreign branching by U.S. banks and branching in the United States by foreign banks are covered in Chapter 11, although this chapter does include a section on Edge corporations, which are organizations that banks may establish to engage in internationally related business.

In the 1981 edition of *Federal Regulation of Banking*, this chapter had a section on branching by mutual savings banks, savings and loan associations, and credit unions. A new chapter, Chapter 12, covering other depository institutions and a number of their characteristics has been added to this, the 1983–84 edition of *Federal Regulation of Banking*. Consequently, the section in this chapter on the branching activities of those institutions has been considerably shortened. So as to contrast the differing branching situations of commercial banks and of other depository institutions, however, the section has not been eliminated entirely.

A branch differs significantly from a unit of a holding company or of a chain in that it is not separately incorporated or capitalized.

Although definitions vary, the most useful for the purposes of this chapter would follow federal law by defining a branch as any office of a bank which receives deposits, pays checks, or makes loans. This broad definition would include what are referred to in some states as limited service facilities or tellers' windows. It would also include several types of electronic banking facilities, principally off-premise automated teller machines (ATMs).

Of the 14,451 insured commercial banks in operation at the end of 1982, only 7,018 operated branch offices. However, the number of banks operating branches has increased markedly over the past two decades; in 1960 there were only 2,386 banks operating more than one office. The number of branch offices has risen even more dramatically. In 1920, when the number of commercial banks reached an all-time high of approximately 30,000, there were only 1,281 branches. By the end of World War II the number of banks had declined to 13,302 but the number of branches had risen to 3,896. In 1963 the number of bank branches exceeded main offices for the first time. Today, the number of branches far exceeds the number of banks; as of December 31, 1982, the total number of banking offices in the United States was 54,235, consisting of 14,451 insured commercial banks with 39,784 branches.

Most branches are formed *de novo;* that is, through the establishment of a new office by the parent bank. However, each year a significant number of branches are formed out of merged institutions. During the year ending December 31, 1982, some 1,394 branches of insured commercial banks were established *de novo;* another 252 were the result of merged banks and their branches being converted to branch offices of the acquiring banks.

BACKGROUND

While branching was to be found early in the development of the American banking system, it did not become a political issue until about the end of the nineteenth century, when the philosophic lines began to harden between the advocates of branching and the proponents of unit banking. The federal government was bound to become intimately involved in this issue, since to the extent that its chartered institutions—national banks—were permitted to branch, state law would almost certainly be forced to conform. However, it was held in 1911 in a ruling of the Attorney General that branching was not a power contained in the National Bank Act.

Various Comptrollers of the Currency in the early decades of the present century urged legislation that would permit national banks to branch, at least to the extent that such privilege was granted state-chartered banks. These efforts finally resulted in passage of the McFadden Act of 1927, which permitted national banks to establish full-service branches within the cities in which they were located, if state banks possessed similar authority. That act introduced a basic principle, namely, that national bank branching privileges would not be greater than those of state banks. It did not, however, give national banks equal branching privileges in those states where state banks had the authority to branch outside of their home office cities.

Although the McFadden Act represented a minor victory for branching advocates, it is probably more correctly viewed as an anti-branching statute. It preserved the unit banking characteristics of much of the nation's banking structure, albeit making some concessions to national banks operating in states that did in fact permit branching. For several years following passage of the McFadden Act, unit banking was reinforced as a number of states, fearful of possible future expansion of national banks through branching, enacted anti-branching statutes. However, with the closing of thousands of banks and the loss of banking services by many small communities during the depression years 1929–33, there was a revival of attempts to expand the branching privilege.

During the five years ending with 1935, 15 states, for the purpose of expanding branching authority, revised their branch laws or enacted such legislation for the first time. Also during this time, national banks obtained wider branching privileges in the Banking Act of 1933, which placed them on a par with state banks with respect to branching within each state.

Resolution of the branching issue in the 1933 legislation, at least so far as federal-state responsibilities were concerned, had two significant consequences. First, it established state boundaries as the ultimate limits for the geographic expansion of full service brick and mortar banking facilities through branching. There were certain "grandfathered" exceptions, such as branches already operated by the Bank of California in Oregon and Washington, but in essence a state boundary was accorded special significance for branching purposes. Second, the federal government in effect turned over to the states the responsibility for deciding what kind of branch banking structure each might have.

As shown in Chart 7, somewhat over one-third of the states currently permit banks to branch statewide. However, in some cases this authority is more apparent than real; under so-called home office protection statutes, branching may be permitted in cities or counties other than that in which the bank is located only if

Chart 7: State Branching Laws as of June 30, 1983

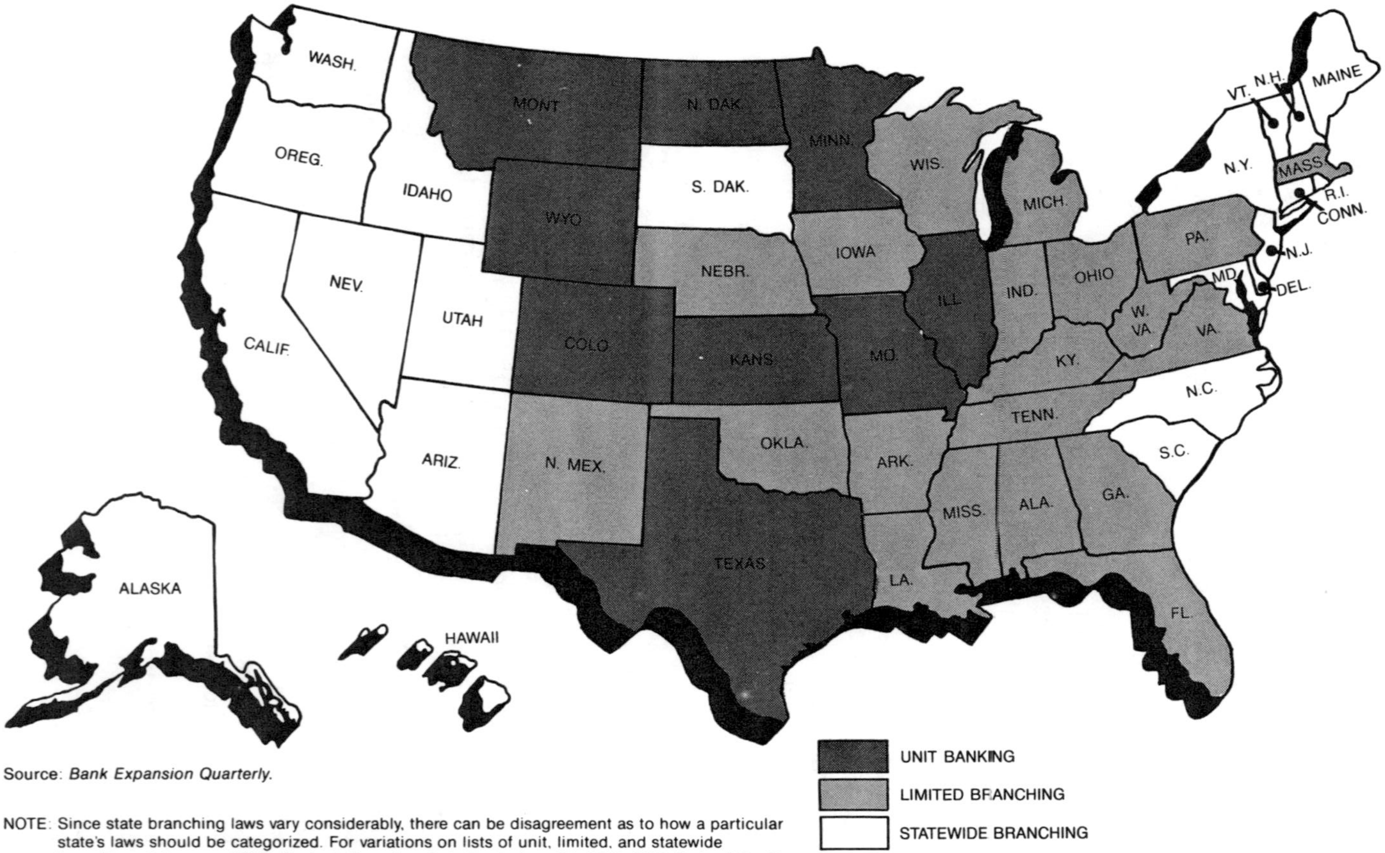

Source: *Bank Expansion Quarterly.*

NOTE: Since state branching laws vary considerably, there can be disagreement as to how a particular state's laws should be categorized. For variations on lists of unit, limited, and statewide branching states, see: FDIC, *Banks & Branches Data Book*, June 30, 1982; CCH, *Federal Banking Law Reporter*, para. 3106; and American Bankers Association, *State Banking Law Service*, Chapter 4, Branching.

there is no head office (or sometimes any office) of another bank.

A slightly smaller group of states permit branching only within specified geographic areas, usually the home office city or county, or within a group of counties. Again, home office protection statutes are found in some limited area branching states, thus further narrowing the branching privilege.

The remaining states prohibit or severely restrict branching, and these are usually characterized as unit banking states. Even here, however, the lines cannot be strictly drawn, since many of the unit banking states permit each bank to have one or several limited service facilities.

BRICK AND MORTAR BRANCHES

The term "brick and mortar branch" is a shorthand way of describing a traditional bank branch that is manned by people. The contrast to a brick and mortar branch is an electronic banking facility, which is discussed in the following section.

National Banks

The Comptroller of the Currency has standard procedures with respect to branch applications by national banks. The application is made by the bank on a prescribed form; there is public notification and an opportunity for interested parties to be heard as well as an examination or other investigation; finally a decision on the particular application is reached by the appropriate official in the Comptroller's office.

Limitations on the ability of the Comptroller to permit branching for national banks arise out of the McFadden Act, which imposes a tie-in with state statutes. The extent of such limitations has generated a series of controversies, particularly since 1960. Indeed, the law in this area is still evolving in a number of respects.

Certain provisions typically found in state law are not applicable to national banks. An example would be the usual requirement that the state supervisor pass on applications by state banks to branch. This kind of provision does not apply to national banks since it would, in effect, give to the state supervisory authorities a veto power over branches of national banks.

On the other hand, state limitations which rather clearly relate to national banks are those having to do with branch locations and capital. As pointed out earlier, states permitting branch banking frequently confine branching by state-chartered banks to specific geographic areas, such as cities, counties, contiguous counties, or regions. Some states permit practically no branching. Whatever the geographic branching situation in a particular state, national banks in the state are subject to it. With respect to capital, if a state has minimum capital requirements for out-of-town branches, such requirements must also apply to national bank branches similarly situated.

In between these two clear-cut situations are several controversial areas, most of which involve the definition of the term "branch." Whether a facility or an office of a national bank is a branch is determined by applying the standards of federal, and not state, law. Once such facility or office falls within the definition of a branch, however, it becomes subject to state branching limitations. As pointed out at the beginning of this chapter, the federal definition of a branch is broad and includes any office of a bank that receives deposits, pays checks, or makes loans. Under this definition, federal courts have found that various types of electronic banking facilities are branches. These facilities are discussed at greater detail in the next section.

Another type of facility or office that has raised the branch definition issue is the loan production office (LPO). These offices solicit or otherwise originate loans but do not actually "make" loans. Such activities as the completion of paperwork or the disbursing of funds constitute the "making" of a loan and are performed at the location of the LPO's parent bank or one of its branches. In 1979, a federal district court ruled that national bank LPOs established under a Comptroller's ruling were branches, but the decision was overturned on appeal. Thus, national bank LPOs currently fall outside the definition of bank branches, and their establishment, either in a bank's home state or in another state, is not restricted by federal law. The 1981 White House McFadden Act Study, *Geographic Restrictions on Commercial Banking In The United States*, contained an estimate that at least 350 LPOs were operating in 20 states.

State law may also place certain limitations on the authority or procedures of the Comptroller of the Currency. If a state law requires a finding of need for a new branch, the requirement may be binding on the Comptroller. For example, in a 1971 North Carolina case, a federal court held that the Comptroller was bound by North Carolina's "need and convenience" and "solvency of the branch" criteria.

State Banks

The basic regulatory authority over state bank branching is exercised by the bank regulatory agency in each of the states. As might be expected, there is wide variance concerning requirements which must be met by state-chartered banks and the procedures which are followed by regulatory authorities. For the purposes of this discussion, we are concerned only with the nature of the federal government's authority in this field.

All state banks with deposits insured by the FDIC are subject to federal government control over branching. For state banks that are members of the Federal Reserve System, the Federal Reserve Act requires that the approval of the Board of Governors "shall be obtained before any State member bank may hereafter establish any branch. . . ." State-chartered banks which are not members of the Federal Reserve System but which are insured are subject to the Federal Deposit Insurance Act provision that no bank shall "establish and operate any new domestic branch unless it shall have the prior written consent of the Corporation. . . ." The FDIC statute goes on to state that in granting or withholding its consent, the Corporation shall consider the factors set forth for approval of a newly organized bank, which include the financial history and condition of the bank, capital adequacy, earnings prospects, the general character of management, and the convenience and needs of the community.

In essence, therefore, the federal government's regulatory authority over domestic branch expansion is complete with respect to all banks with deposits insured by the FDIC—which means, in effect, virtually all commercial banks and a substantial portion of the mutual savings banks. Concerning state-chartered banks, the Federal Reserve and the FDIC have what amounts to a veto power over the action of state authorities in authorizing branches. As a practical matter, this veto is rarely exercised since the federal and state agencies generally work closely with each other with respect to branch applications and would not under ordinary circumstances differ in their assessment of the merits of a branch application from a state-chartered bank.

ELECTRONIC BANKING FACILITIES

Electronic funds transfer (EFT) technology is significantly altering the manner in which banking services are provided. Bank customers can now receive a number of banking services through electronic terminals that do not have to be located at a bank or at one of its brick and mortar branches. These services include making deposits, obtaining cash withdrawals, transferring funds between savings and checking accounts, making balance inquiries, and making loan payments.

Electronic banking facilities come in a variety of forms with varying capabilities. The terminology in this rapidly developing area can be bewildering to the uninitiated. Four terms frequently encountered are customer-bank communications terminal (CBCT), automated teller machine (ATM), electronic funds transfer (EFT) system or terminal, and point-of-sale (POS) terminal. CBCT is the term in the Comptroller's regulation pertaining to the application procedure for establishing remote—that is, not on a bank's premises—electronic banking facilities. ATM is a term of general usage applied to electronic terminals that perform one or more of the functions, such as dispensing cash or accepting deposits, traditionally performed by human tellers. An ATM may or may not be connected to a computer system and may be on or off the premises of a depository institution.

EFT is also a term of general usage. Applied to a system, it describes a computerized network that processes financial transactions or information about financial transactions. EFT terminals are parts of such networks. POS terminals are communication and data capturing devices located where goods or services are purchased. They may serve the accounting and inventory needs of a merchant, and they may operate as part of a financial transactions processing system. For example, a cashier through a POS terminal may be able to verify the status of a customer's credit card or actually debit the customer's bank account and credit the store's account for the price of a purchase.

The courts and the regulators have struggled with an obvious question of federal law presented by electronic banking facilities: are such facilities bank branches and thus subject to federal branching limitations? The question has generally been answered in the affirmative for bank-owned facilities that appear to perform one or more of the functions of receiving deposits, paying checks, or making loans. One of the most notable court decisions was rendered in 1976 by the U.S. Court of Appeals, District of Columbia, in *Independent Bankers Association of America v. Smith*, 534 F2d 921. In that decision, the court struck down a Comptroller's regulation providing that CBCTs did not constitute branches within the meaning of the McFadden Act. The court stated that any facility performing

the traditional bank functions of receiving or disbursing funds is a "branch" of a national bank . . . if (1) the facility is established (i.e., owned or rented) by the national bank, and (2) it offers the bank's customers a convenience that gives the bank a competitive advantage over other banks (national or state) that do not operate similar facilities.

Although the general issue of whether CBCTs are branches has thus been resolved, a number of related issues exist. One that received considerable attention for a time arose from the fact that many states have laws permitting the wider establishment of electronic terminals than of brick and mortar facilities. The extent to which national banks may make use of more liberal electronic terminal limitations in a state that imposes different limitations on different types of facilities was for a while unclear. The consensus now seems to be, however, that national banks can fully use these more liberal state provisions concerning electronic terminal facilities.

A second, and more far-reaching, issue concerns the growing use of shared facilities, even across state lines. The holding in *IBAA v. Smith* was limited to facilities "established (i.e., owned or rented) by" a bank. The implication of this limitation is that facilities not owned or rented by a bank but available to the bank's customers on a transaction fee basis—the fee being paid by either the bank or the customers—are not branches of that particular bank. Relying on this reasoning, both the Comptroller of the Currency and the FDIC have taken the position that an application for an electronic branch need not be made by a bank if the terminal is not owned or leased by the bank but merely utilized by the bank's customers. Thus, banks may establish an electronic terminal network in which terminals owned by one bank are available to the other banks in the network on a transaction fee basis. A large number of such multi-institution EFT networks have come into existence, a number of which involve institutions in more than one state and several of which are nationwide in scope.

A number of commentators and high level commissions have argued that electronic banking facilities should be subject to less stringent branching requirements than brick and mortar branches. For example, the 1981 White House McFadden Act Study recommended that as part of the first phase of a liberalization of interstate banking restrictions, EFT terminals for all banking services, including deposit taking, should be permitted on a statewide basis and within Standard Metropolitan Statistical Areas ("SMSAs") which cross state lines. The study further recommended that this initial phase be followed by terminal deployment on a nationwide basis.

OTHER DEPOSITORY INSTITUTIONS

Other depository institutions are not subject to federal branching restrictions as pervasive as those applicable to commercial banks. The major institutions other than commercial banks that offer federally insured deposits are savings banks, savings and loan associations, and credit unions. Chapter 12 deals in general with these other depository institutions. A few comments concerning their branching activities are appropriate here, however.

State-chartered mutual savings banks have long been eligible for deposit insurance from the FDIC. Such banks that obtain FDIC insurance become subject to many of the same statutory and regulatory provisions that govern state-chartered FDIC-insured commercial banks. As in the case of state-chartered commercial banks—and national banks as a result of the McFadden Act's tie-in to state statutes—the states establish the branching criteria for state-chartered mutual savings banks.

State-chartered mutual savings banks are found mostly in the northeastern part of the country. At the end of 1982, there were 315 federally insured state-chartered mutual savings banks in existence. These 315 banks had a total of 2,418 branches. The number of state-chartered mutual savings banks that were not federally insured at the end of 1982 was 103. These had 248 branches. The number of state-chartered mutual savings banks has not changed much in the last decade, but the number of branches has increased substantially. In 1970, there were 328 federally insured state-chartered mutual savings banks, with 894 branches. Thus there has been a 171 percent increase in branches but a fractional decrease in banks.

Federally chartered mutual savings banks were first authorized in 1978 by the Financial Institutions Regulatory and Interest Rate Control Act (FIRIRCA). Until late 1982, they could only be created by the conversion of existing state-chartered mutual savings banks. Conversion was subject to the approval of the Federal Home Loan Bank Board, and the converted banks had their deposits insured by the Federal Savings and Loan Insurance Corporation. Only six federally chartered mutual savings banks were in existence at the end of 1982.

Prior to the passage of the Garn-St Germain Act in late 1982, federally chartered mutual savings banks had a slight advantage regarding branching. Such an institution was not subject to state numerical limitations on the number of branches and could, with the approval of the FHLBB, establish offices in its own Standard Metropolitan Statistical Area, its own county, or anywhere in its home state within 35 miles of its home office. This rather contrived situation became a footnote to banking history with the passage of the Garn-St Germain Act.

This act expanded the way in which federal savings banks can come into being by authorizing the establishment of new, or *de novo,* institutions. Moreover, federal savings banks can now be in stock as well as mutual form. The act deleted the branching provision described in the preceding paragraph, thus placing federal savings banks in the same branching situation as federally chartered savings and loan associations. This situation currently is that these federally chartered thrift institutions may branch statewide, regardless of state law.

Prior to the Garn-St Germain Act, federal statutory law was silent regarding branching by federally chartered thrifts. In the past, the FHLBB generally allowed federal S&Ls to branch within 100 miles of their home offices unless state policy was more permissive or unless the state prohibited branching by all major depository institutions. If either of these situations existed, the FHLBB attempted to follow state policy. Since January 1, 1980, however, the FHLBB has permitted statewide branching by federally chartered S&Ls in all states regardless of state policy. Since federally chartered savings banks are now joined for most statutory and regulatory purposes with federally chartered S&Ls, the former, as noted in the preceding paragraph, can also branch statewide. In May of 1983, the FHLBB published for comment a proposal to allow interstate mergers, acquisitions, and establishment of branches by federal S&Ls and savings banks where state law specifically permits entry by out-of-state institutions. The Garn-St Germain Act of 1982 confirmed the FHLBB's power to regulate interstate branching by federal institutions subject to its jurisdiction.

In March of 1981, the FHLBB announced a policy of allowing interstate S&L mergers and acquisitions in certain supervisory cases, which are cases involving troubled or failed institutions. This policy has resulted in a number of significant interstate S&L organizations. Approximately 20 interstate S&L transactions were approved by the FHLBB from March of 1981 to May of 1983.

In addition to confirming the FHLBB's general power over interstate branching by federal S&Ls and savings banks, the Garn-St Germain Act gave this regulator the specific power to allow interstate mergers and acquisitions in situations involving failed thrift institutions. Regarding federally chartered thrift institutions, the new power was little more than what the FHLBB had been doing on its own since March of 1981. Regarding state-chartered institutions, however, the new authority was an increase in the powers of the FHLBB. Previously, that agency had little voice regarding the branching—either intrastate or interstate—of state-chartered thrift institutions, whether solvent or failing.

The number of S&L branches has increased sharply since 1970. At the end of that year, there were 4,654 federally insured S&Ls with 8,498 branches. As of September 30, 1982, the number of S&Ls had decreased 27 percent to 3,420, but the number of branches had increased 113 percent to 18,060.

As in the case of federally chartered S&Ls prior to the Garn-St Germain Act, federal statutory law is silent as to the branching of credit unions. Historically, this silence has been interpreted both by the National Credit Union Administration and by the courts as meaning there are no geographic restrictions on federal credit union branching. Both the agency and the courts have also held that any state laws regarding credit union branching (either intrastate or interstate) cannot be applied to federally chartered credit unions. The logic behind this is that credit unions are organized by common bond, either of occupation or association, and consequently need no added restrictions based on geography. As a result, a number of federal credit unions operate nationwide, while several operate literally around the globe, with offices in many foreign nations.

EDGE ACT CORPORATIONS

Edge Act Corporations are authorized by Section 25(a) of the Federal Reserve Act. They are federally chartered institutions whose purpose is to engage in international banking activities. Chapter 11 covers international banking, and Edges and their powers are included in that discussion. Edges also deserve mention in the present chapter, however, because they provide a means for banks to establish out-of-state branches, although for international banking purposes only.

There are two basic types of Edges: banking Edges and investment Edges. The major function of the latter is to acquire or invest in overseas activities that are permitted by the Federal Reserve Board. Since their major activities are overseas operations, investment Edges have little need for a significant domestic presence and are usually colocated with their parent bank.

Banking Edges, however, are concerned with the financing of international trade and the handling of international banking transactions. They accept deposits and make loans, and geographic location is a factor in their ability to carry out their functions. Non-

New York City banks have established Edges in that city to clear international transactions and to have a presence in one of the world's financial centers. Such international trade centers as Miami, Houston, Chicago, Los Angeles, and San Francisco have attracted banks interested in financing international trade.

In the International Banking Act of 1978, Congress instructed the Federal Reserve Board to modify its regulations concerning Edges to increase their competitiveness, to make them more accessible to regional and small banks, and to eliminate any discriminatory provisions concerning foreign banks in Edge matters. A major modification made by the Board in response to Congress' mandate was to permit branching by Edge corporations. Previously, each Edge office had to be separately chartered with a capitalization of $2 million. A number of banks have taken advantage of the branching option. As of December 31, 1982, there were 78 banking Edges with a total of 103 domestic branches.

NOTES

Data on branching are contained in the annual reports of the FDIC and the Federal Reserve Board and the OCC's *Quarterly Journal*. The FDIC's *Annual Report* is particularly useful. A recent discussion of the branching question is the *Geographic Restrictions On Commercial Banking In The United States: The Report of the President* (U.S. Treasury Department, 1981).

Relevant statutory provisions are located at the following sections of Title 12 of the U.S. Code: §36 (branching by national banks; the principal provision of what is referred to as the McFadden Act); §321 (applies the branching restrictions on national banks to state member banks and gives the Federal Reserve the approval authority for branching by state member banks); §1828(d) (gives the FDIC the approval authority for branching by state nonmember insured banks); §1464(a) (chartering of federal savings banks and S&Ls); §1464(r) (interstate branching by federal savings banks and S&Ls); §1730a(m) (power of FHLBB to allow interstate mergers and acquisitions in situations involving failed thrifts); and §§611–631 (Edge Act corporations).

9

Bank Mergers

Although the large majority of branches opened each year consists of *de novo* offices, expansion via the merger route, when a feasible alternative, has distinct advantages to the bank seeking to extend the reach of its activities. One of the most important advantages is the simple fact that the price of the acquisition is definite. Moreover, the location of the merged bank has been tested as a place of business, customers are actually using the facility, and the operating record furnishes as solid a basis as can be obtained for estimating the market potential in the area.

When an expansion-minded bank contemplates the alternative of establishing a completely new branch office, the business problem is much more complex. Then the prospective location is untested, a nucleus of business has not been assembled, and the data for estimating market potential cannot be based on the records of a "going concern." All of these elements have a bearing upon the cost a bank is willing to incur for a new establishment, and the process of estimation cannot be expected to yield results as precise as the acquisition cost figure in a merger case.

Because one effect of a merger is to give the surviving institution additional offices, the ability to merge is partly dependent on state branching laws. Data on mergers bear this out. For example, in 1982, by one count, the federal regulatory agencies approved merger applications from 239 domestic banks. Of these, 85 were located in statewide branching states, 144 were located in states

Table 6: Merger Applications Received by the FDIC, the OCC, and the Federal Reserve Board during 1981–82

	1981	1982
Alabama	6	8
Alaska	2	—
Arizona	2	—
Arkansas	—	3
California	9	8
Colorado	—	—
Connecticut	6	10
Delaware	1	1
District of Columbia	—	—
Florida	22	36
Georgia	10	14
Hawaii	—	1
Idaho	—	—
Illinois	2	3
Indiana	1	6
Iowa	4	8
Kansas	—	—
Kentucky	—	7
Louisiana	—	—
Maine	7	6
Maryland	4	1
Massachusetts	4	6
Michigan	—	2
Minnesota	2	5
Mississippi	5	5
Missouri	2	1
Montana	—	—
Nebraska	—	—
Nevada	—	1
New Hampshire	4	4
New Jersey	17	20
New Mexico	—	—
New York	14	11
North Carolina	7	4
North Dakota	—	—
Ohio	6	11
Oklahoma	—	—
Oregon	2	2
Pennsylvania	6	7
Rhode Island	—	—
South Carolina	2	8
South Dakota	—	—
Tennessee	3	1
Texas	—	1
Utah	4	5
Vermont	—	—
Virginia	9	15
Washington	3	3
West Virginia	—	8
Wisconsin	—	7
Wyoming	—	—
Total	**166**	**239**

Note: The table gives only the approximate number of applications received. It does not give the number acted on by the regulators.

Source: *Banking Expansion Reporter*, February 1, 1982, and April 18, 1983.

permitting limited branching, and only 10 were located in unit banking states. Table 6 gives a state-by-state breakdown of bank merger applications received by the three federal banking agencies for 1981–82.

The federal government plays an extremely important role in the regulation of expansion through bank mergers. There is a specific federal statute relating to mergers, and both the Department of Justice and the banking agencies have a hand in its enforcement.

BACKGROUND

As bank mergers are now so closely regulated, it often comes as something of a surprise to find that this regulation is a relatively new development. Before 1960, the major Congressional interest in bank mergers was to make certain that the resulting institution was, in terms of capital, at least as strong as the two independent institutions had been prior to the merger. In the case of a merger that might have resulted in less capital in the combined institution than the sum of the capital in the two institutions, any questions raised by the banking agencies were usually quickly answered by adjusting the terms of the merger agreement.

So far as the antitrust laws were concerned, it did not appear that they applied in any significant fashion to bank mergers. (Pertinent sections of the antitrust laws are set out in an appendix to this chapter.) Whether the Sherman Act applied at all was occasionally debated, but the question was considered of no particular importance or relevance in an industry where the major problem for many years prior to 1960 had been thought to be one of too many banks rather than too few. The Celler-Kefauver Act of 1950 amended the original Section 7 of the Clayton Act (1914) to include within its purview asset acquisitions (which also happened to be the usual form of a bank merger), but the wording of the amendment was thought to exclude bank mergers.

During the 1950s, however, there was growing uneasiness, both in and out of Congress, over the apparent exemption of bank mergers from significant antitrust review. The number of such mergers began to increase, with several involving banks of particularly large size. The uneasiness culminated in the Bank Merger Act of 1960.

Initially, that act was viewed as a victory by the three federal banking agencies over the Department of Justice, which had been seeking to persuade Congress to further amend the Clayton Act to cover bank mergers. The 1960 legislation did not contain a single reference to the antitrust laws; moreover, the Department of Justice received only advisory responsibilities concerning the competitive aspects of bank mergers. The banking agencies themselves were to weigh the competitive and banking factors and, it was thought, would exercise the final judgment on mergers.

This view of the Bank Merger Act of 1960 had a short life. In 1963, in a landmark decision involving the merger of two Philadelphia banks, *U.S. v. Philadelphia National Bank*, 374 U.S. 321, the Supreme Court held that the Clayton Act did, after all, apply to bank mergers. As one of the dissenting Justices put it, the passage of the 1960 Act "turns out to have been an exorbitant waste of congressional time and energy."

The decision quickly gave rise to attempts by the banking industry, and to some extent by the banking agencies, to alter its results. One bill that was introduced in Congress would have specifically lodged all authority in the banking agencies and exempted bank mergers from the Sherman and Clayton Acts. When legislation finally emerged in 1966, however, authority was divided between the banking agencies and the Department of Justice, and much of the language tracked the two antitrust statutes.

The key provision of the Bank Merger Act of 1966 specifies that the appropriate banking agency must decide whether a bank merger might substantially lessen competition. If so, the merger shall not be approved unless the agency "finds that the anticompetitive effects of the proposed transaction are clearly outweighed in the public interest by the probable effect of the transaction in meeting the convenience and needs of the community to be served." As under the 1960 Act, the agency handling the case is required to seek the opinions of the other banking agencies and the Department of Justice on the competitive factors. If, after approval by the agency, the Department of Justice nevertheless desires to bring antitrust action, it must take this step within 30 days of the agency's approval or be forever barred, except as to Section 2 of the Sherman Act (the section which prohibits monopoly or attempts to monopolize). In any judicial determination of an antitrust action, the courts must apply the same standards as the banking agencies; that is, the courts cannot consider the competitive issue to the exclusion of the public's needs and convenience.

MERGER PROCEDURES

The primary exit route from banking in all but extraordinary years is the merger route. For the period 1976 through 1982, the average number of insured banks per year that ceased operations as a result of absorptions, consolidations, or mergers was 194.

Under the Bank Merger Act of 1966, jurisdiction over a bank merger belongs to the federal banking agency that would regularly supervise the resulting bank. Thus if the resulting bank would be a national bank, the agency responsible for passing on the merger is the Comptroller of the Currency; if a state-chartered member bank, the Federal Reserve Board; and if a state nonmember bank, the FDIC. In the rare situation where the acquired institution is a noninsured bank or other type of institution, the FDIC is the responsible agency.

Application to absorb or merge with another bank is made by the acquiring bank to the responsible federal banking agency on forms that call for information on the competitive and public interest factors, as well as for information of the kind required for ordinary regulatory purposes. Opinions on the competitive factors are asked of the other two banking agencies and the Department of Justice. If the merger is approved by the banking agency, it may not be consummated, except in emergency situations, for 30 days. It is during this period that the Department of Justice may seek to bring action under the antitrust laws; if it fails to do so, the merger "may not thereafter be attacked in any judicial proceeding on the ground that it alone and of itself constituted a violation of any antitrust laws other than [Section 2 of the Sherman Act.]" Of course, the resulting bank must comply with all antitrust laws in the future.

BANK HOLDING COMPANY ACQUISITIONS

The Bank Holding Company Act was also amended in 1966 to apply virtually the same criteria to acquisitions of banks by bank holding companies and to mergers between bank holding companies as the 1966 Bank Merger Act applies to bank mergers. Thus, an application by a bank holding company to acquire an additional bank or to merge with another holding company must be rejected if it is anticompetitive unless the anticompetitive feature is offset by a sufficient showing of advantages to be gained by the public. An important difference between bank mergers and bank holding company mergers and acquisitions, however, is that only the Federal Reserve Board has approval authority concerning holding company transactions. Therefore, regardless of whether a bank to be acquired by a holding company is a national bank, a state member bank, or a state nonmember bank, the approving authority is the Board. As in the case of bank mergers, the Department of Justice has a 30-day period in which to decide whether or not to attack bank holding company mergers and acquisitions in court.

It should be noted, however, that a bank holding company may acquire another bank without Federal Reserve approval if the holding company elects to have a subsidiary bank which is a national or a nonmember bank acquire the additional bank directly, that is, through merger. In such a case the Comptroller or the FDIC would be the responsible agency, as called for in the Bank Merger Act. Such a step is only feasible, however, where the acquired bank can be continued as a branch. The ability of bank holding companies to avoid applying to the Federal Reserve in these kinds of cases has occasionally been questioned, but seems now to be firmly established. Thus, a bank holding company seeking to acquire a bank may engage in a certain amount of "forum shopping." There has even been at least one instance where a holding company had an application to acquire a bank disapproved by the Federal Reserve, restructured the acquisition as a merger between a subsidiary bank and the bank to be acquired, and had the restructured transaction approved by another agency.

THE STATE OF THE LAW

It is difficult to summarize the law with respect to bank mergers or bank holding company mergers and acquisitions because it is still evolving. Since (1) the Supreme Court's decision of 1963 that the Clayton Act's merger provisions apply to banks and (2) Congress' final statutory determination in 1966, each of the banking agencies, the Department of Justice, and the courts have been developing approaches to the subject. Moreover, in recent years, banks and bank holding companies have been less reluctant to seek court review of adverse agency opinions, thus allowing the courts still additional opportunity to participate in the evolving legal and administrative framework.

An area in which there was broad agreement until fairly recently concerns direct competition. Bank mergers, or bank holding company acquisitions, involving two banks in the same service area generally were not permitted to take place. Unless the institutions involved had extremely small market shares, or the bank to be acquired was in serious financial difficulties, favorable public interest factors usually were not found to outweigh the loss of direct competition. Guidelines updated by the Department of Justice in 1982 relating to mergers in general give some indication of the unfavorable attitude toward mergers between direct competitors, commonly called horizontal mergers. According to these guidelines, in a market which is moderately concentrated, an acquiring bank with only 7 percent of the market should usually not be able to acquire another bank unless the latter's market share is less than 7 percent. The guidelines were first published in 1968, and although not being law themselves, are commonly used to judge the competitive aspects of mergers and acquisitions.

Although bank mergers between direct competitors have by no means become easy to bring about, there does seem to have been a relaxation in some quarters in the standards by which such transactions are judged. The Comptroller of the Currency in particular appears willing to countenance horizontal combinations if the evidence indicates that competition in the relevant geographic market will not be reduced.

Parenthetically, a term in the aforementioned Department of Justice's 1982 update of its merger guidelines deserves mention because it has rapidly become commonplace in the banking world. That term is the Herfindahl-Hirschman Index ("HHI"). This is a way of measuring market concentration. Table 7 describes how the HHI is calculated. The other common way of measuring market concentration is by the amount of a market's deposits controlled by the top few firms in the market. For example, a four-firm concentration ratio would be the percentage of the market controlled by the four firms holding the largest share of deposits.

Unlike the area of direct competition where until recently there seemed to be general agreement as to what was and what was not

Table 7: Computing the Herfindahl-Hirschman Index

The Herfindahl-Hirschman Index is computed by adding together the squares of the market shares of a market's participants. For example, if there are six firms in a market, and the market shares of the firms are 30 percent, 25 percent, 20 percent, 15 percent, 5 percent, and 5 percent, the HHI would be computed as follows:

$$30^2 + 25^2 + 20^2 + 15^2 + 2(5^2) = 2200$$

As another example, if a market consists of 14 firms with market shares of 60 percent, 8 percent, 7 percent, 5 percent, and 10 firms with 2 percent each, the HHI would be computed as follows:

$$60^2 + 8^2 + 7^2 + 5^2 + 10(2^2) = 3778$$

When evaluated based on the HHI, the second market is much more highly concentrated than the first market. The three-firm concentration ratio of both markets, however, is the same, 75 percent. That is, the top three firms in each market hold 75 percent of the market's deposits.

acceptable, there are other areas that have long been characterized by disagreement. These areas concern geographic markets, line of commerce, potential competition, and bigness *per se*. The dispute over geographic markets revolves around whether standard geographic areas, such as cities, counties, and SMSAs, are the appropriate areas within which to judge the competitive effects of transactions, or whether the service areas of the institutions involved must be individually determined. The courts have generally opted for the latter approach, requiring that the geographic markets in horizontal competition cases be where the banks are in direct and immediate competition. The bank regulator that has most often accepted this approach is the OCC, and the regulator that has accepted it the least is the Federal Reserve Board.

Line of commerce refers to what institutions are viewed as competing with banks and to what products and services, or combinations thereof, are to be the focus of attention. While one might suppose that competitive effects of transactions would be analyzed on the basis of each of the services offered—commercial loans or savings deposits, for example—the Supreme Court in the *Philadelphia* decision held that commercial banking itself was a distinct line of commerce, in that the "cluster" of services provided by commercial banks is unique. Strictly interpreted, the rule requires that in computing market shares, only commercial banks be taken into consideration even though the market may contain thrift or other financial institutions which compete vigorously with commercial banks. This stance has not been altered, although in a more recent case (in 1974, involving two Connecticut banks) the Court noted the possibility that at some point other financial institutions might offer meaningful competition to banks.

In the view of several lower courts and the banking regulators, this point has been reached. The development of new financial instruments and services by nonbank organizations and legislation expanding the banking powers of thrift institutions have led courts and the regulators, particularly the OCC and the FDIC, to consider competition from other sources when judging bank mergers and acquisitions. It would seem to be only a matter of time before the Supreme Court is called upon to review the approach of the *Philadelphia* decision.

The issue of potential competition arises in situations in which the banking organizations are located in different geographic markets and the market to be entered is highly concentrated, that is, where several organizations hold a very high percentage of the market's deposits. Two theories concerning potential competition have developed.

The first concerns the possibility that the organization seeking to enter a highly concentrated market already influences the actions of banks actually in the market in that the latter price their products and adjust their services to prevent the market from appearing too attractive. If the feared entrant, previously exercising its influence merely by "waiting in the wings" as it were, actually enters the market through an acquisition of one of the larger market participants, the incentive for the banks in the market to act in a procompetitive manner is reduced. Procompetitive effects would more likely be maintained, the "wings" theory continues, if the organization seeking to enter does so by opening a *de novo* office or by acquiring one of the smaller participants in the market.

In the second theory, often called the probable future competition theory, the organization outside the market exerts no present competitive effect, as in the "wings" theory. The argument, however, is that the organization might in the future enhance competition and contribute to deconcentration in the market by opening a *de novo* office or by acquiring a smaller market participant. This possibility would be eliminated if the organization were allowed to acquire one of the larger market participants.

The bank regulatory agencies, the Department of Justice, and the courts have been wrestling for some time with the proper legal scope and the evidentiary requirements of potential competition theories. In general, the courts and the Comptroller of the Currency have been hesitant to engage in much speculation in this area. On the other hand, the Department of Justice and the Federal Reserve Board have in a number of cases in the past found a possible loss of potential competition and consequently concluded that a merger or an acquisition should not take place. These two bodies, however, have never been successful in asserting potential competition theories in the courts in bank merger and acquisition cases. Following two significant judicial setbacks in 1981, the Board backed off considerably from potential competition theories. Under guidelines it proposed in 1982 and has generally followed in analyzing mergers and acquisitions, only a very few transactions raise potential competition concerns.

A logical companion of the potential competition theory, at least to some theoreticians, is the contention that bigness *per se*—size itself—is bad. The Federal Reserve Board showed the most interest in this idea in the past by habitually discussing, in decisions on mergers and acquisitions, the effect on statewide banking structure. Concern about statewide concentration has not been as much in evidence in recent Board decisions, and bigness *per se*, like the potential competition theory, has not found favor in the courts.

NOTES

Bank merger decisions by the FDIC and the Federal Reserve Board are reported in their annual reports. The Board also publishes decisions in the *Federal Reserve Bulletin*. The OCC's merger decisions are reported in its *Quarterly Journal*. A thorough treatment of the development of banking antitrust law is contained in Douglas V. Austin's "The Evolution of Commercial Bank Merger Antitrust Law," *Business Lawyer* 36 (January 1981): 297. A 1980 evaluation of the concept of commercial banking as a distinct line of commerce is contained in *Commercial Banking as a Line of Commerce,* a study prepared by Golembe Associates, Inc., for the Association of Bank Holding Companies.

Several relevant statutory provisions are set out in the appendix to this chapter. The Bank Merger Act is located at §1828(c) of Title 12 of the U.S. Code. Procedural provisions concerning conversions, consolidations, and mergers by national banks are located at §§214-215b of Title 12. Bank holding company mergers and acquisitions are covered by §1842 of Title 12.

APPENDIX—CHAPTER 9

Section 1 of the Sherman Act of 1890, as amended, 15 U.S.C. §1 (in part):

> Every contract, combination in the form of trust or otherwise, or conspiracy, in restraint of trade or commerce among the several States, or with foreign nations, is declared to be illegal.

Section 2 of the Sherman Act of 1890, as amended, 15 U.S.C. §2 (in part):

> Every person who shall monopolize, or attempt to monopolize, or combine or conspire with any other person or persons, to monopolize any part of the trade or commerce among the several States, or with foreign nations, shall be deemed guilty of a felony.

Section 7 of the Clayton Act of 1914, as amended by, *inter alia*, the Celler-Kefauver Act of 1950, 15 U.S.C. §18 (in part):

> No person engaged in commerce or in any activity affecting commerce shall acquire, directly or indirectly, the whole or any part of the stock or other share capital and no person subject to the jurisdiction of the Federal Trade Commission shall acquire

the whole or any part of the assets of another person engaged also in commerce or in any activity affecting commerce, where in any line of commerce or in any activity affecting commerce in any section of the country, the effect of such acquisition may be substantially to lessen competition, or to tend to create a monopoly.

Bank Merger Act of 1966, 12 U.S.C. §1828(c) (in part):

(5) The responsible agency shall not approve—

(A) any proposed merger transaction which would result in a monopoly, or which would be in furtherance of any combination or conspiracy to monopolize or to attempt to monopolize the business of banking in any part of the United States, or

(B) any other proposed merger transaction whose effect in any section of the country may be substantially to lessen competition, or to tend to create a monopoly, or which in any other manner would be in restraint of trade, unless it finds that the anticompetitive effects of the proposed transaction are clearly outweighed in the public interest by the probable effect of the transaction in meeting the convenience and needs of the community to be served.

In every case, the responsible agency shall take into consideration the financial and managerial resources and future prospects of the existing and proposed institutions, and the convenience and needs of the community to be served.

U.S. v. Philadelphia National Bank, 374 U.S. 321, 356 (1963):

We agree with the District Court that the cluster of products (various kinds of credit) and services (such as checking accounts and trust administration) denoted by the term "commercial banking" . . . composes a distinct line of commerce.

10

Bank Holding Companies

Until the late 1960s, bank holding companies were simply another form of multi-office banking, and except for brief periods during the 1920s and the early 1950s, a relatively quiet form at that. In the years since the late 1960s, however, bank holding companies have emerged as a most significant element in both geographic and product expansion by banks and, as might be expected, have become subject to a considerable measure of government control.

As of December 31, 1982, there were 4,557 bank holding companies. These had 6,659 bank subsidiaries with consolidated assets of $1,861 billion, or 85 percent of all commercial bank consolidated assets. Twelve companies, five of which were foreign controlled, operated in more than one state as a result of being grandfathered under the 1956 Bank Holding Company Act. As noted later in the chapter, recent changes in state laws have permitted a number of other bank holding companies to commence interstate banking operations.

BACKGROUND

The date at which companies first began to acquire bank stock and exercise control over those institutions cannot be established with precision. Early in the nation's history it usually was not possible under state corporation laws for one corporation to own stock in another. This limitation, however, began to ease by the end of the nineteenth century, and by the 1920s bank holding companies had acquired some significance. Some measure of federal control over bank holding companies was provided in the Banking Act of 1933. For example, those companies owning banks that were members of the Federal Reserve System had to register with the Federal Reserve Board in order to vote their stock interests in affiliated banks.

During the depressed years of the 1930s and into the 1940s, bank holding companies grew at about the same rate as the banking industry as a whole and did not attract any special attention. In the early 1950s, however, the activities of a few large holding companies caused concerns about the concentration of banking resources and about the control of banking and nonbanking businesses by a single entity. The concerns culminated in passage of the Bank Holding Company Act of 1956, which remains today as the basic federal regulatory measure affecting bank holding companies. The principal purposes of the 1956 Act were to define bank holding companies, to control their formation and expansion, and to require divestment of their nonbanking interests.

The Board of Governors of the Federal Reserve System was made the sole regulatory authority for bank holding companies at the federal level—an action that represented a departure from the traditional division of bank regulatory authority among the three banking agencies. Holding companies subject to regulation by the Board, and therefore required to register, were defined as those which owned or controlled two or more banks, with ownership or control of 25 percent or more of the voting shares of a bank serving as the principal criterion for determining control.

For about a decade after passage of the 1956 Act, the number of bank holding companies and their relative position in the banking industry remained virtually unchanged. In 1956, for example, there were 47 companies registered with the Board of Governors, holding 5.7 percent of the banking offices in the nation and 7.6 percent of total deposits. By 1965 the number of companies had increased only by one, to 48, and there had been only small changes in the proportion of banking offices and of total deposits in the registered companies (6.6 percent and 8.3 percent respectively.)

Although the 1956 Act contained a variety of exemptions from federal regulation of bank holding companies, the most significant was the exemption of companies owning only one bank. In 1965 there were an estimated 548 such companies, with more than $13 billion in deposits in their affiliated banks.

By the middle 1960s, expansionary pressures on banks had

reached a point where important structural changes in the industry were inevitable. After World War II the American economy had entered a period of remarkable economic growth, characterized by only minor recessions and giving rise to ever larger and more complex demands upon commercial banks. Technological change was bringing increasingly heavy capital costs to banks but, at the same time, bringing the prospects of significant economies of scale. Competitor depository institutions were pushing vigorously into areas previously reserved for commercial banks, while commercial banks had begun an aggressive solicitation of savings and time money that was rapidly changing the composition of commercial bank liabilities. And all of this was taking place within a set of laws and regulatory attitudes that had been constructed during the depression of the 1930s and that were essentially hostile to bank expansion.

The first indication that something quite significant was likely to occur in the banking structure and in the nature of banking powers had appeared early in the 1960s when major banks across the country began to desert the state banking system and convert to national charters. It was during this time that the Comptroller of the Currency was moving vigorously to give national banks greater operational freedom and was interpreting provisions of the National Bank Act in a liberal and expansionary manner. By the middle of the decade, however, conversions from state to national charter became less attractive. The Comptroller's liberal policies regarding the activities of national banks were being largely nullified by court actions instituted on the part of those industries that felt themselves threatened by the movement of banks into new product and service areas.

In the mid-1960s the organization of a one-bank holding company appeared to be a way of avoiding suits that had been brought against national banks or the Comptroller of the Currency for the purpose of limiting the nonbank activities of such banks. One-bank holding companies were exempt from federal regulation. In addition, so far as the offering of new banking-type services was concerned, it appeared possible to avoid difficulties that might arise under state banking laws. For example, a one-bank holding company might be able to open a finance company at a location where if the holding company were a bank it could not open a branch. The finance company could perform the banking function of making loans. The movement in the 1960s by banks to the one-bank holding company organization form began about 1967 and reached a peak in 1968–1969.

Some one-bank holding companies were organized for the purpose of expansion and some were organized, primarily by smaller institutions, to obtain certain tax advantages. It appears that from 1967 through 1969 approximately 120 major banks organized one-bank holding companies for the purpose of being able to expand more rapidly than was possible under their national or state bank charters. Although the number of banks involved was less than one percent of all commercial banks, their deposits were approximately $125 billion, accounting at the time for roughly one-third of all commercial bank deposits.

Given the magnitude of this structural change, together with indications that the organization of one-bank holding companies would continue at a rapid clip, it was inevitable that Congress would be asked to extend the scope of the 1956 Act to one-bank companies. Such legislation had been proposed several times prior to 1969, but on those earlier occasions one-bank holding companies were comprised mainly of small and usually rural banks. By 1969 there was clearly a new situation.

Congress quickly agreed to extend federal control to one-bank holding companies. But the major issue with which it wrestled for the better part of two years, 1969–70, concerned the extension of bank holding company activities to areas related to banking. In the legislation that finally emerged from the Congress and was signed into law by the President on the last day of 1970 (the Bank Holding Company Act Amendments of 1970), the issue was resolved by giving the Federal Reserve Board authority for interpreting a revised and expanded Section 4(c)(8). This was the section of the 1956 Act authorizing a bank holding company to own the shares of organizations engaged in certain nonbanking activities.

In the course of reaching the decision in 1970 to expand Section 4(c)(8), the Congress rejected efforts to divide the regulatory authority among the three federal banking agencies. Also rejected were attempts to spell out in the statute specific activities deemed not to be properly part of the banking business and therefore not permissible for bank holding companies. Instead, the amended Section 4(c)(8) permitted bank holding companies to hold:

shares of any company the activities of which the Board after due notice and opportunity for hearing has determined (by order or regulation) to be so closely related to banking or managing or controlling banks as to be a proper incident thereto. In determining whether a particular activity is a proper incident to banking or managing or controlling banks the Board shall consider whether its performance by an affiliate of a holding company can reasonably be expected to produce benefits to the public, such as greater conve-

nience, increased competition, or gains in efficiency, that outweigh possible adverse effects, such as undue concentration of resources, decreased or unfair competition, conflicts of interest, or unsound banking practices. In orders and regulations under this subsection the Board may differentiate between activities commenced de novo *and activities commenced by the acquisition, in whole or in part, of a going concern; . . . .*

This was still in 1983 the language of a portion of Section 4(c)(8). The Congress, however, had retreated somewhat from the principle of not setting forth specific prohibited activities. In the Garn-St Germain Act of 1982, Section 4(c)(8) was amended to prohibit, with several exceptions, bank holding companies from participating in the insurance business. Whether this response to the entreaties of a powerful lobbying group will remain a unique situation or will be the precursor of other restrictions on bank holding company activities remains to be seen.

In addition to the significant change made in the portion of the 1956 Act relating to the permissible nonbanking activities of bank holding companies, the 1970 amendments were important in another regard. The extension of federal regulation to one-bank companies meant that there was no longer any advantage for such companies to have only one bank as a subsidiary. Since federal regulation after 1970 applied to all bank holding companies, there was no reason for the one-bank companies—assuming state law permitted—to refrain from acquiring additional banks.

GEOGRAPHIC EXPANSION

A bank holding company is one of several forms of multi-office banking. Often it is thought of as an alternative to branching, but there are significant differences. The banking "offices" of bank holding companies are separately chartered and capitalized banks, and their branches. These banks have their own boards of directors, and they distribute earnings to their stockholders, which in some instances include other owners in addition to the parent company.

In addition to bank subsidiaries, a holding company may have other subsidiaries, to the extent permitted by federal laws and regulations. This situation is not unique to bank holding companies; national banks and most state banks may have wholly owned operating subsidiaries that engage in those kinds of businesses which the banks themselves might engage in directly. Bank holding companies, however, would seem to have somewhat greater freedom to conduct banking-related businesses through subsidiaries. Moreover, unlike operating subsidiaries of banks, the nonbank subsidiaries of bank holding companies are not constrained by branching laws. Thus, the geographic expansion of bank holding companies may take the form of additional banking offices or of offices of permissible nonbanking firms. Each subject is considered in the following discussion.

Bank Subsidiaries

Although the Bank Holding Company Act provides for the federal regulation of bank holding companies, the states still have a good deal of concurrent jurisdiction over these entities. Moreover, each state has a right to prohibit bank holding companies entirely or to limit their operations. One form of limiting statute is a "cap" law. Such a law puts an upper limit on the percentage of a state's banking operations, usually determined by reference to some measure of bank deposits, that any single bank holding company may control. Chart 8 classifies state bank holding company laws.

From 1956 until recently, federal law had the effect, as in the case of branching, of restricting to state lines bank holding company expansion through bank establishments and acquisitions. The 1956 Act provides, in Section 3(d), called the Douglas Amendment, that the Federal Reserve Board may not approve an application by a bank holding company to acquire any voting shares of, interest in, or all or substantially all of the assets of any bank located outside of the holding company's home state,

unless the acquisition of such shares or assets of a State bank by an out-of-State bank holding company is specifically authorized by the statute laws of the State in which such bank is located, by language to that effect and not merely by implication.

Prior to 1980, the preceding language was of little import. Almost no action had been taken by any of the states that would have allowed banking operations to be conducted within their borders by out-of-state bank holding companies. Since that time, however, state activity has picked up considerably. As of May, 1983, no less than fifteen states had laws allowing banking operations to be conducted by out-of-state bank holding companies. These laws fall into five categories.

First, three states—Florida, Iowa, and Illinois—permit out-of-state bank holding companies with grandfathered in-state operations to expand such operations. This category is the least significant since it directly benefits only those out-of-state holding com-

Chart 8: State Bank Holding Company Laws as of June 30, 1983

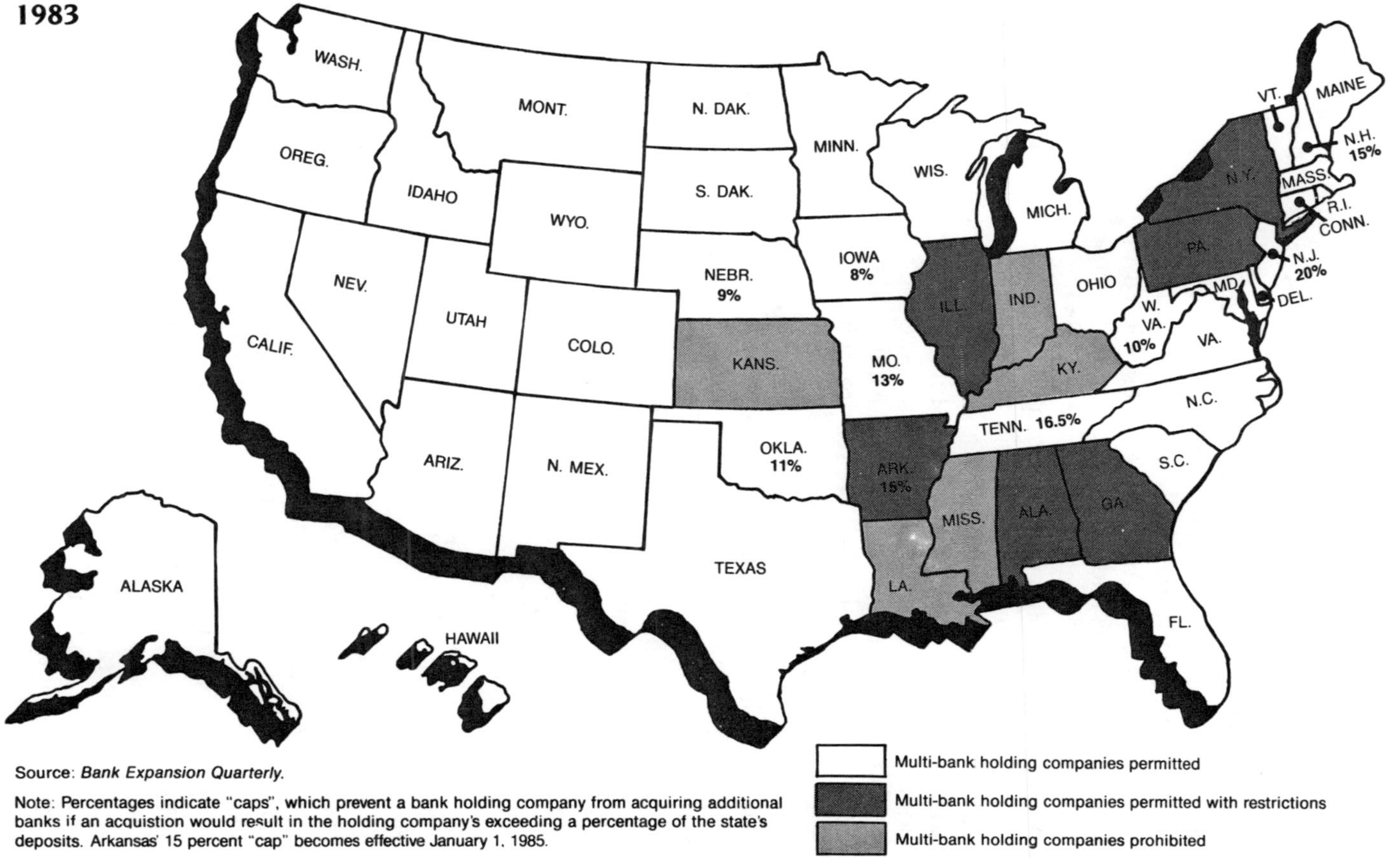

Source: *Bank Expansion Quarterly.*

Note: Percentages indicate "caps", which prevent a bank holding company from acquiring additional banks if an acquistion would result in the holding company's exceeding a percentage of the state's deposits. Arkansas' 15 percent "cap" becomes effective January 1, 1985.

panies fortunate enough to have had in-state banking operations as of the grandfather date set forth in the particular state's law. Three bank holding companies are able to make acquisitions under the Florida law, one under the Iowa law, and one under the Illinois law.

Second, five states—Delaware, Maryland, Nebraska, South Dakota and Virginia—permit out-of-state holding companies to establish limited purpose in-state banks. The limited purposes include such functions as credit card operations and correspondent banking. Activities that are generally not permitted are those falling in the retail banking area. As of May, 1983, eleven out-of-state bank holding companies had established limited purpose banks in Delaware, and one had established such a bank in South Dakota. In the spring of 1983, South Dakota amended its banking code to allow state-chartered banks to engage in the insurance business and to permit banks so engaged to be acquired by out-of-state holding companies. Several out-of-state holding companies quickly announced interest in this possible route into the insurance field.

Third, five states—Connecticut, Maine, Massachusetts, New York, and Rhode Island—have reciprocal interstate banking laws. Reciprocity means that these states will allow out-of-state bank holding companies to conduct banking operations within their borders if the holding companies' home states also have such laws. The Connecticut, Massachusetts, and Rhode Island laws only extend reciprocity to other New England states, although the New England limitation in Rhode Island's law expires in 1986. As of May, 1983, state and federal regulatory approvals had been given for the acquisition of one Maine bank holding company by a New York bank holding company.

Fourth, one state—Washington—passed a law in the spring of 1983 authorizing the state banking superintendent to permit an out-of-state banking organization to acquire an in-state banking organization in danger of closing, failing, or insolvency. The purpose of the law was to permit a particular troubled Washington bank holding company, Seafirst Corporation, to receive out-of-state aid. California's BankAmerica was the acquiring organization.

Finally, one state—Alaska—allows out-of-state bank holding companies to acquire in-state banks to the same extent, with one exception, as in-state bank holding companies are able to do. There is no reciprocity requirement regarding the law of the out-of-state organization's home state. The only exception is that the in-state bank must have been in existence for at least three years.

The proliferation of state laws permitting out-of-state banking organizations to establish or acquire in-state banks has not been the only area of interstate banking activity in recent years. The Douglas

Amendment's interstate restrictions only apply to voting shares and are not triggered until control of five percent or more of such shares are acquired. A number of bank holding companies have acquired nonvoting shares or less than five percent of the voting shares of out-of-state banking organizations, thus making interstate banking investments falling outside the scope of the Douglas Amendment.

The Garn-St Germain Act made one small dent in the Douglas Amendment's interstate banking restrictions. Whenever an insured bank with total assets of $500 million or more is closed, the FDIC, as receiver, may arrange for the sale of its assets to and the assumption of its liabilities by an insured depository institution located in the same state but established by an out-of-state bank or bank holding company. The FDIC can authorize such a transaction only if an appropriate in-state acquisition partner is not available. As of May, 1983, no interstate acquisitions had taken place under this provision, which in any event expires in 1985.

It was pointed out in Chapter 9 that the basic antitrust provisions of the 1966 Bank Merger Act were added by amendment in the same year to the Bank Holding Company Act. The primary antitrust provision directs the Federal Reserve Board to disapprove bank holding company formations, bank acquisitions by bank holding companies, and mergers between bank holding companies,

> *whose effect in any section of the country may be substantially to lessen competition, or to tend to create a monopoly, or which in any other manner would be in restraint of trade, unless it finds that the anticompetitive effects of the proposed transaction are clearly outweighed in the public interest by the probable effect of the transaction in meeting the convenience and needs of the community to be served.*

Also added to the Bank Holding Company Act in 1966 were the provisions limiting the time within which the Department of Justice could institute antitrust action against a transaction approved by the Federal Reserve. As in the case of a bank merger, Justice has 30 days after approval to bring suit or be forever barred from doing so with respect to that particular transaction. The only exception is that Justice retains the authority to bring action at any time under Section 2 of the Sherman Act. This section prohibits the establishment of a monopoly.

Chapter 9 contained a discussion of the state of the law regarding bank mergers, including a brief review of the principal subjects that are currently in issue: direct competition, geographic markets, line of commerce, potential competition, and bigness *per se*. That dis-

Table 8: Bank Holding Company Acquisition Applications Received by the Federal Reserve Board during 1981–82

	1981	1982
Alabama	5	11
Alaska	—	—
Arizona	—	—
Arkansas	—	1
California	7	2
Colorado	3	11
Connecticut	1	2
Delaware	1	—
District of Columbia	—	—
Florida	22	24
Georgia	10	9
Hawaii	—	—
Idaho	—	—
Illinois	7	42
Indiana	—	1
Iowa	11	15
Kansas	2	19
Kentucky	—	—
Louisiana	1	—
Maine	—	1
Maryland	4	1
Massachusetts	5	5
Michigan	17	7
Minnesota	4	5
Mississippi	—	—
Missouri	19	20
Montana	4	2
Nebraska	2	9
Nevada	—	—
New Hampshire	3	1
New Jersey	4	2
New Mexico	3	2
New York	4	1
North Carolina	—	1
North Dakota	2	1
Ohio	10	16
Oklahoma	1	—
Oregon	2	—
Pennsylvania	—	5
Rhode Island	—	1
South Carolina	1	—
South Dakota	3	3
Tennessee	2	9
Texas	76	73
Utah	3	1
Vermont	1	1
Virginia	2	6
Washington	—	1
West Virginia	—	—
Wisconsin	9	11
Wyoming	1	4
Total	**252**	**326**

Note: The table gives only the approximate number of applications received. It does not give the number acted on by the Federal Reserve Board.

Source: *Banking Expansion Reporter*, February 1, 1982, and April 18, 1983.

cussion is equally relevant to bank holding company acquisition and merger activity. Indeed, a number of the important court cases in the banking antitrust field have involved holding companies. Therefore, Chapter 9 should be referred to for further discussion on the antitrust problems surrounding the expansion of banking activities by bank holding companies. Table 8 gives a state-by-state breakdown of bank holding company merger and acquisition applications received by the Federal Reserve Board for 1981–82.

Nonbank Activities

Historically, geographic expansion of banking organizations was usually considered in the context of the acquisition or establishment of additional banking offices. The Bank Holding Company Act Amendments of 1970, however, made the provision of services over a broad geographic area by nonbank subsidiaries of bank holding companies an equally important expansion method.

In announcing the initial set of activities permissible under the amended Section 4(c)(8) in 1971, the Federal Reserve Board made the following comment:

The regulation as proposed does not limit the location at which permissible activities may be conducted to any state or other geographical area. Such limitations might be imposed by regulation or by order in particular cases.

Thus the Board at the initial stage of the development of the current Section 4(c)(8) removed nonbank activities from the interstate restrictions applicable to the banking activities of bank holding companies. The effect was to enable bank holding companies to conduct a wide range of business across state lines. The effect was also to increase competition, in that a holding company entering a market distant from its home base brings additional competition to that market with respect to the activity concerned.

Some states have not looked favorably upon the so-called nonbank activities conducted within their boundaries by out-of-state bank holding companies, particularly since many of the activities are almost indistinguishable from banking. In 1980, those opposing the expansion of bank holding company nonbank activities across state lines won a small victory when Congress imposed a moratorium, which expired in 1981, on the establishment or acquisition of trust companies by out-of-state bank holding companies. On the other hand, the ability of a state itself to discriminate against out-of-state holding companies was dealt a blow in 1980 in *Lewis v. BT Investment Managers, Inc.*, 447 U.S. 27. In that decision, the U.S.

Supreme Court struck down a Florida statute that prevented out-of-state bank holding companies from establishing investment advisory businesses in Florida. In-state holding companies could establish such businesses, and the Court could perceive no legitimate reason to allow the state to treat out-of-state organizations in a manner different than it treated in-state organizations.

Of the applications made to the Board by holding companies under Section 4(c)(8), a good many involve activities to be conducted out-of-state. During the fourth quarter of 1982, for example, 53 percent of all applications or notifications involved out-of-state activities.

PRODUCT EXPANSION

As the reader should have discerned by now, the principal legal provision regarding the nonbanking activities of bank holding companies is Section 4(c)(8) of the Bank Holding Company Act. This section does not provide the only means for the expansion of a banking organization's nonbank activities, however. After first discussing Section 4(c)(8), this portion of the chapter will mention a few of the other nonbanking expansion possibilities.

Section 4(c)(8)

One of the most important aspects of the Bank Holding Company Act Amendments of 1970 was the fact that the federal government, through the Board of Governors of the Federal Reserve System, injected itself in a significant fashion into determining the scope of the banking business. With the exception of the Banking Act of 1933, which separated the banking business from certain aspects of the securities business, there is no comparable situation to be found earlier in American banking development. This power of the Federal Reserve Board to determine the scope of the banking business arises from Section 4(c)(8) of the Bank Holding Company Act. Under that section, the Board determines for bank holding companies those activities that are (1) closely related to banking and (2) a proper incident thereto. The closely related test is often presented as requiring the proposed activity to meet one of the following criteria:

1. Banks generally have in fact provided the proposed services.
2. Banks generally provide services that are operationally or functionally so similar to the proposed services as to equip them particularly well to provide the proposed services.

3. Banks generally provide services that are so integrally related to the proposed services as to require their provision in a specialized form. (*National Courier Association v. Board of Governors*, 516 F2d 1229 (D.C. Cir. 1975).)

The proper incident test is set forth in Section 4(c)(8) itself, which was quoted earlier, and requires a finding that benefits to the public, such as greater convenience, increased competition, or gains in efficiency, resulting from the holding company's performance of the activity must outweigh possible adverse effects, such as undue concentration of resources, decreased or unfair competition, conflicts of interest, or unsound banking practices. The proper incident test is usually, though not always, applied to the particular factual situation presented in an application by a bank holding company. That is, the test is most often an individualized one, used to decide whether approval of a specific application will be beneficial to the public. The closely related test, on the other hand, is usually limited to a determination as to whether a proposed activity should be permissible for bank holding companies in general.

Bank holding companies may engage in bank-related activities either through the acquisition of an existing firm or on a *de novo* basis. The latter method rarely poses anticompetitive problems and thus presents less danger of failing the proper incident test, an event that usually occurs because adverse competitive effects are not found to be outweighed by public benefits. Partly because of this absence of competitive problems, applications to engage in previously approved activities on a *de novo* basis have generally been handled at the Reserve Bank level. In May of 1983, the Federal Reserve Board proposed, among other things, a substantial easing of the procedures a bank holding company must follow in certain cases in which it seeks to open new offices to engage in a Section 4(c)(8) activity. The cases are when the expansion is limited to states where the bank holding company has previously received permission to engage in that particular activity.

Since 1970, the Federal Reserve Board has ruled—by regulation or interpretation or in individual decisions—on the permissibility of a number of activities under Section 4(c)(8). Undoubtedly, the lists of those activities that are permissible and those that are not will continue to grow. Activities that had been ruled on by the Board as of May 31, 1983, are listed in the appendix to this chapter. In the proposals of May 1983 mentioned in the preceding paragraph, the Board suggested a relaxation of the procedures under which it considers applications to add activities to the list of activities that bank holding companies may engage in.

The product expansion of bank holding companies under Section 4(c)(8) has not gone unchallenged. Trade associations in such fields as data processing and insurance have fought strenuously any intrusions by the banking industry into their respective areas of interest. The battles have been waged in both the judicial and legislative forums.

In the judicial forum, those opposing bank holding company expansion enjoyed until a few years ago a fair amount of success, at least to the extent of tying up expansion efforts in lengthly litigation proceedings. This was particularly true concerning insurance activities. A 1981 Supreme Court decision, however, may signal a change in this situation. In *Board of Governors v. Investment Company Institute*, 450 U.S. 46, discussed in Chapter 6, the Court, in upholding a Federal Reserve Board regulation permitting bank holding companies to sponsor closed-end investment companies, indicated that the Board has a great deal of leeway in determining the range of permissible nonbank activities for bank holding companies.

In the legislative forum, the anti-expansion forces have had a bit more success. In 1980, they obtained from Congress an eighteen-month moratorium on the establishment or acquisition by bank holding companies of out-of-state trust companies. And in 1982, they won, as part of the Garn-St Germain Act, restrictions on the insurance activities of bank holding companies.

Other Nonbank Expansion Methods

Section 4(c)(8) is only one of a number of provisions in Section 4, the nonbanking section, of the Bank Holding Company Act. Most of the other nonbanking activities permitted in Section 4 are rather limited in scope, although they should be examined closely by bank holding companies investigating expansion alternatives. What may turn out to be a significant exception, however, was added by the Export Trading Company Act of 1982. Title II of that act permits bank holding companies to own the shares of export trading companies. These are organizations whose purpose is to facilitate the exportation of U.S. goods and services. Letting bank holding companies own or control such organizations certainly blurs the distinction that is often considered to exist between commerce and trade on one hand and banking on the other. It is too soon to discern the nature and extent of bank holding company involvement in export trading activities, and consequently to predict the changes that might result in the financial industry from this involvement.

The extensive list of so called "nonbank" activities that bank holding companies may engage in can be misleading. Many of these activities are not really "nonbank" because banks themselves may engage in them. They are perhaps classified as "nonbank" because their financial intermediary aspects are not predominant. But the fact that banks themselves conduct many "nonbank" activities should not be overlooked.

The Comptroller of the Currency has at times had national banks ahead of bank holding companies in the provision of nonbank services. For example, in 1982, the OCC permitted national banks to conduct both futures commission merchant and discount brokerage activities before the Federal Reserve Board permitted bank holding companies to do so. The national banks established or acquired subsidiaries to conduct the activities. OCC regulations permit national banks to engage through operating subsidiaries in any activities that the banks themselves can engage in.

Thus a bank holding company may not only engage in nonbank activities directly or through a nonbank subsidiary, primarily a Section 4(c)(8) subsidiary. It may also engage in nonbank activities through a subsidiary bank. And for certain activities, the subsidiary bank's regulator, whether it be the OCC in the case of a national bank or a state authority in the case of a state-chartered bank, may be more permissive. At least a few state banking codes permit banks to engage in a comparatively wide range of activities. The recently enacted South Dakota law, mentioned earlier in the chapter, permitting banks to participate in the insurance business is an example.

NOTES

One of the earliest and still relevant authoritative works on the history of bank holding companies is Gerald C. Fischer's *Bank Holding Companies* (New York: Columbia University Press, 1961). A more recent Federal Reserve Staff study reviewed many aspects of the holding company movement: *The Bank Holding Company Movement to 1978: A Compendium* (1978). Pauline B. Heller's *Handbook of Federal Bank Holding Company Law* (New York: Law Journal Press, 1976) is a comprehensive review of, as its title suggests, bank holding company law. The Association of Bank Holding Companies, 730 Fifteenth Street, N.W., Washington, D.C. 20005, makes available a variety of studies and reports on bank holding companies. The Association also publishes the highly useful *Bank Holding Companies: A Compilation of State Laws*.

The Bank Holding Company Act is codified at 12 U.S.C. §§1841-1850. Specific sections referred to in the text are:

§1843(c)(8) (the nonbank activity provision, Section 4(c)(8), which includes the insurance restrictions added by the Garn-St Germain Act); §1842(d) (the Douglas Amendment's interstate restrictions on bank holding company expansion); §1846 (reservation of rights to the states); §1842(c) (antitrust provisions); §1849(b) (requirement that Department of Justice act within thirty days in order to contest Board approval of an application); §1843 (overall nonbanking section of the Bank Holding Company Act); and §1843(c)(14) (authorization for bank holding companies to own export trading companies).

APPENDIX—CHAPTER 10

ACTIVITIES PERMITTED AS "CLOSELY RELATED TO BANKING" UNDER §4(C)(8) OF THE BANK HOLDING COMPANY ACT

By Regulation

1. Making or acquiring loans or other extensions of credit for own account or account of others, such as would be made by mortgage, finance, credit card, or factoring companies [§225.4(a)(1); 57 FRB 512 (June 1971)].

2. Operating as an industrial bank or industrial loan company [§225.4(a)(2); 57 FRB 513 (June 1971)].

3. Servicing loans or other extensions of credit [§225.4(a)(3); 57 FRB 513 (June 1971)].

4. Conducting trust or fiduciary activities [§225.4(a)(4); 57 FRB 513 (June 1971); 60 FRB 447 (June 1974)].

5. Acting as investment or financial adviser to the extent of (1) serving as advisory company to a mortgage or real estate investment trust, (2) serving as investment adviser to mutual funds, (3) providing portfolio investment advice to other persons, (4) furnishing general economic information, general statistical forecasting, and industry studies, and (5) providing financial advice to state and local governments on matters such as issuing securities and financ-

Note: Unless otherwise indicated, citations are to the Board's Regulation Y and to the volume number, page number, month, and year of the Federal Reserve Bulletin (FRB).

ing real estate projects [§225.4(a)(5); 57 FRB 513 (June 1971); 58 FRB 149 (February 1972); 58 FRB 571 (June 1972); 59 FRB 701 (September 1973); 66 FRB 984 (December 1980); *Board of Governors v. Investment Company Institute*, 450 U.S. 46 (1981)].

6. Leasing personal and real property provided the transaction is the functional equivalent of an extension of credit, i.e., a full payout lease [§225.4(a)(6); 57 FRB 513 (June 1971); 57 FRB 725 (September 1971); 62 FRB 930 (November 1976)].

7. Making equity or debt investments in corporations designed to promote community welfare or rehabilitation [§225.4(a)(7); 57 FRB 513, 515 (June 1971); 58 FRB 572, 595 (June 1972); 62 FRB 639 (July 1976); 64 FRB 45 (January 1978); Board staff letter BHC—180 (June 25, 1979)].

8. Providing data processing and data transmission services, data bases, or facilities (including data processing and data transmission hardware, software, documentation, and operating personnel), or access to such services, data bases, or facilities by any technologically feasible means, where the data to be processed are financial, banking, or economic [§225.4(a)(8) and §225.123(e); 57 FRB 513, 515 (June 1971); 61 FRB 245 (April 1975); 68 FRB 505 (August 1982); 68 FRB 552 (September 1982)].

9. Acting as agent for sale of insurance (including property and casualty insurance) directly related to certain extensions of credit or the provision of other financial services by a bank or bank-related firm; and acting as agent for sale of any insurance in communities not exceeding 5,000 population [§225.4(a)(9); 57 FRB 674 (August 1971); 58 FRB 800 (September 1972); *Alabama Association of Insurance Agents v. Board of Governors*, 533 F2d 224 (5th Cir. 1976), rehearing denied 558 F2d 729, cert. den. 435 U.S. 904; 65 FRB 924 (November 1979); 66 FRB 987 (December 1980); 67 FRB 629 (August 1981); §601 of the Garn-St Germain Act (Pub. L. No. 97–320) made significant alterations in the insurance powers of bank holding companies].

10. Underwriting credit life and credit accident and health insurance directly related to credit extensions by the bank holding company system [§225.4(a)(10); 59 FRB 20 (January 1973); 62 FRB 537 (June 1976); §601 of the Garn-St Germain Act (Pub. L. No. 97–320) made significant alterations in the insurance powers of bank holding companies].

11. Operating courier services for time-critical bank or financially-related instruments, documents, records, and processing media [§225.4(a)(11); 59 FRB 892 (December 1973); *National Courier Association v. Board of Governors*, 516 F2d 1229 (D.C. Cir. 1975); 61 FRB 588 (September 1975)].

12. Providing management consulting advice to nonaffiliated banks and nonbank depository institutions [§225.4(a)(12); 60 FRB 223 (March 1974); 60 FRB 446, 470 (June 1974); 68 FRB 237, 248 (April 1982)].

13. Issuance and sale of travelers checks [§225.4(a)(13); 65 FRB 250 (March 1979); 67 FRB 912 (December 1981)].

14. Retail sales of money orders ($1,000 maximum face value) and U.S. savings bonds [§225.4(a)(13); 65 FRB 250 (March 1979); 67 FRB 912 (December 1981)].

15. Performing real estate appraisals [§225.4(a)(14); 66 FRB 975, 984 (December 1980)].

16. Conducting discount brokerage and certain margin lending activities [69 FRB 105 (February 1983); 69 FRB __(September 1983)].

By Order

1. Operating a "pool-reserve plan" for the pooling of loss reserves of banks with respect to their loans to small business [57 FRB 1037 (December 1971)].

2. Operating a savings and loan type business in Rhode Island [58 FRB 313 (March 1972); 58 FRB 417 (April 1972); 66 FRB 665 (August 1980); see also entry No. 15].

3. Operating a guaranty (stock) savings bank in New Hampshire [61 FRB 901 (December 1975); 66 FRB 590, 594 (July 1980); 66 FRB 917 (November 1980)].

4. Buying and selling gold and silver bullion and silver coin; dealing in exchange and silver futures and arbitraging gold and silver internationally [Board Order September 27, 1973, re Standard and Chartered Banking Group, Ltd., 38 Federal Register 27552, October 4, 1973; 67 FRB 635 (August 1981)].

5. Acting as futures commission merchant for futures contracts covering bullion, foreign exchange, U.S. government securities, negotiable U.S. money market instruments, and certain other money market instruments [63 FRB 951 (October 1977); 68 FRB 514 (August 1982); 68 FRB 651 (October 1982); 68 FRB 776 (December 1982); 69 FRB 216, 220 (March 1983)].

6. Operating an Article XII New York Investment Company [63 FRB 595 (June 1977)].

7. Issuance of money orders and general purpose variable denominated payment instruments primarily of use to consumers [63 FRB 414, 416 (April 1977)].

8. Providing consumer-oriented financial management courses, counseling, and related financial materials [65 FRB 265 (March 1979)].

9. Providing check authorization, verification, or guarantee services for subscribing merchants [65 FRB 263 (March 1979); 66 FRB 64 (January 1980); 67 FRB 740 (September 1981)].

10. Underwriting and dealing in obligations of the United States, general obligations of States and their political subdivisions, and other obligations eligible for that purpose to member banks [62 FRB 928 (November 1976); 64 FRB 222, 223 (March 1978); 65 FRB 363 (April 1979); 68 FRB 249 (April 1982); 69 FRB 465 (June 1983)].

11. Executing unsolicited purchases and sales of securities as agent solely on the order and for the account of customers [67 FRB 635 (August 1981)].

12. Dealing in certain money market instruments, including bankers acceptances and certificates of deposit [68 FRB 249 (April 1982); 69 FRB 465 (June 1983)].

13. Performing commercial banking functions at offshore locations; such functions include funding domestic operations through the offshore wholesale money market [68 FRB 251 (April 1982); 69 FRB 36 (January 1983)].

14. Offering NOW accounts, provided they are subject to the same federal interest rate limitations and reserve requirements that apply to a federally insured depository institution [68 FRB 253 (April 1982)].

15. Operating a savings and loan association, provided the powers of the S&L are no broader than the powers of bank holding companies and the S&L acquired is threatened with financial harm [68 FRB 316 (May 1982); 68 FRB 382 (June 1982); 68 FRB 656 (October 1982); 69 FRB ___ (July 1983)].

16. Arranging equity financing, which involves arranging for the financing of commercial or industrial income-producing real estate through the transfer of the title, control, and risk of the project from the owner/developer to one or more investors [68 FRB 647 (October 1982); 69 FRB 34 (January 1983); 69 FRB 225 (March 1983)].

17. Providing advice concerning foreign exchange operations, policies, and procedures and arranging for the execution for foreign exchange transactions [69 FRB 221 (March 1983)].

ACTIVITIES PROHIBITED UNDER §4(c)(8)

1. Insurance premium [equity] funding—that is, the combined sale of mutual funds and insurance [58 FRB 905 (October 1972)].

2. Underwriting life insurance that is not sold in connection with a credit transaction by a bank holding company or a subsidiary thereof [58 FRB 905 (October 1972)].

3. Real estate brokerage [58 FRB 427 (April 1972); 58 FRB 905 (October 1972)].

4. Land investment or development [58 FRB 428 (April 1972); 58 FRB 905 (October 1972); 61 FRB 325 (May 1975)].

5. Real estate syndication [58 FRB 905 (October 1972); Board letter re BankAmerica Corp., April 4, 1972)].

6. Management consulting [58 FRB 674, 676 (July 1972); 58 FRB 905 (October 1972)].

7. Property management services generally [58 FRB 652 (July 1972); 58 FRB 905 (October 1972); 64 FRB 415 (May 1978)].

8. Underwriting mortgage guaranty insurance [60 FRB 681 (September 1974); 60 FRB 727 (October 1974)].

9. Operation of a travel agency [62 FRB 148 (February 1976); *Association of Bank Travel Bureaus v. Board of Governors*, 568 F2d 549 (7th Cir. 1978)].

10. Operation of a savings and loan association [63 FRB 280 (March 1977); Board letter March 16, 1981, re National Detroit Corporation/Landmark Savings & Loan; 68 FRB 316 (May 1982); 68 FRB 382 (June 1982); 68 FRB 656 (October 1982)].

11. Underwriting home loan life mortgage insurance [66 FRB 660 (August 1980)].

12. Contract key entry services [66 FRB 666 (August 1980)].

13. Underwriting property and casualty insurance, and adjusting claims and making appraisals relative thereto [64 FRB 506 (June 1978); *NCNB Corp. v. Board of Governors*, 599 F2d 609 (4th Cir. 1979)].

14. Dealing in platinum and palladium and other commodities [Board Order, September 27, 1973, re Standard and Chartered Banking Group, Ltd., 38 Federal Register 27552, October 14, 1973].

15. Issuance of market rate intrastate notes [68 FRB 198 (March 1982); see also 12 C.F.R. §217.156, §250.221].

16. Underwriting group mortgage life insurance (credit life insurance directly related to real estate loans) [68 FRB 319 (May 1982)].

17. Pit arbitrage (an activity conducted in connection with futures commission merchant functions) [68 FRB 776 (December 1982)].

18. Issuance and sale of money orders with a face value of $50,000 or higher [Board letter dated April 28, 1983].

11

Multinational Banking

International operations of financial institutions are a reflection of international economic activity. Thus, there has been a need for international banking as long as there has been international trade and investment. As far back as the days of the Egyptian Pharaohs, bankers operated branches and subsidiaries outside their home countries and issued letters of credit and check-type instruments. During the Middle Ages and the Renaissance periods, Italian bankers established offices throughout Europe. In the nineteenth century, the British merchant banks played a major role in financing the westward expansion of the United States.

In this century, the international operations and capabilities of financial institutions have kept pace with the growing interdependence, particularly since the end of World War II, of the world's national and regional economies. A major aspect of the growth of international banking has been the operation by banking organizations of offices outside their home countries, an activity more precisely referred to as multinational banking. In the U.S. banking industry, domestic banking organizations have gone overseas, and foreign banking organizations have entered the United States, both events occurring in a variety of forms. Congress and the bank regulatory agencies have attempted to control these movements, most recently in the International Banking Act of 1978 and the regulations promulgated thereunder.

This chapter is divided into two sections. The first discusses the establishment of international offices by U.S. banking organizations. The second deals with the movement of foreign banks into the United States.

Although the chapter is primarily concerned with the statutory and regulatory environment governing the establishment and operation of an actual physical presence, it should not be inferred that the internationalization of the banking industry is solely dependent upon the growing number of banks with multinational offices. Banking internationalization has taken other routes as well. International correspondent banking has become, with the aid of technological improvements and innovations, increasingly sophisticated. The Euromarkets have broken down barriers to the international movement of funds and securities. Lending and underwriting syndicates made up of banking organizations from more than one country have become a common part of the international financial scene. And banking transactions with foreign parties may take place at, and the results may be reflected on the books of, domestic rather than foreign offices.

The worldwide economic problems of the early 1980s led to a retrenchment in the international activities of U.S. banking organizations in 1982–83. This was reflected mostly in a slowdown of international lending. Provided that the international economic environment improves, the retrenchment should only be temporary. There are likely to be changes in the regulation of international banking in the years ahead, however. First, national authorities are paying greater attention to the international activities of their banking organizations. And second, such international organizations as the International Monetary Fund and the Bank for International Settlements are assuming an increasing number of leadership and coordinating functions. Indeed, the IMF has been in the forefront of many of the debt rescheduling efforts of 1982–83. Nevertheless, although there are likely to be changes in the supervisory environment concerning the international activities of banking organizations over the years ahead, the nature of such activities and the organizational structures through which they are conducted will probably remain fairly constant.

U.S. BANKS IN THE INTERNATIONAL ARENA

This section covers the various structural forms available for the international activities of U.S. banking organizations and what those activities may consist of. The forms include foreign branches, investments in foreign banks, Edge and Agreement corporations, bank holding company Section 4(c)(13) subsidiaries, international banking facilities, and export trading companies.

Foreign Branches

Branching is the principal way that U.S. banking organizations engage in international activities. As of December 31, 1982, foreign branches of U.S. banks had total assets of $315 billion, which constituted 60 percent of the international banking assets of U.S. banks and Edge corporations. (See Table 9.) International banking assets include not only assets located outside the United States but also loans at domestic offices to foreign parties and international trade financing as evidenced by customers' liabilities on acceptances outstanding.

Federal Reserve member banks—both national banks and state member banks—may establish foreign branches with the approval of the Federal Reserve Board. Subsequent to their establishment, branches of national banks are subject to the Office of the Comptroller's supervision, although the Board may also require reports. The Board supervises branches of state member banks. As of the

Table 9: International Assets of U.S. Banking Organizations and Edge Corporations, December 31, 1982

Type of Office	*Total Assets[1] (billions)*	*Percent of Total*
U.S. Banks:		
Domestic offices[2]	$140	26.6%
Foreign branches	315	59.9
Foreign subsidiaries of U.S. banks and investment Edge corporations[3]	55	10.5
Edge corporations:		
Banking Edge corporations	16	3.0
Total	$526	100.0%

[1]Amounts adjusted to eliminate "intrafamily" transactions. Balances also exclude assets of U.S. branches and agencies of foreign banks ($204 billion as of September 30, 1982) and foreign subsidiaries owned directly by U.S. bank holding companies ($13.1 billion as of year-end 1981).
[2]Represents amount of credit extended by domestic offices of U.S. banks to foreign parties plus the amount of international trade financing indicated by customers' liabilities on acceptances outstanding.
[3]The figure for foreign subsidiaries reflects controlled companies and includes assets of certain companies of which the U.S. bank is not majority owner.

Source: Estimates by James V. Houpt, Senior Financial Analyst, Federal Reserve Board, based on Federal Reserve preliminary data for 1982.

end of 1982, 163 national and state member banks had a total of 877 foreign branches.

The establishment of foreign branches by state nonmember banks was brought under the authority of the FDIC by the Financial Institutions Regulatory and Interest Rate Control Act of 1978. Prior to the enactment of that law, commencement of overseas operations by a state nonmember bank was solely a matter of state concern, although both the FDIC and the states exercised supervisory authority once operations were begun. The FDIC and the states continue to exercise this supervisory authority. As of December 31, 1982, 23 state nonmember banks had a total of 28 overseas branches.

Investments in Foreign Banks

One alternative to establishing overseas branches for U.S. banks is to invest directly in foreign banks. The approval authority for the acquisition of stock in foreign banks is the same as for the establishment of foreign branches: the Federal Reserve Board for member banks, both national and state, and the FDIC for state nonmember banks. In Table 9, the major portion of the $55 billion entry for foreign subsidiaries of U.S. banks and investment Edge corporations is accounted for by investments of U.S. banks in foreign banks.

Edge and Agreement Corporations

Both member banks and bank holding companies may establish Edge Act corporations. Named after the U.S. Senator who sponsored the authorizing legislation in 1919, Edge corporations are chartered by the Federal Reserve Board to engage in international banking and financing operations. Edges are located in the United States but may have overseas branches, subsidiaries, and investments. An important characteristic of Edges is that they are not subject to the interstate restrictions of the McFadden Act. Thus Edges provide a way for banks to establish out-of-state banking offices, although such offices are limited to internationally-related business. The attractiveness of Edges for interstate operations was increased by a 1979 regulatory amendment permitting branching. Prior to the amendment, which was in response to the International Banking Act (IBA) of 1978, each domestic Edge office had to be separately incorporated and capitalized.

Edges are of two types: banking Edges and investment Edges. The dichotomy was at one time required by regulation, but this is no longer the case. The distinction remains because the two types are functionally different. Banking Edges perform functions similar to the international departments of banks, such as financing international trade, dealing in foreign exchange, and accepting internationally-related deposits. Investment Edges are essentially holding companies for investments outside the United States. Since they are principally conduits for investments overseas, investment Edges are generally located where investment decisions are made: at the home office of the parent bank or bank holding company. Banking Edges, on the other hand, are attractive as a means for providing banking services and thus are likely to be located where international banking opportunities are found. New York and Miami have the most banking Edge offices; other locations include Chicago, Miami, Houston, San Francisco, and Los Angeles.

As of December 31, 1982, there were 78 banking Edges with a total of 103 domestic branches and 9 foreign branches. Assets at year-end 1982, after netting out intrafamily transactions, were $16.3 billion. Sixteen of these Edges, and one of the branches, were owned directly by foreign banking organizations, which have been permitted to own Edges since the passage of the IBA in 1978. Several other Edges were owned by U.S. banking organizations which were owned or controlled by foreign banking organizations. Investment Edges totalled approximately 54 at year-end.

Very similar to Edge corporations are Agreement corporations. These are federal or state chartered corporations which have entered into an agreement with the Board that they will not exercise any powers impermissible for an Edge corporation. As is the case with Edge corporations, both member banks and bank holding companies may invest in Agreement corporations. There were only three such organizations in existence as of December 31, 1982, two of which were owned by foreign banking organizations.

Bank Holding Company §4(c)(13) Subsidiaries

In addition to conducting foreign operations through Edge and Agreement corporations, bank holding companies may invest directly in foreign companies under Section 4(c)(13) of the Bank Holding Company Act. This section permits a bank holding company, with Board approval, to own shares of any company that does no business in the United States except as may be incident to its international or foreign business. A disadvantage of direct ownership by a bank holding company under Section 4(c)(13) is that Section 23A of the Federal Reserve Act limits the amount of credit a bank can extend to subsidiaries of its parent bank holding company. Section 23A exempts from its coverage extensions of credit by a bank to one of its own subsidiaries.

International Banking Facilities

In December, 1981, the Federal Reserve Board authorized the establishment of international banking facilities (IBFs) in the United States. IBFs can be established by U.S. banks or other U.S. depository institutions, Edge and Agreement corporations, and U.S. branches and agencies of foreign banks. An IBF is not a separate physical or corporate entity but is merely a separate set of accounts.

As of April 20, 1983, 270 IBFs with assets of more than $50 million each were in existence. Their total assets were $177 billion. Agencies and branches of foreign banks accounted for 181 of the IBFs and $96 billion, or more than half, of the total assets.

An IBF can accept deposits from foreign sources, other IBFs, and its parent institution without being subject to reserve requirements or interest rate ceilings. It may extend credit only to foreign residents, other IBFs, and its parent institution. The minimum deposit amount that may be accepted is $100,000. States can encourage the establishment of IBFs within their borders by giving them favorable tax treatment.

Foreign Activities

Member banks, bank holding companies, and Edge and Agreement corporations, which account for the major portion of the international activities of the U.S. banking industry, are subject to the Federal Reserve Board's Regulation K. The only organizations in the U.S. banking industry that escape Regulation K coverage are state nonmember banks, but these institutions, with a total of 28 foreign branches at the end of 1982, have a relatively minor international presence.

Regulation K was promulgated in substantially its present form in June of 1979. Prior to that date, overseas activities subject to Board jurisdiction were covered in several separate regulations. Much of the motivation for consolidating the regulations pertaining to overseas activities of U.S. banking organizations was provided by the passage of the IBA in 1978.

The activities that may be engaged in overseas under Regulation K must generally be of a financial nature. Member banks' direct overseas investments in foreign companies are limited to foreign banks. Bank holding companies and Edge and Agreement corporations, on the other hand, can directly invest in foreign companies engaged in certain nonbank activities, as well as in foreign banks. Member banks can only invest in foreign nonbank companies by doing so indirectly through Edge or Agreement corporations.

The precise scope of permissible overseas activities of bank holding companies and Edge and Agreement corporations is dependent on the extent of the U.S. organization's ownership or control of the entity directly engaging in the activities. Regulation K defines three ownership or control categories:

1. Subsidiaries—ownership or control of more than 50 percent of the voting stock;
2. Joint ventures—ownership or control of 20 to 50 percent of the voting stock; and
3. Portfolio investments—ownership or control of less than 20 percent of the voting stock.

Subsidiaries may engage in banking and in certain financially-related activities. The more important of these financially-related activities are:

1. financing;
2. leasing, of both real and personal property;
3. acting as fiduciary;
4. underwriting credit life insurance and credit accident and health insurance;
5. providing investment, financial, or economic advisory services;
6. general insurance brokerage;
7. data processing;
8. managing a mutual fund if the fund's shares are not sold in the United States or to U.S. residents and the fund does not exercise managerial control over the firms in which it invests;
9. performing management consulting services provided that such services with respect to the U.S. market are restricted to initial entry;
10. underwriting, distributing, and dealing in debt and equity securities outside the United States, provided that no underwriting commitment for shares of an issuer may exceed $2 million or represent 20 percent of the capital and surplus or voting stock of an issuer unless the underwriter is covered by binding commitments from subunderwriters or other purchasers; and
11. other activities that the Board has determined are permissible under Section 4(c)(8) of the Bank Holding Company Act.

Joint ventures may engage in a small proportion of additional types of activities. To be precise, not more than 10 percent of a joint venture's consolidated assets or revenues can be attributable to activities that are not permissible for a subsidiary.

The limitation on portfolio investments depends on the investing organization's capital structure. Portfolio investments in organizations engaged in activities that are not permissible for joint ventures cannot exceed 100 percent of the investor's capital and surplus.

In addition to offices that are engaged in activities subject to the control and supervision of U.S. banking regulators, U.S. banking organizations may establish representative offices abroad. Such offices cannot conduct banking transactions, but they offer opportunities for establishing foreign contacts and for making a banking organization's name known in foreign markets.

Export Trading Companies

In the fall of 1982, Congress passed the Export Trading Company Act. Title II of the act is the Bank Export Services Act. This law allows bank holding companies, Edge and Agreement Corporations, and bankers' banks to invest in export trading companies. These are organizations whose purpose is to export or to facilitate the export of U.S. goods and services.

An investment in an export trading company may not exceed 5 percent of the investing organization's consolidated capital and surplus, except that the limit for an Edge or Agreement corporation not engaged in banking is 25 percent. Joint ventures between banking organizations and nonbank firms are specifically encouraged. One of the Congressional purposes is to enable the trade expertise of nonbank firms to be combined in one corporate entity with the financing services of banking organizations.

The list of permissible services for export trading companies is fairly extensive. It includes, but is not limited to: consulting; international market research; advertising; marketing; the provision of warehouse-to-warehouse insurance; product research and design; legal assistance; transportation, including trade documentation and freight forwarding; communication and processing of foreign orders to and for exporters and foreign purchasers; warehousing; foreign exchange; financing; and taking title to goods.

The first banking investment in an export trading company passed Federal Reserve Board scrutiny in May of 1983, and final implementing regulations were issued in June.

FOREIGN BANKING IN THE UNITED STATES

Foreign banking in the United States can be categorized as the banking activities of (1) foreign banking organizations and (2) other foreign residents, primarily foreign individuals. As of September 30, 1982, both categories owned or had interests in U.S. banks or banking offices with assets of $322.8 billion, or 17.2 percent of total U.S. commercial bank domestic assets. (See Table 10.) Foreign banking organizations, the first category, accounted for almost 90 percent of the $322.8 billion. This section discusses the various forms that foreign banking activity in the United States may take and reviews the changes wrought by the IBA.

Foreign Individuals

Foreign individuals become part of the U.S. banking environment by ownership of stock of U.S. banks or bank holding companies. As is the case with U.S. citizens, foreign individuals may either purchase stock in an existing institution or establish a bank *de novo*. In either case, the applicable federal laws do not distinguish between foreign individuals and U.S. citizens. A study by the Comptroller of the Currency's office showed that from 1970 through the first quarter of 1980 foreign individuals acquired 56 existing U.S. banking organizations and foreign individuals and nonbank companies established 9 *de novo* banks. As of September 30, 1982, foreign individuals had a 10 or more percent interest in 75 U.S. banking organizations.

The establishment of a *de novo* institution requires approval of the appropriate regulatory agency: the Office of the Comptroller of the Currency for national banks, the Federal Reserve Board for bank holding companies, and state authorities for state banks. As

Table 10: Foreign Investment in the U.S. Banking Industry, September 30, 1982

Type of Organization	*Number*	*U.S. Assets (billions)*
U.S. chartered insured commercial banks owned or invested in by:[1]		
Foreign individuals	75 banks	$ 23.0
Foreign bank holding companies	55 banks	84.4
Other foreign entities	33 banks	10.7
Edge and Agreement corporations with direct or indirect foreign owners or investors	28 corporations	1.0
U.S. branches of foreign banks	240 branches	150.1
U.S. agencies of foreign banks	186 agencies	53.6
Total		$322.8

[1]Foreign investments of less than 10 percent are not included.

Source: Federal Reserve Board, "Foreign Investment in U.S. Banking Institutions," September 30, 1982.

noted in Chapter 3, the Federal Reserve Board and the FDIC can also play a significant role in the establishment process for state banks. The Federal Reserve Board rules on applications by state banks that wish to become members of the Federal Reserve System; and the FDIC rules on applications for deposit insurance by state nonmember banks, deposit insurance for new national banks and state member banks being automatic.

Since 1978, the acquisition by an individual or individuals of control of an existing banking institution has been subject to review by the appropriate bank regulatory agency under the Change in Bank Control Act. The criteria for review under the law include antitrust standards, the financial condition of the acquiring person, and the competence, experience, and integrity of the proposed new management.

Foreign Banking Organizations

The banking offices of foreign banking organizations in the United States may be in the form of branches, agencies, commercial lending companies, Edge or Agreement corporations, bank subsidiaries or international banking facilities. As noted earlier in the chapter, IBFs are not separate offices but are merely sets of accounts. A foreign banking organization may also have a less than 25 percent interest in a U.S. bank, in which case the U.S. bank would not necessarily be classified as a subsidiary.

Branches, and of course banks, generally have full deposit-taking powers. Agencies cannot accept deposits from U.S. citizens or residents. Agencies and commercial lending companies may accept credit balances, which are obligations that are incidental to the exercise of other lawful banking powers, serve a specific purpose, are not solicited from the general public, are not used to pay routine operating expenses in the United States, are withdrawn within a reasonable period of time after the specific purpose for which they were placed has been accomplished, and are drawn upon in a manner reasonable in relation to the size and nature of the account.

"Commercial lending company" is a term defined in the International Banking Act of 1978 and intended primarily to refer to investment companies chartered in New York under the New York State Investment Company Act. These organizations engage in wholesale international commercial banking activities.

As discussed earlier in the chapter, Edge and Agreement corporations are organizations whose purpose is to engage in an international banking business or to make foreign investments. Edges are federally chartered and Agreements are generally state chartered.

The IBA in 1978 first permitted foreign ownership of Edges; foreign ownership of state-chartered Agreement corporations is dependent on state law. Although foreign banking organizations have no need for them as a vehicle for making foreign investments, Edge and Agreement corporations provide foreign organizations with alternative forms for U.S. banking offices.

The main locations in the United States for the banking activities of foreign banking organizations are New York, California, Illinois, Texas, and Florida. As of September 30, 1982, foreign banking organizations had in the United States 186 agencies, 240 branches, 64 investments of 10 percent or more in U.S. banks, and 7 commercial lending companies. Sixteen Edge corporations, one with a branch, were directly owned by foreign banking organizations, and there were two foreign-owned Agreement corporations. Foreign banking organizations held indirect interests in several other Edges through investments in U.S. banks. In addition to such banking offices, foreign banking organizations have a number of representative offices, which do not receive deposits or make loans. As of the end of 1982, there were almost 300 such representative offices in the United States.

As in the case of foreign individuals, foreign banking organizations may establish a presence in the United States either *de novo* or by the acquisition of an existing institution. Branches, agencies, and commercial lending companies are ordinarily established *de novo*. Subsidiary banks may be either established *de novo* or acquired as going concerns. From 1970 through the first quarter of 1980, according to an OCC study, foreign banking organizations acquired 36 U.S. banks.

Federal Licensing and Interstate Restrictions

The IBA of 1978 made significant changes in the regulatory environment within which foreign banking organizations operate in the United States. Although foreign banking organizations with U.S. bank subsidiaries were, and are, bank holding companies and thus subject to the Bank Holding Company Act, prior to the enactment of the IBA the federal government had little involvement with the U.S. branches and agencies of foreign banks. Such branches and agencies were established under state laws and supervised by state authorities. According to a 1980 General Accounting Office study, twenty-four states permitted foreign banks to establish agencies and twelve allowed foreign banks to establish branches. Moreover, prior to the IBA a foreign bank could establish deposit-taking branches in more than one state because it was not a "bank" subject to the McFadden Act restrictions on interstate branching.

The IBA gave the Comptroller of the Currency authority to license federal branches and agencies of foreign banks. Thus foreign banks wishing to open a branch or an agency in the United States now have the option of proceeding under state or federal law. If a foreign bank has no U.S. branch or bank subsidiary and the statutes of a particular state do not specifically forbid the establishment of a branch or agency by a foreign bank, the Comptroller will grant a federal license for such establishment in that state. If a foreign bank has a U.S. branch or bank subsidiary, the IBA authorizes a federal branch or a federal agency to be opened in another state only if that state expressly permits such establishment. Moreover, the deposit-taking activities of a branch in a second state must be limited to those that are permitted to Edge corporations; that is, to those that are incidental to international banking activities.

This inability to open a full-service deposit-taking branch in a second state is a facet of a major purpose of the IBA: to impose as nearly as possible the same interstate restrictions on the U.S. banking activities of foreign banking organizations as domestic banking organizations are subject to. Under the IBA, each foreign banking organization with a branch or bank subsidiary in the United States has a "home state," and the organization's U.S. deposit-taking offices that are not grandfathered are limited to that state. Offices established or applied for as of July 27, 1978, are grandfathered.

Equalizing the interstate restrictions imposed on domestic and foreign banking organizations is an implementation of the concept of "National Treatment." This concept calls for imposing the same duties on and giving the same privileges to foreign organizations as are imposed on and given to domestic organizations. Other attempts to implement National Treatment in the IBA were (1) the requirement that foreign bank branches engaged in retail banking have deposit insurance, (2) the permission granted to foreign banking organizations to own stock in Edge corporations, and (3) the authorization to the Federal Reserve Board to impose reserve requirements on U.S. branches and agencies of foreign banking organizations with worldwide assets in excess of $1 billion. The Depository Institutions Deregulation and Monetary Control Act of 1980 extended reserve requirement coverage to U.S. branches and agencies of foreign banking organizations with less than $1 billion in worldwide assets by requiring reserves of all institutions eligible for deposit insurance.

Nonbank Activities

Another provision of the IBA implementing the concept of National Treatment was the extension of the nonbank provisions of the Bank Holding Company Act to foreign banks with U.S. branches, agencies, or commercial lending companies. Prior to the enactment of the IBA, the only foreign organizations subject to the Bank Holding Company Act were those that were bank holding companies as a result of having a U.S. bank subsidiary. A foreign bank with only, for example, a branch in the United States was not subject to the constraints on nonbank activities in the United States that U.S. banking organizations are subject to. As a result of the IBA, however, all foreign organizations with a U.S. banking presence are limited, with certain grandfathered exceptions, by the nonbanking provisions of the Bank Holding Company Act. The principal such provision is Section 4(c)(8), which is discussed in Chapter 10.

On the other hand, the IBA added a nonbanking provision to Section 2(h) of the Bank Holding Company Act that permits foreign organizations to engage in the United States in nonfinancial activities not permitted U.S. banking organizations. A qualifying foreign organization may own a foreign company that engages, either directly or through a U.S. company, in U.S. nonbank activities as long as the foreign company is principally engaged in business outside the United States. The provision is not available if the U.S. activities involve the securities business or are of the type that are covered by Section 4(c)(8). As of June, 1983, Section 2(h) did not appear to be a significant factor in the U.S. activities of foreign banking organizations.

CONCLUSION

As a result of its wealth and economic strength, the United States has been an important factor in the growth of a worldwide economy. The banking industry in the United States has been an integral part of this process. U.S. banks have established a substantial presence overseas, and foreign banking organizations have established a substantial presence in the United States. It seems safe to predict that the national and regional economies of the world will become increasingly interdependent and that the internationalization of the banking industry will continue.

NOTES

A most valuable source pertaining to foreign acquisition and control of U.S. banks is a series of fourteen staff papers that the

Comptroller of the Currency released in 1980 and 1981. Other informative works include: Department of the Treasury, *Report to the Congress On Foreign Government Treatment of U.S. Commercial Banking Organizations*, September 17, 1979; James V. Houpt, "Performance and Characteristics of Edge Corporations," *Staff Studies*, No. 110, Board of Governors of the Federal Reserve System, 1981; James V. Houpt and Michael G. Martinson, "Foreign Subsidiaries of U.S. Banking Organizations," *Staff Studies*, No. 120, Board of Governors of the Federal Reserve System, 1982. In 1980, the Federal Reserve Board began a quarterly report, "Foreign Investment in U.S. Banking Institutions," that gives a listing of foreign investments by type of institution. Finally, the *American Banker* periodically provides a listing of banking offices owned and activities conducted by foreign banks in the United States and U.S. banks overseas.

The International Banking Act of 1978 amended a number of provisions of Title 12 of the U.S. Code and added Chapter 32 (§§3101-3108), entitled "Foreign Bank Participation in Domestic Markets." The note to §3101 contains a list of the Title 12 provisions that were amended. Specific statutory provisions referred to in the text are located at the following sections of Title 12 of the U.S. Code: §§601-604(a) (foreign branching by national banks; investments in foreign banks by national banks; Agreement corporations); §321 (application of §§601-604(a) to state member banks); §§1813(o) and 1828(d)(2) (foreign branching by state nonmember insured banks); §§611-631 (Edge Act corporations); §1843(c)(5) (authority under which bank holding companies own Edge and Agreement corporations); §1843(c)(13) (foreign direct investments by bank holding companies); §371c (Section 23A of the Federal Reserve Act limiting the amount of credit a bank can extend to affiliates but exempting bank subsidiaries from the limitation); §1843(c)(14) (Bank Export Services Act); §1817(j) (Change in Bank Control Act); §§3101-3108 (Chapter 32 on foreign bank activities generally in the U.S.); §3102 (establishment of federal branches and agencies); §3103 (interstate banking limitations on foreign banks); §3105 (reserve requirements on U.S. branches and agencies of foreign banks; see also §461(b)(5)); §§3104 and 1815(b) (deposit insurance for branches of foreign banks); §619 (ownership of Edges by foreign banking organizations); and §§1841(h), 1843(c)(9), and 3106 (nonbank activities of foreign banks and bank holding companies).

PART V

The New Environment

A blurring of the distinctions between the different types of financial institutions has been a major trend in the financial industry in the United States over the last decade or so. In large measure, this trend is a reflection of entrepreneurial vigor, prompted or compelled by the computer-communications revolution and sustained by periods of high interest rates. The trend, however, has been facilitated by changes in law or regulation, and by an unceasing awareness of the opportunities (or "loopholes") available in existing law.

A consequence of the blurring of the distinctions is that each type of institution has felt increased competitive pressures from other types of institutions. Thus the participants in the financial industry have become more aware of each other's presence and have sought to increase their knowledge of their competitors.

This part has two chapters. Chapter 12 covers depository institutions other than commercial banks. There are three traditional categories of institutions in this area: mutual savings banks, savings and loan associations, and credit unions. Recent legislation has expanded the savings bank category to include federal stock savings banks. A phenomenon of the 1970s and early 1980s, money market mutual funds, has also been included in the discussion.

Chapter 13 approaches the blurring of distinctions from the perspective of the changes that have been taking place in the packaging of financial services and products. This results in consideration of several topics. One is the legal quirk known as the nonbank bank. Another is the financial supermarket concept. A third is the money management account. And a fourth is networking, or the growing number of affiliations and arrangements between commercial banks and nondepository institutions.

In future editions of *Federal Regulation of Banking,* Chapter 13 is likely to change the most, for at least two reasons. First, nondepository institutions are just beginning to offer competition to banks; the next several years should see either a rapid expansion of these operations, or significant retrenchments. Second, technology and deregulation might enable even more nondepository institutions to offer products or services in competition to commercial banks. Thus Chapter 13 is an appropriate predecessor to the final chapter of this book, which is entitled "Winds of Change."

12

Nonbank Depository Institutions

Mutual savings banks, savings and loan associations, and credit unions have long offered the public, or various segments thereof, depository alternatives to commercial banks. Indeed, mutual savings banks have been in existence since at least the 1820s, and savings and loan associations since the 1830s. Competition for deposits is competition on the liabilities side of the balance sheet. For most of the period of coexistence of commercial banks and nonbank depository institutions, the liabilities side of the balance sheet was the only side on which they competed to any significant extent.

Over the last several decades or so, however, competition has spread to the assets side of the balance sheet. Commercial banks have expanded their lending operations into areas traditionally the province of the nonbank depository institutions. In the case of mutual savings banks and savings and loan associations, this area is real estate-related lending. In the case of credit unions, the area is consumer loans. At the same time, mutual savings banks and savings and loan associations have sought to acquire lending and investment powers beyond the real estate area.

As competition between commercial banks and nonbank depository institutions was developing on the assets side of the balance sheet, competition on the liabilities side, where it has long existed, was increasing. As noted in Chapter 6, all of the principal depository institutions in New England received federal authorization by 1976 to offer NOW accounts. The authorization was extended to New York and New Jersey in 1978 and 1979, respectively, and nationwide in 1980. As a result of the Garn-St Germain Act of 1982, federal savings and loan associations and federal savings banks can now offer checking account services to customers with whom they have a business, corporate, commerical, or agricultural loan relationship.

As competition was increasing between commercial banks and the traditional nonbank depository institutions, another player was making its appearance. Money market mutual funds, a form of investment company, began by the mid-1970s to attract a fair amount of funds that otherwise probably would have been in deposit accounts subject to interest rate ceilings in commercial banks, mutual savings banks, S&Ls, or credit unions. The funds offered a much higher return than could be obtained by most depositors in the regulated interest rate environment. Moreover, many of the funds could be accessed by checks or check-like instruments.

By the early 1980s, the mutual fund presence was substantial. In November of 1982, the balances in these funds amounted to $241.0 billion. The total has since been reduced as depositors have been attracted to the money market deposit accounts authorized for depository institutions in December of 1982.

SAVINGS BANKS

The origins of mutual savings banks in the early nineteenth century were discussed in Chapter 1. As of the end of 1982, there were 418 state-chartered mutual savings banks. They operated in 15 states, although most of their number were located in New York, Connecticut, and Massachusetts. (See Table 11.) Until 1978, all savings banks were state-chartered. The Financial Institutions Regulatory and Interest Rate Control Act (FIRIRCA) of that year authorized the conversion of existing mutual savings banks to federal charter. At the end of 1982, there were six federally chartered mutual savings banks. The Garn-St Germain Act of 1982 authorized the federal chartering of new savings banks. Its provisions also permit federal savings banks to exist in stock as well as mutual form.

Mutual savings banks developed as institutions that channeled individual savings into long-term investments, mainly mortgages. State-chartered mutual savings banks are similar to state-chartered

Table 11: Mutual Savings Banks by State December 31, 1982

Massachusetts	155
New York	95
Connecticut	62
Maine	24
New Hampshire	25
New Jersey	19
Washington	9
Pennsylvania	8
Vermont	6
Indiana	5
Maryland	4
Wisconsin	3
Alaska	3
Delaware	2
Oregon	2
Minnesota	2
Total	424

Note: Figures include six federal mutual savings banks.

Source: The National Association of Mutual Savings Banks.

S&Ls, but there are differences. The former generally have had broader lending and investment powers than S&Ls have had. For example, some states have permitted their mutual savings banks to invest in corporate bonds but generally have denied S&Ls the ability to do so. Also, mutual savings banks usually have had fewer restrictions placed upon them as to where they can acquire mortgages. And finally, the mortgage portfolios of mutual savings banks usually have included more varied types of properties than have the portfolios of S&Ls. One-to-four family residential mortgage loans have constituted the bulk of the assets of S&Ls.

The "mutual" in the term mutual savings banks indicates that these institutions are owned by their depositors. Indeed, depositors are actually creditors of their savings banks. As creditors, they in theory have a higher legal standing than if they were considered mere shareholders. In the past, somes states also chartered stock savings banks. For legal and practical purposes, these are generally indistinguishable from state-chartered commercial banks, and in fact are included with commercial banks in banking statistics.

Mutual savings banks were included among the institutions eligible for deposit insurance from the Federal Deposit Insurance Corporation when that agency was formed in 1933. Since the early 1940s, the majority of mutual savings banks have had insurance from the FDIC. For example, of the 424 mutual savings banks at the end of 1982, the deposits of 315, or 75 percent, were insured by the FDIC. These FDIC-insured institutions held 93 percent of all mutual savings bank assets. The savings banks that converted to federal charter following the passage of FIRIRCA in 1978 received insurance from the Federal Savings and Loan Insurance Corporation. As noted earlier, there were six such FSLIC-insured savings banks at the end of 1982.

The Garn-St Germain Act of 1982 made significant changes in the legal environment concerning savings banks. Before discussing the provisions of that act, however, the economic troubles that mutual savings banks encountered in the early 1980s should be mentioned.

Most of the assets of both mutual savings banks and savings and loan associations have long-term maturities. The liabilities of these organizations, however, as in the case of the liabilities of commercial banks, are generally short-term in nature. When interest rates skyrocketed in the early 1980s, mutual savings banks and S&Ls suffered substantially because their low interest rate long-term assets were funded with high rate short-term liabilities. Significant losses resulted, and had to be absorbed by charges against capital or net worth. For example, in 1981, the mutual savings bank industry lost in the aggregate $1.4 billion. In 1982, it lost $1.3 billion. The savings and loan industry for those years lost $4.6 billion and $3.4 billion, respectively.

The weaker institutions, those with insufficient capital to tide them over the period of losses, began to fall by the wayside. And even the stronger institutions began looking for merger partners as a way to maintain their strength. In 1981, 1982, and the first half of 1983, there were a number of savings bank mergers, some under the close guidance of the FDIC. As a result of the activity, the number of mutual savings banks declined from 463 at the end of 1980 to 424 at the end of 1982.

In the Garn-St Germain Act, Congress sought to alleviate some of the difficulties facing depository institutions in general and thrift institutions in particular. As short-term help, the act authorized the FDIC and the FSLIC to provide notes to institutions in exchange for net worth certificates. The notes serve as capital for the institutions. Eligibility to issue net worth certificates and consequently receive notes from a federal insurer depends on an institution's having a capital-to-asset ratio below a certain level specified in the act. Authority for the net worth program expires in 1985.

Congress also provided for the longer term viability of thrift institutions in two ways. First, it greatly expanded the chartering options. Federal charters for *de novo* savings banks can now be obtained, and federal savings banks can be in either stock or mutual form. S&Ls can convert to federal savings banks, and savings banks can convert to federal S&Ls. Federal savings banks are chartered by the Federal Home Loan Bank Board and insured by the Federal Savings and Loan Insurance Corporation, although FDIC-insured savings banks that convert to federal charters remain insured by the FDIC for a transition period, whose length is unspecified.

The second action taken by Congress was to expand the powers of federal thrifts, both S&Ls and savings banks. As of January 1, 1984, these institutions will be able to invest up to 10 percent of their assets in commercial loans. Another 40 percent of assets can be invested in loans backed by nonresidential real property. Thirty percent can be invested in consumer loans, a category that includes inventory and floor-plan financing for dealers in consumer goods. And 10 percent can be invested in personal property leasing activities.

The expansion of the lending and investment powers of federal thrifts has been matched, as noted in the introductory portion of this chapter, by some increase in their deposit taking powers. The Depository Institutions Deregulation and Monetary Control Act of 1980 permitted all depository institutions—commercial banks, savings banks, S&Ls, and credit unions—to issue NOW accounts or their equivalent. Initially, the accounts could be offered only to individuals or to certain non-profit organizations, but the Garn-St Germain Act expanded the eligible account holders to include governmental units. The Garn-St Germain Act also permitted federal S&Ls and federal savings banks to offer checking accounts to customers with whom they have a business, corporate, commercial, or agricultural loan relationship.

The FHLBB issued regulations effective in January, 1983, promulgating the federal thrift organizational powers of the Garn-St Germain Act. Federal savings banks were an immediate success. During the first three months of the year, 96 federal savings bank charters were granted. Forty-six were granted as a result of the conversion of S&Ls, and fifty were granted as the result of the conversion of existing savings banks.

As noted in Chapter 8, savings banks are not necessarily limited by the branching constraints that apply to commercial banks. State-chartered mutual savings banks branch according to state law, and many states have the same branching laws for mutual savings banks as for commercial banks. Federal savings banks, however, are subject to the more liberal branching situation enjoyed by federally chartered S&Ls, which are the subject of the next section.

SAVINGS AND LOAN ASSOCIATIONS

Historically, savings and loan associations developed as institutions receiving deposits from their members and investing the funds in mortgages on residences of the members. S&L lending powers eventually came to include loans to non-depositors, but the residential real estate focus of the loans was largely maintained. S&Ls arose as mutual institutions, or institutions owned by their depositors. There was, and probably still is, a slight legal distinction between depositors in S&Ls and those in mutual savings banks. Depositors in the latter are creditors, while depositors in the former are shareholders. In theory, certain distinctions differentiate the two types of ownership. In view of the pervasiveness of deposit insurance, however, the distinctions probably have little practical significance.

A number of savings and loan associations are now in stock form. Of the 3,343 federally insured S&Ls at the end of 1982, 755, or 23 percent, were stock institutions. Conversion of mutual S&Ls to stock form has been permitted since 1975 under detailed regulations of the Federal Savings and Loan Insurance Corporation. From the fourth quarter of 1975 through March of 1983, there were 181 such conversions.

The stock form enables S&Ls to increase their equity, or net worth, through sales of shares. It also enables them to be owned by other organizations and to be bought and sold. Corporate owners of S&Ls are called S&L holding companies and are subject to the Savings and Loan Holding Company Act. There are two kinds of S&L holding companies: unitary companies and multiple companies. The former type owns only one S&L. Little restriction is imposed on the activities in which unitary S&L holding companies and their non-S&L subsidiaries may engage. Unitary S&L holding companies include such organizations as National Steel and Sears, Roebuck and Company. Multiple S&L holding companies, on the other hand, are limited to engaging in S&L-related activities.

At the end of 1982, there was a total of 3,833 savings and loan associations. Of these, 3,343 were either federally chartered or federally insured. The latter figure was broken down into 1,727 federally chartered S&Ls and 1,616 federally insured state-chartered S&Ls.

The supervisory authority for federal S&Ls is the Federal Home Loan Bank Board, which was established in 1932. The FHLBB has three members, who are appointed by the President. It is headed by a chairman, who is named by the President. The FHLBB supervises the Federal Home Loan Bank System and the Federal Savings and Loan Insurance Corporation, which is the federal deposit insurer for S&Ls and, except for those converting state-chartered savings banks that remain insured by the FDIC for a transition period, federally chartered savings banks. The S&Ls insured by the FSLIC include both federally chartered institutions and those state-chartered institutions that either desire or are required by their states to have federal deposit insurance.

The FHLB System has 12 geographic districts, in each of which there is a district Federal Home Loan Bank. The FHLBB's expenses are met by assessments on the district Federal Home Loan Banks and the FSLIC and by fees charged to the institutions it examines.

As noted in the preceding discussion on savings banks, the economic events of 1981 and 1982 were hard on thrift institutions. During those years, there were 70 assisted mergers involving distressed S&Ls. "Assisted" means the FSLIC provided financial support in some form. A number of mergers of healthy institutions also took place during the period, continuing a trend that had been going on for some time. As a result of the events of 1981 and 1982, the FSLIC insurance funds dropped from $6.5 billion at the end of 1980 to $6.4 billion at the end of 1982. The number of S&Ls during that time period fell from 4,613 to 3,833, or 17 percent.

As also noted in the preceding discussion on savings banks, both the asset and liability powers of federal S&Ls have been substantially expanded in recent years. In 1980, Congress permitted S&Ls in all states to issue NOW accounts. The 1980 legislation also authorized federally chartered S&Ls to invest a certain percentage of their assets in consumer loans, in commercial paper, and in corporate debt securities. The Garn-St Germain Act of 1982 authorized federal S&Ls to invest, as of January 1, 1984, up to 10 percent of their assets in commercial loans. It also authorized them to invest up to 40 percent of their assets in loans secured by non-residential real property, up to 30 percent in consumer loans, including inventory and floor-plan financing for dealers in consumer goods, and up to 10 percent in personal property leasing.

An important development concerning S&Ls in the last few years has been the growing interstate nature of the industry. In March of 1981, the Federal Home Loan Bank Board adopted a policy of allowing interstate S&L mergers in supervisory situations. Such situations are where one or more of the merger partners are troubled or failing institutions. From March of 1981 to May of 1983, there were approximately 20 interstate S&L combinations. When an out-of-state S&L merges with an in-state institution, the out-of-state organization acquires the in-state institution's ability to branch in the state. The growing number of interstate S&L mergers and the subsequent expansion by out-of-state institutions once they enter a state should result in more pressure to remove the barriers to interstate banking.

In the spring of 1983, the FHLBB put forth for comment a proposal to allow federal S&Ls to merge, make acquisitions, and establish branches on an interstate basis in other than supervisory situations. The only major restraint would be that the target state would have to permit such transactions. Currently, the FHLBB allows a federal S&L to branch anywhere within the borders of the state where it is located. Branching by S&Ls and savings banks is discussed more thoroughly in Chapter 8.

A current issue concerning S&Ls is their relationship with banking organizations. For a long time following the passage of the Bank Holding Company Act Amendments of 1970, the Federal Reserve Board resisted letting bank holding companies acquire S&Ls as a permissible nonbanking activity under Section 4(c)(8) of the Bank Holding Company Act. In 1982, the Board relaxed its ban enough to allow two failing S&Ls to be acquired by bank holding companies. One of the acquisitions was an interstate transaction. The bank holding company was Citicorp of New York, and the S&L was a California institution.

The Garn-St Germain Act of 1982 specifically permits the emergency acquisition of S&Ls by bank holding companies, provided S&L acquisition partners are not available. This provision of the Garn-St Germain Act will expire in 1985. The issue of the acquisition of healthy thrift institutions by bank holding companies will most likely resurface at that time.

CREDIT UNIONS

Credit unions are cooperative institutions that provide deposit and lending services to their members. They can be state or federally chartered and insured, and some states allow private insurance. Their member shareholders have a common bond or affinity, such as occupation or association. Table 12 gives a percentage breakdown of credit unions by the principal common bond categories as of the end of 1982.

As with mutual savings and loan associations, credit unions are owned by their depositors. Traditionally, credit unions have invested mostly in consumer loans.

Table 12: Distribution of Credit Unions by Common Bond, 1982

Associational	16.9%
Occupational (total)	78.6
Manufacturing	33.5
Wholesale & Retail trade	3.8
Governmental	16.0
Educational	8.6
Other occupational	16.7
Residential	4.5

Note: includes both federally chartered and state-chartered, federally insured credit unions.

Source: Credit Union National Association, Inc., *Credit Union Report*, 1982.

The National Credit Union Administration was created in 1970. Its purposes are to charter, examine, supervise, and provide share insurance for all federal credit unions. As of the end of 1982, there were 11,412 federally chartered credit unions, 5,024 federally insured state-chartered credit unions, and 3,156 state-chartered credit unions that were not federally insured.

The NCUA is the successor to the Bureau of Federal Credit Unions, which was established in 1934. The NCUA is headed by a three member board appointed by the President, who also appoints one member of the board as chairman. The chairman and the board members serve terms of six years. The NCUA is financed by operating fees from federal credit unions and by share insurance premiums. The share insurance fund is called the National Credit Union Share Insurance Fund.

In the early 1980s, the NCUA was in the lead in the deregulation of financial institutions. Although the chairman of the NCUA is a member of the Depository Institutions Deregulation Committee, credit unions are not subject to the interest rate ceiling deregulation schedule of that body. In 1982, the NCUA in effect removed all limitations on the interest rates that federal credit unions may pay on shares.

Although credit unions must have a common bond, in some cases the common bond allows a credit union to expand over a wide geographical area. For example, the Navy Federal Credit Union is made up of employees of the United States Navy and Marine Corps and has facilities worldwide.

Along with savings banks and savings and loan associations, credit unions were permitted in 1980 to offer transaction-type accounts. In the case of credit unions, the accounts are called share draft accounts. From a credit union member's standpoint, these accounts differ little from checking accounts of commercial banks.

MONEY MARKET MUTUAL FUNDS

Money market mutual funds are not normally included in a list of traditional nonbank depository institutions. Nevertheless, their impact on depository institutions, both bank and nonbank, in the latter half of the 1970s and the early 1980s has been such as to justify that they be given special recognition. Money market mutual funds are a form of mutual fund that invests in short-term, usually very safe, debt instruments, such as U.S. Government securities, highly rated commercial paper, and commercial bank certificates of deposit.

Mutual funds, or open-end investment companies, are organized under the Investment Company Act of 1940. Many are creations of securities brokerage firms. The funds sell shares to the public and invest the proceeds. The investment decisions are usually made by investment advisors, which in some cases are commercial banks.

The attraction that money market mutual funds had in the late 1970s and early 1980s was that they were not limited by interest rate ceilings. As short-term interest rates went into double digits, there was a rush into the money market mutual funds. In the years 1980–82, the monthly auction average interest rate on three month Treasury Bills fluctuated between 6.9 percent and 16.2 percent. The commercial bank deposit alternatives that could match high rates required investments of at least $100,000. Money market mutual funds, however, could in effect pass through most of the interest rate of an unregulated obligation. Thus during the period December 1979 to November 1982, the balances of money market mutual funds rose from $45.2 billion to $241.0 billion.

The future of money market mutual funds is uncertain. The Garn-St Germain Act of 1982 called upon the Depository Institutions Deregulation Committee to come up with a money market deposit account that would be competitive with the money market mutual funds. This the DIDC did. From December 14, 1982, to March 31, 1983, the money market deposit accounts attracted $320.5 billion. From the end of November, 1982, to the end of April, 1983, the assets in money market mutual funds declined from $241.0 billion to $187.7 billion. The money market mutual funds probably never would have come into existence without federal interest rate ceilings. These ceilings are rapidly becoming a thing of the past. Whether money market mutual funds can develop an alternative attraction that will enable them to survive remains to be seen.

NOTES

The Federal Home Loan Bank Board and the National Credit Union Administration put out a number of publications and compilations of data on the institutions in their industries.

Many of the changes discussed in this chapter resulted from the provisions of the Garn-St Germain Act of 1982. A partial legislative history of the act may be found at 1983 *U.S. Code Cong. and Adm. News* 3054. Relevant statutory provisions are located at the following sections of Title 12 of the U.S. Code: §1464(a) (authorizes the FHLBB to issue charters for federal associations, which are federal savings and loan associations and federal savings banks); §1464(b) (concerns capital stock and demand deposits of federal associations); §1464(c) (lists the permissible investments of federal associations); §1464(i) (allows conversions from state to federal charters and the reverse, from savings bank charters to savings and loan charters and the reverse, and from mutual to stock form and the reverse; for the latter also see §1725(j)); §1464(o) (provides for the temporary continuance of FDIC insurance for federal savings banks created by the conversion of FDIC-insured state savings banks); §1464(r) (concerns interstate branching by federal associations); §1729(f)(5) (authorizes the net worth certificate program for S&Ls); §1730a(m) (allows interstate and interindustry acquisitions of distressed S&Ls, including acquisitions by bank holding companies); §1823(i) (authorizes the net worth certificate program for insured banks); §3503(c) (directs the Depository Institutions Deregulation Committee to authorize money market deposit accounts); and §1730a (the Savings and Loan Holding Company Act).

In general, the activities of the FHLBB are governed by the Home Owners' Loan Act, which is codified at Chapter 12 of Title 12. The National Housing Act, codified at Chapter 13, concerns both the FHLBB and its subsidiary insurer, the FSLIC. The activities of the National Credit Union Administration are governed by the Federal Credit Union Act, codified at Chapter 14 of Title 12.

13

Focus on Competition

Throughout this volume, but particularly in the last chapter, it has been stressed that the regulation of banking, while still a discrete body of regulation, is nonetheless being affected by the blurring of distinctions between what were once institutions solely engaged in banking and institutions that, even if deposit takers, were engaged in a related but not a true banking business. This chapter looks at the changing nature of the banking business from a different viewpoint: the kinds of services and delivery systems that are evolving, in part as a response to regulatory distinctions and in part as a response to market forces. Whatever the cause, the implications for banking regulation are important.

Another way to describe this chapter is to say that it focuses on competition, in particular on the nature of the competitive environment that has emerged in the last few years. The focus of what has preceded in this book has been regulation. A theme of the chapter is that few of the products and services being offered in the new competitive environment are totally new themselves. What is new is how they are being repackaged for delivery to the ultimate consumers. A large part of the change is due to technology. Computers and related improvements in communications have enabled participants in the financial industry to substantially alter the way in which they deliver their products and services and have opened up the industry to others who were previously not considered participants.

The chapter discusses repackaged products and services, and

their delivery, under four headings: nonbank banks, financial supermarkets, money management accounts, and networking. There is a fair amount of overlap among the topics, but sufficient distinctions exist to provide some categorization. The inclusion of nonbank banks may seem at first glance to be adding a topic to the chapter that more properly belongs elsewhere, say in Chapter 10's discussion of bank holding companies. Indeed, nonbank banks are mentioned in the discussion in Chapter 6 on how a few firms in the securities industry have become affiliated with banks without running afoul of the Glass-Steagall and Bank Holding Company Acts. Nevertheless, nonbank banks would seem to have a place in this chapter because they are a means by which nondepository institutions, both those in the financial industry and those in other industries, are adding the products and services of depository institutions to their repertoire. Thus a form of repackaging is occurring, and repackaging is a theme of this chapter.

What is not covered in the chapter are the economic causes and ramifications of the new competitive environment. Traditional concepts of money and of commercial banks' role in the payment mechanism are being buffeted. The structure of the financial industry is ultimately dependent on the function of money, the items that are accepted as money, and the means by which these items move from place to place. Therefore, readers should keep in mind that the discussion in this chapter, and indeed in the entire book, deals with legal and institutional arrangements whose financial underpinnings are considered in more theoretical texts.

NONBANK BANKS

"Nonbank banks" is a term that came into prominence in the financial industry during the early 1980s. It refers to an entity that is a bank under some criteria, but not that of the Bank Holding Company Act, which defines a bank as an institution that both accepts demand deposits and makes commercial loans. Some have referred to the ability of an entity to be a bank for some purposes but not those of the Bank Holding Company Act as a "loophole". This is a misnomer to the extent that it implies an oversight in legislative drafting. One of the reasons bank holding company regulation was thought necessary was to restrain the particular power of banks that supposedly results from the combination of their control of large amounts of the public's funds with their role as lenders to business. Institutions not characterized by this combination were viewed as not requiring the regulation and supervision called for in the Bank Holding Company Act.

An organization that owns a bank as defined in the act is a bank holding company and subject to the Federal Reserve Board's supervision and to the restrictions on nonbanking activities contained in the act and the Board's Regulation Y. Activities that the Board has held to be permissible or not permissible for bank holding companies are listed in the appendix to Chapter 10. The organization is also subject to the interstate banking restrictions of the Douglas Amendment. These restrictions are described in Chapter 10.

If an organization takes demand deposits but does not make commercial loans, or makes commercial loans but does not take demand deposits, it is not a bank for the purposes of the Bank Holding Company Act. Consequently, a company owning such an organization is not a bank holding company and not subject to the Bank Holding Company Act and Federal Reserve Board supervision. In the early 1980s, a number of entities entered or considered entering the banking business, in limited fashion, by owning a nonbank bank. These entities included an oil company, a furniture store, finance companies, securities firms, insurance companies, a retailer, and a pen manufacturer. The Comptroller of the Currency seemed particularly willing to charter nonbank banks. The regulator would issue a charter for a national bank, but the bank would make a commitment not to accept demand deposits or, alternatively, not to make commercial loans.

The nonbank bank situation was given a curious twist by the Garn-St Germain Act. A provision of that act added an exemption to the Bank Holding Company Act's definition of a bank. The exemption is for any institution insured by the Federal Savings and Loan Insurance Corporation or chartered by the Federal Home Loan Bank Board. The exemption was added to preclude any uncertainty about (1) the status of federal S&Ls, and of federal savings banks, as they began to exercise the powers they received in the Garn-St Germain Act, and (2) the status of federally insured state S&Ls as they might be granted additional powers by state legislatures and regulators in response to the expanded powers of federal S&Ls. The expanded powers granted to federal S&Ls and savings banks by the Garn-St Germain Act were described in the preceding chapter.

In the absence of the added exemption, the argument could be made that federally chartered or insured S&Ls and federally chartered savings banks are banks under the definition in the Bank Holding Company Act. Consequently, any corporate owner of such an institution would be a bank holding company. With the exemption, a company, without becoming a bank holding company, can own a deposit-taking federally insured or chartered institution that can exercise powers almost identical to those of commercial banks.

As a result of accelerating interest in nonbank banks on the part of both the private sector and the Congress, the Comptroller of the Currency announced in April of 1983 a partial moratorium on the chartering of these institutions. The Federal Reserve Board, at the same time, was seeking a statutory moratorium, which would include several ways of creating nonbank banks not covered by the OCC's effort. Whether the nonbank bank becomes a mere footnote in financial history or will be an important part of the financial scene in the years ahead is now unknown. The significance of the nonbank bank phenomenon, however, is that it demonstrates the problem of applying a functional definition to banking at the same time that similar functions are being performed by nonbanking organizations.

FINANCIAL SUPERMARKETS

The term "financial supermarkets" has come into common usage over the last several years. The precise meaning of the term is somewhat elusive, however. The concept would seem to apply to two situations. The first concerns the actual physical colocation of different types of financial services. And the second refers to organizations that offer a variety of financial services, but not necessarily at the same physical locations.

The leading example thus far of the first type of financial supermarket is provided by Sears, Roebuck and Company. This organization, the nation's largest retailer, owns an insurance company, a savings and loan association, a national real estate firm, and a securities firm. The insurance company is Allstate Insurance; the S&L is Allstate Savings and Loan Association; the real estate firm is Coldwell Banker & Co.; and the securities firm is Dean Witter Reynolds Inc.

In 1982, Sears set up financial service centers in several of its stores. Each center has a Dean Witter office, an Allstate Insurance office, and a Coldwell Banker office. Centers in California, where Allstate Savings and Loan Association is located, also have S&L facilities. As of the spring of 1983, Sears had not released any figures concerning the profitability of its financial service centers. However, the retailer had announced plans to open additional centers, which would seem to indicate that the project is achieving at least some level of success.

Sears' financial service centers are perhaps the most widely known example of the physical colocation of different types of financial products and services. But they are not the only efforts in this area. Another example is afforded by the growing number of banks and savings and loan associations that are offering discount brokerage facilities on their premises. One notable program of this type is the INVEST Program. Originated as a joint venture by three savings and loan associations in 1982, this program was enabling a number of thrift institutions to provide discount brokerage services by the spring of 1983.

The second type of situation to which the term "financial supermarket" attaches is the organization that offers a variety of financial products and services, but not necessarily at the same physical location. Two large organizations of this type are American Express Company and Prudential Insurance Company of America. American Express has a number of financial products and services. It has the American Express credit card and American Express travelers checks. It owns Hartford Insurance Company. It has a banking business outside the United States; the banking business has U.S. offices in New York and Florida. In 1981, it acquired what is now Shearson/American Express, a large securities firm. And in the spring of 1983, it was reported to have reached an agreement to acquire an Indiana S&L.

Prudential is one of the nation's largest insurance companies. In 1981, it acquired the parent of Bache Halsey Stuart Shields, Inc., a large securities firm. In early 1983, it was reported to have reached an agreement to acquire a national bank in Georgia. The bank would divest either its demand deposits or its commercial loans and thus be a nonbank bank.

Neither American Express nor Prudential appears as yet to have made extensive efforts to physically colocate different types of financial services. Instead, the efforts seem to have been in other areas. The exchange of customer lists among subsidiary corporations of a financial conglomerate is one way to take advantage of common ownership. Perhaps at some point in the future, it will be commonplace for an employee of a financial conglomerate to sell products and services from more than one of the conglomerate's subsidiaries. For example, an account executive with a conglomerate's securities firm subsidiary might also sell insurance products. At the very least, there will probably be substantial efforts by the financial conglomerates to ensure that the employees of one subsidiary make efforts to apprise customers of the products and services of other subsidiaries.

The verdict is not yet in on the financial supermarket, either the actual physical supermarket such as Sears' financial centers, or the financial conglomerate supermarket, represented by such firms as Prudential and American Express. If the concept does have a fair measure of success, the next edition of *Federal Regulation of Banking* might be substantially different.

MONEY MANAGEMENT ACCOUNTS

In 1977, Merrill Lynch Pierce Fenner & Smith introduced its Cash Management Account. Since then, a number of similar services, which will be referred to here as money management accounts, have appeared. Brokerage houses and banking organizations are the most common offerors of these accounts. As of this writing, Merrill Lynch was attempting to assert a proprietary right to the computer software being used in money management accounts. Merrill Lynch's judicial action is based on patent law.

The major characteristic of money management accounts is that they combine several traditionally separate financial services. Idle funds in a money management account are placed in some sort of investment vehicle. This could be a money market fund or one of the recently authorized money market deposit accounts. The investment vehicle is usually accessible by check. One access method is that a checking account is maintained at a zero balance. When a check is presented for payment, funds are transferred from the investment vehicle to the checking account.

A plastic card, either a credit or a debit card, or even both, can be part of a money management account. If the card is a debit card, funds to meet obligations arising from the card's use may be transferred out of the investment vehicle in the same manner as funds are transferred to meet check obligations.

Another common element of money management accounts is securities services. An account holder is likely to have a good portion of the total value of his money management account invested in securities. If funds in the money market fund or other investment vehicle are insufficient to meet obligations arising from the use of checks or the plastic card, loans may be made automatically against the value of the securities. Alternatively, securities may be sold.

As the number of organizations offering money management accounts has grown, attempts to differentiate the accounts have increased. Some money management accounts offer discount brokerage services rather than full brokerage services. Others may offer access to travelers checks and to certain insurance products.

From an economic standpoint, a characteristic of money management accounts is the increase in liquidity they provide. Through a check or a plastic card, an account holder can have instant access to the value of a sizeable securities portfolio. The ramifications of this increase in liquidity on the velocity of money and on concepts of what constitute money are only beginning to be studied by economists.

A characteristic of most money management accounts is that more than one institution is involved in their delivery. For example, the checking account and debit card services of a Merrill Lynch Cash Management Account are provided by a commercial bank. For those money management accounts offered by banking organizations, the securities services portions are most likely provided by securities firms. One of the main reasons for more than one institution being involved in a money management account is Section 21 of the Glass-Steagall Act. That section prohibits firms engaged in the business of issuing, underwriting, selling, or distributing securities from also offering deposit accounts accessible by check.

Another important legal consideration is the Bank Holding Company Act, which was discussed in Chapter 10. That act and the Federal Reserve Board's Regulation Y promulgated thereunder limit the activities of companies that own banks. One general category of activities in which bank holding companies cannot participate to any great extent is insurance. Consequently, insurance companies cannot be bank holding companies and thus cannot own commercial banks. If an insurance company wants to offer a money management account that has as one component a commercial bank checking account, the company must make a contractual arrangement with a bank.

Such contractual arrangements and other types of alliances between financial organizations are discussed in the final section of this chapter, on networking.

NETWORKING

A general term that encompasses the two preceding topics—financial supermarkets and money management accounts—is networking. In the context of the financial services industry, the meaning of the term is that the offering of many financial products and services involves the efforts of more than one organization. Involvement of two or more organizations in a product or service is not something new. For example, the correspondent banking system has been a mainstay of commercial banking in the United States. Under this system, larger banks in urban areas support the activities of smaller banks in rural areas. Larger banks take portions of loans that are too big for the smaller banks. And they provide a number of other services that smaller banks are unable to provide for themselves.

In recent years, however, cooperative action seems to have become more pervasive. The arrangements among participants in the financial arena are covering a number of products and services previously viewed as separate. For example, securities services are being offered in conjunction with services by depository institutions. As another example, insurance products are turning up in a variety of combinations with the products of the securities industry and the trust industry.

Moreover, the delivering of financial products and services appears at times to be almost a separate product. The operation of electronic funds transfer systems, both the terminals and the connections with and among financial institutions, requires enormous capital investments. A number of organizations willing to make these investments have come into being. These organizations play an important role in the operation of many EFT systems. Providers of financial products and services through the systems must make arrangements with these EFT specialty organizations. In other instances, EFT systems are operated as joint ventures by traditional providers of financial products and services. The joint venture form is a type of networking. In still other instances, EFT joint venture participants may include, along with traditional providers of financial products and services, such organizations as retailers or supermarkets.

Is networking an anomaly due to legal requirements mandating the separation of various types of organizations? The legal reasons for separate organizations are only part of the explanation. Specialization is also due to technology and economics, particularly high capital requirements. The relaxation of legal barriers, which certainly seems to be the trend, will probably not erase the technological and economic reasons for specialization and the separation of functions. Financial conglomerates combining a number of different organizations under one corporate umbrella seem to have achieved an important niche in the financial world. But within or without the same corporate umbrella, the provision of financial products and services will continue to require the cooperation of a number of different specialty organizations.

NOTES

The Bank Holding Company Act is codified at Chapter 17 of Title 12 of the U.S. Code. The definition of a bank for purposes of the act is at 12 U.S.C. §1841(c). The principal provisions of the Glass-Steagall Act are at 12 U.S.C. §§24 (Seventh), 78, 377, and 378.

PART VI

The Future of Federal Bank Regulation

No account of the federal government's involvement in banking regulation can afford to overlook the changing characteristics of this regulation and the likelihood of major alterations in the future. Whether viewed in terms of structure, scope of authority, or method of operation, there is little reason to believe that federal regulation of banking will remain unchanged. Indeed, the substantial changes that occurred between the first edition of this book in 1975 and this third edition in 1983–84 are evidence of a dynamic federal statutory and regulatory structure. To cite one example, in the past eight years, four major federal banking laws were passed: the Financial Institutions Regulatory and Interest Rate Control Act of 1978, the International Banking Act of 1978, the Depository Institutions Deregulation and Monetary Control Act of 1980, and the Garn-St Germain Act of 1982. Chapter 14 discusses recent trends which may influence the shape of federal bank regulation in the years ahead.

14

Winds of Change

New developments in banking, as in any industry, are difficult to foresee. Nevertheless, this chapter makes a few general predictions in the context of commenting on broad trends in federal banking regulation as they have been evidenced over recent years and as they promise to develop. These comments relate to the scope and nature of such supervision, to the structure of the supervisory system, and to the changing balance between government and private supervision.

SCOPE AND NATURE OF SUPERVISION

In the years ahead there should be no significant lessening in the interest of the federal government in banks and their performance. So long as banks occupy a central position in the monetary system, the federal government must concern itself with their soundness and stability. And so long as banks remain one of the major mobilizers and allocators of credit, the federal government must, if it is to act in a manner consistent with basic principles underlying the business structure of the nation, be concerned with maintaining a reasonably competitive system. Finally, it is unlikely that the federal government will attach less importance in the future to protecting consumers against possible injustices, real or perceived, on the part of banks and other financial institutions.

This is not to say, however, that the scope and nature of federal supervision of banks will remain unaltered. On the contrary, significant changes are already under way and more are to be expected. Indeed, changes in the nature and scope of supervision are inevitable as the banking system itself changes in response to a wide variety of forces, including but not limited to technological advances, competitive pressures, and consumer interests.

There are several important kinds of changes under way in the banking system that seem especially significant. One of these stems from the fact that the federal government's interest in the competitiveness of the banking system conflicts with the continued applicability of measures adopted in the early 1930s to protect the solvency of banks by placing constraints on competition. It is the latter set of constraints that is giving way. Deposit interest regulation, discussed in Chapter 6, is the most obvious illustration. As of mid-1983, this particular constraint appeared to be fast disappearing.

Geographic constraints on bank expansion, which at the federal level apply primarily to commercial banks, are also under heavy pressure. In part, this is for the same reason that interest rate controls are being dismantled. Both types of constraints serve to protect individual banks against incursions into their markets by other competitors and are therefore, by their very nature, anticompetitive and inconsistent with the public policy goal of maintaining a competitive banking system.

There are, however, other reasons why serious criticism is being directed at the continuation of restraints on geographic expansion by commercial banks. Competitor institutions, particularly nonbank institutions offering a wide and competitive range of financial services, such as securities firms and insurance companies, are not constrained by federal law with respect to the geographic areas over which they may operate. The antitrust laws are believed by many to provide sufficient protection against undue concentrations of banking power. And technological change, making distance an irrelevant consideration in the provision of many banking services, points up the archaic nature of geographic constraints. On the other hand, because these constraints have been in place for more than a half-century, there are strong economic interests tied to their continuation. Thus their elimination is likely to be gradual and, possibly, accompanied by the development of new federal standards or guidelines on geographic expansion.

Finally, the product mix of commercial banks is changing. So long as commercial banks were the sole providers of third-party transaction account services (i.e., demand deposits subject to check) the boundaries of the banking business could be fairly well limited by statute or regulation. But commercial banks no longer hold this exclusive franchise. Transaction account services for individuals may now be provided by thrift institutions. Federal savings and loan associations can offer demand deposit services to their business customers. And nondepository institutions are discovering ways to make similar services available. It may be expected, therefore, that as nonbank financial firms and depository thrift institutions take on more of the powers of commercial banks, commercial banks will be able to offer and package a broader range of services. This in turn will place a high premium on professional, highly-skilled regulation by federal agencies—regulation that will focus most importantly on management capabilities and management planning.

FEDERAL BANK REGULATORY STRUCTURE

The present tripartite system of bank regulation at the federal level, wherein most regulatory authority is divided among the three banking agencies (the FDIC, the Federal Reserve Board, and the Comptroller of the Currency), had scarcely been put in place in 1933 when recommendations were made concerning reorganization. In the first edition of this book, in 1975, it was suggested that proposals for change would continue to be made but that there seemed to be no special reason to believe that any would be adopted. Today, that judgment must be modified. Before commenting on recent developments, however, it may be useful to readers, and serve also as a possible indicator of the future, if there is a brief review of the principal recommendations made in the past for change in the federal regulatory structure.

One of the first such recommendations was made by the Brookings Institution in 1937 and would have abolished the Office of the Comptroller of the Currency and placed all bank examination authority in the FDIC. In the immediate post-World War II years the task forces of the Hoover Commission made several recommendations, of which one would have moved the FDIC to the Federal Reserve, a second would have placed the Office of the Comptroller of the Currency in the Federal Reserve, while still another would have unified all bank regulatory authority in the Federal Reserve. The final report of the Hoover Commission adopted none of these approaches but instead recommended that the FDIC be transferred to the Treasury Department, thereby presumably effecting some kind of uniformity of regulation by placing the FDIC in the same cabinet agency in which the Office of the Comptroller of the Currency was already located.

The Commission on Money and Credit in its report in 1961 stated that there should be only one federal examining authority for commercial banks and this should be the Federal Reserve. Among the proposals made in the Congress during the 1960s was one that would have established a single federal bank regulatory agency outside of the Federal Reserve System; another would have consolidated all regulatory authority in the Treasury Department.

The Conference of State Bank Supervisors in 1970 recommended that much of the regulatory authority now exercised by the Federal Reserve and the FDIC be transferred to the states. That organization has continued to press such proposals.

A sweeping proposal for change in the federal bank regulatory system was made by President Nixon's Commission on Financial Structure and Regulation, often referred to as the Hunt Commission. That body recommended that the bank regulatory authority of the Federal Reserve be transferred to the FDIC and that the new combined agency be retitled "Office of the Administrator of State Banks." The Federal Reserve would retain, under this plan, regulatory authority over holding companies and foreign operations of domestic banks. The Office of the Comptroller of the Currency would remain essentially unchanged, although given more formal independence from the Treasury Department and retitled "Office of the National Bank Administrator."

Another recommendation by the Hunt Commission was to split insurance functions from the regulatory functions and establish a new federal agency, to be known as the "Federal Deposit Guarantee Administration." This new agency would be concerned primarily with insurance activities rather than with regulation and would exercise the insurance functions located in the Federal Deposit Insurance Corporation, the Federal Savings and Loan Insurance Corporation, and the National Credit Union Administration.

By the latter part of the 1970s, the same forces for change that were impacting on banks and other financial institutions compelled federal authorities to consider new ways of coordinating their activities. One illustration involves the relaxation of deposit interest regulation. Because of the differing impact on commercial banks and thrift institutions, it appeared that deregulation of interest rate controls could not proceed through unilateral action by each of the federal agencies that had some authority in this area. Therefore, a coordinating committee made up of representatives of the agencies was created.

Chapters 2 and 6 have already described in some detail the nature of the coordinating steps taken at the federal level in recent years. It is almost (but not quite) possible to say that two new federal regulatory agencies have been created for all depository institutions, bank and nonbank—the Federal Financial Institutions Examination Council and the Depository Institutions Deregulation Committee. Whether either or both of these bodies will evolve into a new, consolidated financial institutions regulatory agency—with the present federal bank regulatory agencies or powers incorporated therein—is still too early to tell.

The trend toward centralization was given added impetus in 1982 by the creation of a special task group, under the direction of the Vice President, to study reorganization of the federal regulatory structure. The Bush Task Group is to report in September of 1983 and may suggest new approaches to regulation, such as functional rather than institutional regulation, or possibly broad consolidation extending beyond the traditional banking agencies.

In the 1975 edition of this book, it was suggested that the centralization trend seemed to be pointing toward making the Federal Reserve Board the eventual "single banking agency." At the time that edition was prepared, the Congress had only recently insisted on retaining all bank holding company regulation in the Board. Moreover, the Congress seemed to be establishing a pattern of giving the Board certain other kinds of regulatory responsibilities, such as the drawing up of regulations to implement truth-in-lending legislation.

Because of the Board's increasing preoccupation with monetary policy, it is possible that what appeared in 1975 to be a trend toward centering bank regulatory authority in the Federal Reserve Board has been slowed or perhaps even reversed. It is still too early, however, to render any confident judgment on this matter. What seems in 1983 to be clear is that in the future the regulation of banks will be conducted on a more coordinated basis at the federal level and that this coordination will extend beyond the traditional bank regulatory agencies to include, at the very least, other federal agencies regulating nonbank depository institutions.

THE LOCUS OF REGULATION

Banks and other depository institutions have two sets of regulators: government agencies and the private market. The latter is a loose collection of concerned persons and institutions, including creditors (depositors and others) and investors, plus those who serve them, such as rating agencies and market analysts. Regulation accorded banks by the market is not as easily or precisely defined as government agency regulation, but it can be as effective, and at times overpowering. When, for example, the market judges a bank to be headed for dire trouble, it may act so as to compel a substantial loss of deposits or a drastic fall in the price of the bank's stock, events that usually will result in quick changes in management or ownership, or even in the closing of the bank.

As one looks ahead to the future of bank regulation, the most puzzling question is how these two sets of regulators will interface. Will a new balance be struck and, if so, what are the implications for federal regulation of banking or, indeed, for the banking structure itself?

For a long period, the regulatory balance was moving away from the market and towards the government. The reason was the increasing scope of deposit insurance. The federal insuring agencies have followed practices that result in almost 100 percent insurance coverage. Recently, Congress furthered the result of these agency practices by providing, in the Garn-St Germain Act, for capital assistance to distressed depository institutions. This assured the continued viability of most of these institutions and thus the full protection of their depositors. In such a situation, the market regulators could afford to relax somewhat, with the growing, though not complete, assurance that they could rely on government to oversee the operations of depository institutions, and to make creditors, and possibly even investors, whole should problems arise.

Deregulation could alter the equation. Banks and other depository institutions may soon be free to pay whatever interest is required to obtain funds, and to offer a broader variety of services over broader geographic areas. Can government be relied upon to continue to underwrite new risks that result?

In mid-1983 two schools of thought are emerging. One would look for some form of re-regulation, beginning with a better definition of "banking" and the exercise of strict, though possibly new and different, controls over institutions that offer services that meet the definition. The other school of thought looks toward the possibility of the market assuming a greater part of the regulatory burden. This school would alter insurance practices to put depositors, particularly those with large accounts, at greater risk in the event of bank failure, thus compelling the private market to be more attentive to its historic regulatory duties.

Deregulation of depository institutions poses other issues of significance to the subject of this volume. Will regulation, in the pure sense, be diminished, to be replaced by greater *supervision* of depository institutions by federal agencies? Will risk-adjusted insurance premiums take the place of regulatory restrictions, and if so how much additional auditing and supervision will be required?

The problem of achieving a proper balance between government and private regulation of banks will likely affect future editions of this volume. But the problem is unlikely to be fully resolved when the next edition appears.

Statistical Section

The tables in this section are intended to provide a quantitative backdrop to the discussions in the text. Much of the data are from the annual reports of the federal banking agencies, particularly the Federal Deposit Insurance Corporation. Nationwide data are prepared by the FDIC on two bases: (1) for the 50 states and the District of Columbia and (2) for the 50 states, the District of Columbia, and other U.S. controlled jurisdictions, such as Puerto Rico. Unless otherwise indicated, nationwide data from the FDIC in the following tables are for the second category, referred to by the FDIC as "states and other areas." The term "n.a." in the tables means "not available."

Table 1
Numbers of Offices of Commercial Banks, 1920, 1930, 1940, 1950, 1960, and 1965–1982[1]

Year	*Total Offices*	*Banks—Main Offices*	*Branches[2]*
1920	31,572	30,291	1,281
1930	27,201	23,679	3,522
1940	17,899	14,361	3,538
1950	18,966	14,121	4,845
1960	23,954	13,471	10,483
1965	29,556	13,803	15,753
1966	30,673	13,766	16,907
1967	31,652	13,721	17,931
1968	32,691	13,678	19,013
1969	33,858	13,661	20,197
1970	35,330	13,686	21,644
1971	36,903	13,783	23,120
1972	38,538	13,927	24,611
1973	40,620	14,171	26,449
1974	42,890	14,458	28,432
1975	44,609	14,630	29,979
1976	45,795	14,673	31,122
1977	47,600	14,710	32,890
1978	49,286	14,711	34,575
1979	51,280	14,708	36,572
1980	53,333	14,836	38,497
1981	55,427	14,880	40,547
1982	54,492	14,960	39,532

[1]50 States and D.C.
[2]Domestic branches only.
Source: FDIC, *Annual Report*, 1940, 1950, 1960, and 1965–1981; FDIC, *Changes Among Operating Banks and Branches*, 1982; Federal Reserve Board, *All Banks Statistics* 1896–1955.

Table 2
Numbers of Commercial Banks and Offices by Class of Bank, 1940, 1950, 1960, and 1970–1982[1]

Year	National Banks			State Federal Reserve Member Banks			Nonmember Insured Banks			Noninsured Banks		
	Banks	Branches[2]	Total Offices	Banks	Branches[2]	Total Offices	Banks	Branches[2]	Total Offices	Banks	Branches[2]	Total Offices
1940	5,144	1,542	6,686	1,342	1,003	2,345	6,952	941	7,893	923	52	975
1950	4,958	2,230	7,188	1,912	1,359	3,271	6,562	1,204	7,766	689	52	741
1960	4,529	5,507	10,036	1,641	2,624	4,265	6,948	2,305	9,253	353	47	400
1970	4,620	12,522	17,142	1,147	3,651	4,798	7,735	5,424	13,159	184	47	231
1971	4,599	13,272	17,871	1,128	3,819	4,947	7,875	5,989	13,864	181	40	221
1972	4,612	13,959	18,571	1,092	3,981	5,073	8,017	6,626	14,643	206	45	251
1973	4,659	14,908	19,567	1,076	4,051	5,127	8,229	7,444	15,673	207	46	253
1974	4,708	15,729	20,437	1,072	4,209	5,281	8,438	8,446	16,884	240	48	288
1975	4,741	16,269	21,010	1,046	4,406	5,452	8,586	9,254	17,840	257	50	307
1976	4,735	16,667	21,402	1,023	4,672	5,695	8,639	9,729	18,368	276	54	330
1977	4,654	17,578	22,232	1,015	4,595	5,610	8,734	10,663	19,397	307	54	361
1978	4,564	18,107	22,671	1,000	4,721	5,721	8,814	11,696	20,510	333	51	384
1979	4,448	18,798	23,246	977	4,879	5,856	8,926	12,844	21,770	357	51	408
1980	4,425	19,738	24,163	997	4,771	5,768	9,000	13,949	22,949	414	39	453
1981	4,455	20,710	25,165	1,020	5,173	6,193	8,927	14,617	23,544	365	29	394
1982	4,578	20,232	24,810	1,039	4,979	6,018	8,818	14,274	23,092	408	28	436

[1]50 States and D.C.
[2]Includes domestic branches only.
Source: FDIC, *Annual Report*, 1940, 1950, 1960, and 1970–1982; FDIC, *Changes Among Operating Banks and Branches*, 1982.

Table 3
Composition of Liabilities and Capital of U.S. Commercial Banks, Year-End 1960–1982

		Percentage of Liabilities and Capital[1]										
		Deposits						Capital Accounts			
Year	Total (millions)	Total	Demand	Savings	Other Time	Federal Funds Purchased	Loan Reserves[2]	Total	Notes and Debentures	Equity	Other Liability and Reserves
1960	$ 258,359	89.23%	60.69%	28.54%[3]	n.a.%	n.a.%	0.91%	8.15%	n.a.%	n.a.%	1.71%
1961	279,503	89.27	59.46	22.93	6.88	n.a.	0.93	8.06	n.a.	n.a.	1.74
1962	298,196	88.22	55.10	23.89	9.22	n.a.	0.91	8.10	n.a.	n.a.	2.77
1963	314,056	87.96	52.24	24.40	11.32	n.a.	0.96	8.20	n.a.	n.a.	2.88
1964	348,433	88.52	51.72	23.90	12.90	n.a.	1.02	8.01	n.a.	n.a.	2.45
1965	378,899	88.09	48.91	24.52	14.66	0.64	1.06	8.02	n.a.	n.a.	2.19
1966	406,515	87.36	47.52	22.23	17.61	0.69	1.07	7.92	n.a.	n.a.	2.96
1967	454,603	87.59	46.62	20.85	20.13	1.10	1.04	7.60	0.45	7.15	2.67
1968	504,637	86.69	45.68	19.12	21.89	1.48	1.04	7.36	0.43	6.94	3.43
1969	535,680	82.14	45.20	17.57	19.37	2.75	1.16	7.50	0.38	7.12	6.45
1970	581,536	83.49	42.82	17.05	23.62	2.87	1.09	7.42	0.38	7.05	5.13
1971	646,283	84.01	40.86	17.41	25.73	3.76	1.00	7.34	0.47	6.87	3.89
1972	746,131	83.30	40.02	16.69	26.59	4.54	0.93	7.10	0.56	6.53	4.13
1973	842,865	81.58	36.98	15.21	29.39	6.08	0.93	6.93	0.50	6.43	4.48
1974	927,486	81.26	34.24	14.73	32.29	5.65	0.94	6.90	0.47	6.42	5.25
1975	974,711	81.35	33.39	16.53	31.42	5.53	0.93	7.13	0.47	6.66	5.06
1976	1,040,090	81.25	32.56	19.66	29.03	7.02	0.60	7.54	0.51	7.03	3.59
1977	1,176,608	80.49	32.71	18.76	29.02	7.34	0.58	7.32	0.49	6.83	4.27
1978	1,329,012	78.50	30.74	16.67	31.08	7.24	0.59	7.11	0.45	6.66	6.56
1979	1,437,749	77.11	30.25	14.42	32.44	7.99	0.63	7.22	0.41	6.81	7.05
1980	1,543,545	77.35	28.06	13.04	36.25	8.65	0.64	7.41	0.41	7.00	5.95
1981	1,692,329	75.50	22.78	13.23	39.50	9.67	0.66	7.38	0.37	7.01	5.64
1982	1,878,290	74.86	19.82	16.23	38.82	9.56	0.68	7.25	0.37	6.88	6.11

[1]Percentages may not add to totals due to rounding.
[2]Information unadjusted for changes in accounting procedures between 1969 and 1975.
[3]1960 figures for "Savings" include "Other time."
Source: FDIC, *Annual Report*, 1960–1982.

Table 4
Total Domestic Deposits of Commercial Banks by Class of Bank, Year End 1960–1982[1] (millions)

		National banks		State Federal Reserve members		State insured nonmember		State noninsured[3]	
Year	*Total*	*Amount*	*Percent of total*	*Amount*	*Percent of total*	*Amount*	*Percent of total*	*Amount*	*Percent of total*
1960[2]	$ 230,532	n.a.	n.a.	n.a.	n.a.	n.a.	n.a.	$ 1,538	0.7%
1961	249,504	$123,408	49.5%	$ 66,559	26.7%	$ 35,247	14.1%	1,599	0.6
1962	263,060	133,255	50.7	71,763	27.3	38,301	14.6	1,616	0.6
1963	276,230	144,733	52.4	76,746	27.8	42,591	15.4	1,583	0.6
1964	308,427	158,806	51.5	82,245	26.7	46,938	15.2	2,197	0.7
1965	333,779	185,334	55.5	78,327	23.5	51,982	15.6	2,267	0.7
1966	355,128	207,049	58.3	85,547	24.1	60,244	17.0	2,288	0.6
1967	398,204	232,083	58.3	95,637	24.0	68,075	17.1	2,409	0.6
1968	437,489	258,655	59.1	98,467	22.5	77,529	17.7	2,837	0.6
1969	439,989	257,844	58.6	94,445	21.5	84,701	19.3	3,000	0.7
1970	485,519	285,436	58.8	101,512	20.9	95,566	19.7	3,006	0.6
1971	542,910	315,549	58.1	111,777	20.6	111,858	20.6	3,726	0.7
1972	621,547	360,779	58.0	123,186	19.8	132,942	21.4	4,639	0.7
1973	687,576	397,372	57.8	131,421	19.1	152,827	22.2	5,956	0.9
1974	753,630	433,162	57.5	144,799	19.2	168,453	22.4	7,217	1.0
1975	792,882	450,308	56.8	143,409	18.1	187,031	23.6	12,133	1.5
1976	845,057	472,124	55.9	149,482	17.7	209,318	24.8	14,133	1.7
1977	947,072	523,233	55.2	163,444	17.3	242,492	25.6	17,903	1.9
1978	1,043,250	564,202	54.1	178,205	17.1	273,977	26.3	26,866	2.6
1979	1,108,690	598,860	54.0	186,977	16.9	308,768	27.8	14,085	1.3
1980	1,193,968	656,752	55.0	191,183	16.0	344,311	28.8	1,722	0.1
1981	1,277,785	710,539	55.6	193,459	15.1	372,480	29.2	1,307	0.1
1982	1,406,148	784,589	55.8	217,109	15.4	403,539	28.7	911	0.1

[1]1961 through 1965 are average figures for year.
[2]Data for insured banks not broken down into categories for 1960. Total insured commercial bank deposits equalled $228,993 million or 99.3 percent of total commercial bank deposits.
[3]The decline in figures for State noninsured banks after 1978 reflects, in part, the conversion of many U.S. branches of foreign banks from noninsured to insured status.
Source: FDIC, *Annual Report*, 1960–1982.

Table 5
Shares of Total Credit Market Debt Claims Against Nonfinancial Sectors[1], Five-Year Moving Average[2] 1956–1982, Percent

Year-End	*Commercial Banks*[3]	*Savings Institutions*[4]	*Insurance and Pension Funds*	*Other Financial*[5]	*Nonfinancial*[6]
1956	28.5	11.0	19.6	3.0	37.9
1957	28.0	11.6	20.1	3.2	37.0
1958	27.8	12.3	20.5	3.3	36.1
1959	27.3	12.9	20.8	3.4	35.6
1960	27.0	13.5	21.0	3.5	35.0
1961	26.8	14.1	21.2	3.6	34.3
1962	26.8	14.7	21.2	3.8	33.5
1963	26.8	15.4	21.2	4.0	32.7
1964	27.1	16.0	21.2	4.1	31.6
1965	27.6	16.6	21.1	4.3	30.5
1966	27.9	17.0	21.1	4.4	29.6
1967	28.4	17.2	20.9	4.5	29.0
1968	29.0	17.3	20.7	4.6	28.4
1969	29.3	17.3	20.5	4.7	28.2
1970	29.6	17.2	20.3	4.8	28.1
1971	30.1	17.4	19.8	4.9	27.9
1972	30.5	17.7	19.3	5.1	27.4
1973	31.0	18.1	18.7	5.4	26.8
1974	31.7	18.3	18.2	5.5	26.3
1975	32.0	18.7	17.8	5.5	26.1
1976	32.0	19.0	17.6	5.5	26.0
1977	31.6	19.3	17.6	5.4	26.1
1978	31.1	19.5	17.7	5.4	26.3
1979	30.6	19.7	17.8	5.5	26.5
1980	30.2	19.7	17.9	5.7	26.5
1981	30.0	19.3	18.0	6.3	26.5
1982[7]	29.7	18.6	18.1	6.9	26.8

[1]Includes government securities, domestic and foreign corporate bonds, mortgages, consumer credit, domestic and foreign open market paper, other domestic and foreign bank loans, and other domestic and foreign debt instruments.
[2]The year shown is the final year in the five-year moving average.
[3]Consists of U.S. chartered banks, domestic bank affiliates, Edge Act corporations, domestic agencies and branches of foreign banks, and banks in U.S. possessions. Does not include nonbank affiliates of bank holding companies or foreign affiliates of U.S. chartered banks.
[4]Consists of savings and loan associations, savings banks, and credit unions.
[5]Consists of finance companies, real estate investment trusts, open-end investment companies, money market funds, and security brokers and dealers.
[6]Includes households, businesses, governments, Federal Reserve Banks, and all foreign entities.
[7]End of third quarter.
Source: Federal Reserve Bank of Minneapolis, *Annual Report*, 1982. Source of basic data: Board of Governors of the Federal Reserve System, *Flow of Funds Accounts, Assets and Liabilities Outstanding.*

Table 6
Shares of Total Financial Assets Held by Financial Institutions[1], Five-Year Moving Average[2] 1956–1982
Percent

Year-End	*Commercial Banks*[3]	*Savings Institutions*[4]	*Insurance Companies*	*Pension Funds*	*Other Financial*[5]
1956	45.9	16.1	25.2	6.1	6.7
1957	44.4	16.9	25.1	6.7	7.0
1958	43.0	17.5	24.9	7.3	7.3
1959	41.6	18.2	24.7	7.9	7.6
1960	40.5	18.8	24.4	8.5	7.8
1961	39.4	19.3	24.0	9.1	8.1
1962	38.6	19.8	23.5	9.6	8.4
1963	37.9	20.4	23.1	10.0	8.7
1964	37.4	20.8	22.5	10.4	8.9
1965	37.1	21.2	21.8	10.8	9.1
1966	37.0	21.4	21.3	11.0	9.2
1967	36.9	21.4	20.8	11.5	9.5
1968	37.1	21.1	20.2	11.9	9.8
1969	37.3	20.8	19.8	12.1	10.0
1970	37.5	20.6	19.5	12.4	10.0
1971	37.6	20.6	19.0	12.7	10.1
1972	37.6	20.8	18.6	13.0	10.1
1973	38.0	21.1	18.1	12.9	9.9
1974	38.8	21.6	17.7	12.5	9.6
1975	39.1	22.2	17.3	12.3	9.3
1976	39.2	22.7	17.0	12.1	8.9
1977	39.3	23.4	17.0	11.7	8.6
1978	39.1	23.9	17.0	11.7	8.4
1979	38.3	24.2	17.0	11.9	8.5
1980	37.8	24.2	17.1	12.1	8.9
1981	37.5	23.7	17.0	12.1	9.7
1982[6]	37.0	23.1	16.9	12.3	10.7

[1]Includes credit market debt claims against nonfinancial sectors (Table 5), plus currency, demand and time deposits, security credit, corporate equities, member bank reserves, and miscellaneous assets.
[2]The year shown is the final year in the five-year moving average.
[3]Consists of U.S. chartered banks, domestic bank affiliates, Edge Act corporations, agencies and branches of foreign banks, and banks in U.S. possessions. Does not include nonbank affiliates of bank holding companies or foreign affiliates of U.S. chartered banks.
[4]Consists of savings and loan associations, savings banks, and credit unions.
[5]Consists of finance companies, real estate investment trusts, open-end investment companies, money market funds, and security brokers and dealers.
[6]End of third quarter.
Source: Federal Reserve Bank of Minneapolis, *Annual Report*, 1982. Source of basic data: Board of Governors of the Federal Reserve System, *Flow of Funds Accounts, Assets and Liabilities Outstanding*.

Table 7
Deposits of Major Depository Institutions by Type of Institution and State, Year-End 1981 (billions)

State	Total Deposits	Insured Commercial Banks	Mutual Savings Banks	Savings & Loan Associations	Credit Unions	Insured Commercial Banks as a % of Total Deposits
Alabama	$ 20.5	$15.6	—	$4.4	$0.5	76.1%
Alaska	3.1	1.9	$ 0.3	0.4	0.5	61.3
Arizona	18.3	12.2	—	5.5	0.6	66.7
Arkansas	14.4	10.3	—	4.0	0.1	71.5
California	306.1	208.9	—	91.0	6.2	68.3
Colorado	23.3	14.7	—	7.9	0.7	63.1
Connecticut	31.1	11.9	14.4	4.2	0.6	38.3
Delaware	4.2	3.0	0.9	0.2	0.1	71.4
District of Columbia	12.3	8.0	—	3.6	0.7	65.0
Florida	90.9	43.2	—	45.7	2.0	47.5
Georgia	30.9	20.4	—	9.8	0.7	66.0
Hawaii	8.2	5.4	—	2.1	0.7	65.9
Idaho	5.4	4.4	—	0.9	0.1	81.5
Illinois	160.1	119.8	—	39.6	0.7	74.8
Indiana	39.1	28.3	0.3	9.1	1.4	72.4
Iowa	25.9	19.8	—	6.1	—	76.5
Kansas	21.4	15.2	—	6.1	0.1	71.0
Kentucky	23.4	17.8	—	5.3	0.3	76.1
Louisiana	32.2	23.8	—	7.8	0.6	73.9
Maine	6.6	3.0	2.6	0.6	0.4	45.5
Maryland	24.3	14.7	1.8	6.7	1.1	60.5
Massachusetts	55.1	29.9	21.4	3.2	0.6	54.3
Michigan	63.4	46.1	—	15.9	1.4	72.7
Minnesota	36.7	27.4	0.8	8.3	0.2	74.7
Mississippi	13.6	10.8	—	2.6	0.2	79.4
Missouri	43.1	29.7	—	13.4	—	68.9
Montana	6.1	4.9	—	1.0	0.2	80.3
Nebraska	15.0	10.5	—	4.3	0.2	90.0
Nevada	5.6	3.4	—	1.9	0.3	60.7
New Hampshire	6.7	3.1	2.5	1.0	0.1	46.3
New Jersey	64.6	31.8	9.5	22.4	0.9	49.2
New Mexico	8.4	5.8	—	2.3	0.3	69.1
New York	458.0	353.9	80.2	21.2	2.7	77.3
North Carolina	32.2	22.1	—	9.7	0.4	68.6
North Dakota	7.2	5.2	—	2.0	—	72.2
Ohio	78.8	45.7	—	32.1	1.0	58.0
Oklahoma	29.1	23.6	—	5.1	0.4	81.1
Oregon	16.9	11.0	0.4	5.0	0.5	65.1
Pennsylvania	112.0	75.4	13.2	21.3	2.1	67.3
Rhode Island	8.3	5.8	1.8	0.7	—	69.9
South Carolina	13.2	7.0	—	5.8	0.4	53.0
South Dakota	7.7	6.5	—	1.0	0.2	84.4
Tennessee	28.4	21.3	—	6.5	0.6	75.0
Texas	147.9	114.8	—	29.9	3.2	77.6
Utah	9.7	6.2	—	3.4	0.1	63.9
Vermont	3.3	2.2	0.9	0.2	—	66.7
Virginia	32.7	21.9	—	8.5	2.3	67.0
Washington	32.3	20.3	3.9	7.4	0.7	62.9
West Virginia	11.1	9.3	—	1.5	0.3	83.8
Wisconsin	35.0	23.2	0.9	10.9	—	66.3
Wyoming	4.3	3.3	—	0.9	0.1	76.7

Sources: FDIC, *Banking Operating Statistics*, 1981; National Association of Mutual Savings Banks, *1982 National Fact Book;* FHLBB, *1981 Combined Financial Statements;* NCUA, *1981 Annual Report.*

Table 8
Number and Deposits of Banks Closed Due to Financial Difficulties, 1960–1982

Year	Number of Failed Banks					Deposits of Failed Banks (thousands)				
			Insured					Insured		
	Total	Non-Insured	Total	Without Disburse-ments by FDIC	With Disburse-ments by FDIC	Total	Non-Insured	Total	Without Disburse-ments by FDIC	With Disburse-ments by FDIC
1960–1964	24	8	16	1	15	$70,118	$4,359	$65,759	$3,011	$62,748
1965–1969	33	5	28	0	28	224,963	4,043	220,920	0	220,920
1970	8	1	7	0	7	55,229	423	54,806	0	54,806
1971	6	0	6	0	6	132,058	0	132,058	0	132,058
1972	3	2	1	0	1	99,784	79,304	20,480	0	20,480
1973	6	0	6	0	6	971,296	0	971,296	0	971,296
1974	4	0	4	0	4	1,575,832	0	1,575,832	0	1,575,832
1975	14	1	13	0	13	340,574	1,000	339,574	0	339,574
1976	17	1	16	0	16	865,459	800	864,659	0	864,659
1977	6	0	6	0	6	205,208	0	205,208	0	205,208
1978	7	0	7	0	7	854,154	0	854,154	0	854,154
1979	10	0	10	0	10	110,696	0	110,696	0	110,696
1980	10	0	10	0	10	216,300	0	216,300	0	216,300
1981	10	0	10	0	10	3,826,022	0	3,826,022	0	3,826,022
1982	42	0	42	0	42	9,908,379	0	9,908,379	0	9,908,379

Source: FDIC, *Annual Report*, 1982, Table 122

Table 9
Number of U.S. Banks Failing Between 1970 and 1982 by Class of Bank and Size

Deposit Size (millions)	*Total*	*National Banks*	*State Federal Reserve members*	*State insured nonmembers*	*Non-Insured*
Under $5	32	4	1	24	3
$5–$10	29	6	1	22	0
$10–$25	37	7	2	28	0
$25–$50	14	3	2	7	2
$50–$100	8	1	1	6	0
Over $100	23	7	2	14	0
Total	143	28	9	101	5

Source: FDIC, *Annual Report*, 1970–1982.

Table 10
FDIC Disbursements and Recoveries in Failures of Insured Commercial Banks 1960–1982, as of December 31, 1982 (thousands)

Year	*Pay-Off Cases*			*Purchase and Assumption Cases*			*All Cases*		
	Principal Disbursements Net of Recoveries[1]	*Advances and Expenses*	*Total Net Disbursements*	*Principal Disbursements Net of Recoveries*[1]	*Advances and Expenses*	*Total Net Disbursements*	*Principal Disbursements Net of Recoveries*[1]	*Advances and Expenses*	*Total Net Disbursements*
1960–1964	$ 2,699	$1,184	$ 3,883	$ 0	$ 0	$ 0	$ 2,699	$ 1,184	$ 3,883
1965–1969	4,849	1,218	6,067	637	7,331	7,968	5,486	8,549	14,035
1970	272	702	974	16	1,988	2,004	288	2,690	2,978
1971	193	811	1,004	—	11,578	11,578	193	12,389	12,582
1972	1,226	398	1,624	—	—	—	1,226	398	1,624
1973	—	1,677	1,677	67,597	1,158	68,755	67,597	2,835	70,432
1974	—	—	—	328	171,532	171,860	328	171,532	171,860
1975	82	1,447	1,529	18,613	28,308	46,921	18,695	29,755	48,450
1976	1,900	1,415	3,315	20,614	38,996	59,610	22,514	40,411	62,925
1977	—	—	—	1,160	3,637	4,797	1,160	3,637	4,797
1978	129	50	179	5,756	33,194	38,950	5,885	33,244	39,129
1979	739	299	1,038	7,094	6,458	13,552	7,833	6,757	14,590
1980	1,810	480	2,290	19,150	8,647	27,797	20,960	9,127	30,087
1981	1,217	438	1,655	555,481	67,670	623,151	556,698	68,108	624,806
1982	48,009	2,176	50,185	1,021,121	7,197	1,028,318	1,069,130	9,373	1,078,503

[1]Recoveries are actual recoveries as of year-end 1982 plus additional recoveries expected as of that date.
Source: FDIC, *Annual Report*, 1982.

Table 11
Numbers and Deposits of All U.S. Commercial Banks Failing Between 1960 and 1982 by State

State	Number of Failed Banks Total	Number of Failed Banks Insured Banks	Deposits of Failed Banks Total	Deposits of Failed Banks Insured Banks
Alabama	7	7	$ 99,191,413	$ 99,191,413
Alaska	0	0	0	0
Arizona	2	2	9,793,040	9,793,040
Arkansas	5	5	38,009,806	38,009,806
California	6	6	1,058,592,705	1,058,592,705
Colorado	11	9	39,700,594	38,392,594
Connecticut	1	1	2,790,582	2,790,582
Delaware	0	0	0	0
District of Columbia	0	0	0	0
Florida	5	5	193,064,985	193,064,985
Georgia	11	5	67,892,707	66,322,707
Hawaii	0	0	0	0
Idaho	0	0	0	0
Illinois	17	17	492,808,854	492,808,854
Indiana	0	0	0	0
Iowa	7	7	98,130,275	98,130,275
Kansas	7	6	100,699,576	100,270,576
Kentucky	3	3	7,188,257	7,188,257
Louisiana	3	3	174,629,817	174,629,817
Maine	0	0	0	0
Maryland	0	0	0	0
Massachusetts	5	5	51,069,967	51,069,967
Michigan	7	7	195,493,292	195,493,292
Minnesota	1	1	789,387,775	789,387,775
Mississippi	2	2	45,575,199	45,575,199
Missouri	7	7	39,519,702	39,519,702
Montana	0	0	0	0
Nebraska	4	3	11,691,415	10,595,415
Nevada	0	0	0	0
New Hampshire	0	0	0	0
New Jersey	5	5	645,056,609	645,056,609
New Mexico	0	0	0	0
New York	10	9	10,866,468,000	10,863,810,000
North Carolina	0	0	0	0
North Dakota	2	1	11,428,222	10,428,222
Ohio	1	1	95,615,692	95,615,692
Oklahoma	8	8	230,232,771	230,232,771
Oregon	2	2	9,075,645	9,075,645
Pennsylvania	4	4	1,980,933,450	1,980,933,450
Rhode Island	1	0	800,000	0
South Carolina	1	1	112,702,997	112,702,997
South Dakota	0	0	0	0
Tennessee	6	6	416,318,877	416,318,877
Texas	34	31	607,362,108	570,124,108
Utah	1	1	5,991,999	5,991,999
Vermont	0	0	0	0
Virginia	2	2	19,766,404	19,766,404
Washington	1	1	550,485,712	550,485,712
West Virginia	2	2	48,415,763	48,415,763
Wisconsin	2	2	103,116,151	103,116,151
Wyoming	0	0	0	0
Virgin Islands	2	1	14,679,352	14,256,352
Puerto Rico	4	4	804,562,989	804,562,989
National Total	193	182	$20,038,242,702	$19,991,670,702

Source: FDIC, *Annual Report*, 1960–1982; and *Changes Among Operating Banks and Branches*, 1971 and 1976.

Table 12
Percentages of Total State Commercial Bank Deposits Held by the Largest Five, Ten, and Twenty Banking Organizations in Each State, 1970 and 1982

State	*Total Commercial Bank Deposits (billions)*		*Largest Five Organizations*			*Largest Ten Organizations*			*Largest Twenty Organizations*		
	1970	*1982*	*1970*	*1982*	*Change %*	*1970*	*1982*	*Change %*	*1970*	*1982*	*Change %*
Alabama	$5.0	$15.6	32.2%	54.9%	22.7	45.4%	61.0%	15.6	56.0%	66.2%	10.2
Alaska	0.6	2.1	85.4	80.1	(5.3)	99.0	99.0	0	—	—	—
Arizona	3.5	12.7	96.8	93.4	(3.4)	99.9	98.5	(1.4)	—	99.8	—
Arkansas	3.1	10.5	21.6	16.6	(5.0)	31.0	25.5	(5.5)	42.1	36.4	(5.7)
California	49.3	157.6	77.0	72.4	(4.6)	88.2	79.5	(8.7)	93.0	83.6	(9.4)
Colorado	4.4	14.6	47.2	58.9	11.7	59.6	67.4	7.8	68.2	73.7	5.5
Connecticut	5.2	11.2	61.3	59.2	(2.1)	82.7	83.9	(1.2)	92.3	92.2	(0.1)
Delaware	1.3	3.6	92.3	82.6	(9.7)	97.2	92.4	(4.8)	—	99.1	—
Dist. of Columbia	2.9	6.1	90.2	87.7	(2.5)	98.2	95.7	(2.5)	—	—	—
Florida	14.0	44.5	28.0	38.9	10.9	40.4	54.3	13.9	51.4	69.0	17.6
Georgia	7.3	20.6	48.8	43.8	(5.0)	55.3	54.7	(0.6)	61.1	60.7	(0.4)
Hawaii	1.7	5.1	89.8	92.6	2.8	100.0	99.8	(0.2)	—	—	—
Idaho	1.4	4.4	88.0	85.9	2.1	94.2	93.8	(0.4)	99.0	98.7	(0.3)
Illinois	34.6	91.2	39.3	38.6	(0.7)	44.3	40.4	(3.9)	49.5	44.1	(5.4)
Indiana	10.9	28.3	27.5	20.1	(7.4)	34.2	27.5	(6.7)	44.1	37.0	(7.1)
Iowa	6.6	19.9	17.6	25.6	8.0	24.6	32.9	8.3	32.7	39.5	6.8
Kansas	5.0	15.2	15.4	10.3	(5.1)	22.1	15.5	(6.6)	29.3	22.1	(7.2)
Kentucky	5.4	17.4	32.4	27.3	(5.1)	41.1	33.2	(7.9)	49.2	41.2	(8.0)
Louisiana	6.5	24.3	28.8	18.7	(10.1)	43.0	30.5	(12.5)	58.0	44.7	(13.3)
Maine	1.3	3.0	59.6	76.9	17.3	81.7	91.3	9.6	93.8	99.4	5.6
Maryland	5.4	13.8	61.0	63.0	2.0	75.7	80.2	4.5	83.1	88.0	4.9
Massachusetts	11.0	23.4	64.1	67.1	3.0	73.0	81.8	8.8	80.7	89.7	(9.0)
Michigan	20.8	44.4	45.8	54.4	8.6	57.7	66.4	8.7	67.6	78.1	10.5
Minnesota	9.1	26.4	59.2	56.6	(2.6)	62.1	59.7	(2.4)	65.2	62.7	(2.5)
Mississippi	3.2	11.1	33.3	32.2	(1.1)	40.9	43.5	2.6	51.0	54.6	3.6
Missouri	11.5	28.7	31.1	40.7	9.6	40.5	54.8	14.3	48.5	64.3	15.8
Montana	1.7	4.9	58.4	53.5	(4.9)	65.4	64.1	(1.3)	72.9	72.9	0
Nebraska	3.6	10.4	34.3	23.6	(10.7)	39.0	28.4	10.6	46.2	35.6	10.6
Nevada	1.2	3.6	97.4	95.6	(1.8)	—	99.7	—	—	—	—
New Hampshire	1.0	3.2	42.8	49.0	6.2	58.2	61.8	3.6	73.3	77.2	3.9
New Jersey	15.0	31.6	24.5	37.4	12.9	38.6	53.2	14.6	55.3	73.6	18.3
New Mexico	1.5	6.0	54.2	56.8	2.6	65.8	68.5	2.7	79.0	81.0	2.0
New York	88.3	234.3	56.4	42.9	(13.5)	79.7	57.8	(21.9)	89.1	70.2	(18.9)
North Carolina	7.3	19.8	67.0	68.7	1.7	79.1	84.9	5.8	88.3	93.1	4.8
North Dakota	1.6	4.7	50.5	42.6	(7.9)	59.3	50.7	(8.6)	67.5	61.0	(6.5)
Ohio	21.7	44.7	32.9	38.6	5.7	47.3	58.1	10.8	61.8	73.0	11.2
Oklahoma	5.6	23.5	32.6	26.4	(6.2)	39.7	32.1	(7.6)	46.7	39.5	(7.2)
Oregon	4.1	15.6	86.4	72.4	(14.0)	90.9	89.1	(1.8)	95.1	93.8	(1.3)
Pennsylvania	28.8	68.2	36.6	30.1	(6.5)	51.6	44.3	(7.3)	64.0	58.4	(5.6)
Rhode Island	1.6	5.6	92.4	94.0	(1.6)	99.1	98.7	(0.4)	—	—	—
South Carolina	2.4	7.2	58.3	64.0	5.7	70.2	75.3	5.1	78.9	84.9	6.0
South Dakota	1.6	6.7	47.7	60.2	12.5	55.5	67.7	12.2	66.5	76.9	10.4
Tennessee	7.5	21.7	40.2	38.5	(1.7)	57.1	50.0	(7.1)	64.8	58.3	(6.5)
Texas	26.4	110.1	23.6	40.1	16.5	32.5	54.6	22.1	40.5	61.3	20.8
Utah	1.8	5.9	73.7	76.3	(2.6)	83.4	86.6	3.2	91.0	92.6	1.6
Vermont	0.9	2.2	51.0	63.2	12.2	67.3	80.3	13.0	84.1	95.2	11.1
Virginia	8.0	22.5	50.3	53.6	3.5	68.6	76.4	7.8	76.4	82.0	5.6
Washington	5.7	20.4	77.5	78.4	0.9	87.2	88.1	0.9	92.8	91.4	(1.4)
West Virginia	2.9	9.6	17.6	11.3	(6.3)	26.9	18.5	(8.4)	39.8	30.4	(9.4)
Wisconsin	9.7	22.5	33.9	33.1	(0.8)	39.9	41.6	1.7	47.6	49.0	1.4
Wyoming	0.8	3.3	37.2	49.2	12.0	51.0	60.6	9.6	68.7	75.5	6.8

Source: Federal Reserve Board, "Call Data for Commercial Banks in U.S., Consolidated Within State for Bank Holding Companies," December 31, 1970, and June 30, 1982.

Table 13
Number of Bank Holding Companies by Type, with Percentages Held of All Bank Deposits, 1975–1982

	Total Bank Holding Companies			*One Bank Holding Companies*		*Multibank Holding Companies*		
Year	*Number*	*Number of Subsidiary Banks*[1]	*Percentage of U.S. Commercial Bank Deposits*	*Number*	*Percentage of U.S. Commercial Bank Deposits*	*Number*	*Number of Subsidiary Banks*	*Percentage of U.S. Commercial Bank Deposits*
1975	1,708	3,674	67.07	1,418	29.23	290	2,256	37.80
1976	1,802	3,791	66.04	1,504	31.87	298	2,295	34.18
1977	1,913	3,903	66.45	1,607	31.90	306	2,301	34.55
1978	2,113	4,101	66.77	1,799	34.10	314	2,310	32.67
1979	2,357	4,280	67.80	2,028	34.52	329	2,261	33.28
1980	2,905	4,954	71.01	2,544	36.62	361	2,426	34.39
1981	3,500	5,689	74.13	3,093	36.13	407	2,607	38.00
1982	4,557	6,659	n.a.	n.a.	n.a.	n.a.	n.a.	n.a.

[1]Because of certain eliminations, the number of subsidiary banks under total bank holding companies does not necessarily equal the number of one bank holding companies plus the number of subsidiary banks under multibank holding companies.

Source: Federal Reserve Board, *Annual Statistical Digest*, 1975–1981.

Table 14
Volume of Bank Holding Company Section 4(c)(8) Activities, January 1, 1971–December 31, 1982

Activity	*De Novo Notifications Received*[1]	*Proposed Acquisitions Processed*	
		Approved	*Denied*
Fiduciary and Trust	167	22	2
Mortgage Banking	966	134	11
Leasing	675	42	4
Investment, Financial, and Economic Advisory Services	285	18	3
Insurance Agency or Broker	2,010	307	17
Insurance Underwriting, Credit Life, Accident, and Health	181	77	1
Finance Company[2]			
General	480	15	1
Commercial	342	22	1
Consumer	1,124	127	11
Insurance Premium	13	5	0
Mobile Homes	28	2	2
Agriculture	16	5	1
Data Processing	214	29	1
Factoring	72	17	1
Community Development	36	3	2
Industrial Banking	147	37	4
Management Consulting for Banks	14	16	0
Payment Instruments, Issuance or Selling of	41	2	0
Savings and Loan Association	0	5	5
Underwriting Government Securities	1	2	0
Other	86	30	3
Total	6,898	917	70

[1]This column includes primarily holding company expansion notifications processed by Federal Reserve Banks under delegated authority. Notifications involving multiple activities were counted once for each such activity. For example, if a notification involved mortgage banking and insurance agency activities, it was counted once in each category.

[2]Until March 31, 1973, finance company notifications were placed in a single category. Since then, notifications have been distributed within the subcategories shown. The row labeled "General" includes 123 notifications received through March 31, 1973. For the period subsequent to March 31, 1973, the "General" row includes firms that (1) engaged in both consumer and commercial finance, (2) could not be distinguished as engaging in either consumer or commercial finance, or (3) engaged in a type of financing that could not be placed in a category listed in the table.

Source: *Bank Expansion Quarterly*, Volume XXXII (Fourth Quarter 1982).

Table 15
Number of Savings and Loan Associations, with Offices and Assets, 1940–1982

Year	Number of Associations Total	Number of Associations FSLIC Insured	Total Offices[1]	Assets (Millions) Total	Assets (Millions) FSLIC Insured
1940	7,521	2,277	n.a.	$ 5,733	$ 2,926
1945	6,149	2,475	n.a.	8,747	6,123
1950	5,992	2,860	n.a.	16,893	13,691
1955	4,307	3,554	6,672	37,656	34,198
1960	6,320	4,098	7,931	71,476	67,430
1965	6,185	4,508	9,179	129,580	124,576
1970	5,669	4,365	9,987	176,183	170,645
1971	5,474	4,271	10,435	206,023	199,984
1972	5,298	4,191	11,149	243,127	236,349
1973	5,170	4,163	12,206	271,905	264,797
1974	5,023	4,141	13,798	295,545	288,223
1975	4,931	4,078	15,449	338,233	330,259
1976	4,821	4,044	16,729	391,907	383,172
1977	4,761	4,065	17,848	459,241	449,998
1978	4,725	4,053	18,975	523,542	513,310
1979	4,684	4,039	20,192	578,962	568,107
1980	4,592	4,002	21,325	630,712	608,465
1981	4,347	3,779	22,135	663,844	651,068
1982	3,833	3,343	22,545	706,045	692,663

[1] All associations.
Source: United States League of Savings Associations: *1982 Savings and Loan Sourcebook; 1966 Savings and Loan Fact Book.*

Selected Bibliography

Items in this brief and highly selected bibliography were chosen for the primary purpose of directing attention to certain publications in the field of bank regulation of fundamental importance or of a pervasive nature. The content of the bibliography is heavily weighted toward publications by various sectors of the U.S. government. This is not to denigrate private sector contributions in the field. Government statistics and studies, however, are the basis for much of the analysis by the private sector. Therefore, in the interests of brevity, these official and semi-official sources are emphasized.

Altman, Edward, and Sametz, Arnold, eds. *Financial Crisis: Institutions and Markets in a Fragile Environment*. New York: Ronald Press Company, 1977.

Austin, Douglas V. "The Evolution of Commercial Bank Merger Antitrust Law." *Business Lawyer* 36 (January 1981): 297–396.

Baughn, William H., and Walker, Charls E., eds. *The Bankers' Handbook*. Homewood, Illinois: Dow Jones-Irwin, 1978.

Board of Governors of the Federal Reserve System. *Annual Statistical Digest*, 1981 and previous years.

———. *The Bank Holding Company Movement to 1978: A Compendium,* 1978.

———. *Banking and Monetary Statistics, 1914–1941,* 1943.

———. *Banking and Monetary Statistics, 1941–1970,* 1976.

———. *Annual Report,* 1982 and previous years.

———. *Federal Reserve Bulletin,* 1983 and previous years.

———. *The Federal Reserve System, Purposes and Functions,* 1974.

Carson, Deane, editor. *Banking and Monetary Studies.* Homewood, Illinois: Richard D. Irwin, Inc., 1963.

Clark, Robert C. "The Regulation of Financial Holding Companies." *Harvard Law Review* 92 (February 1979): 789–863.

Comptroller of the Currency. *101st Annual Report: Years of Reform, A Prelude of Progress, 1963.*

———. *Annual Report,* 1980 and previous years.

———. *Quarterly Journal,* 1983–1981.

———. Staff Papers Pertaining to Foreign Acquisition and Control of U.S. Banks:

Longbrake, William A.; Quinn, Melanie, R.; and Walter, Judith A. *Foreign Acquisitions of U.S. Banks: Facts and Patterns.* (1980-1).

Walter, Judith A. *Foreign Acquisitions of U.S. Banks: Motives and Tactical Considerations.* (1980-2).

Goddin, Stewart C., and Weiss, Steven J. *U.S. Banks' Loss of Global Standing.* (1980-3).

Weiss, Steven J. *A Critical Evaluation of Reciprocity in Foreign Bank Acquisitions.* (1980-4).

Smith, William P., and Weiss, Steven J. *Potential Acquisition Partners for Large U.S. Banks: The Discriminatory Effects of Law and Policy.* (1980-5).

Weiss, Steven J. *Competitive Standards Applied to Foreign and Domestic Acquisitions of U.S. Banks.* (1980-6).

Shockey, John E., and Glidden, William B. *Foreign-Controlled U.S. Banks: The Legal and Regulatory Environment.* (1980-7).

Walter, Judith A. *Supervisory Performance of Foreign-Controlled U.S. Banking Organizations.* (1980-8).

Hodgkins, Blair B., and Goldberg, Ellen S. *Effect of Foreign Acquisition on the Balance Sheet Structure and Earnings Performance of American Banks.* (1980-9).

Goldberg, Ellen S. *Analysis of Current Operations of Foreign-Owned U.S. Banks.* (1980-10).

______. *Comparative Cost Analysis of Foreign-Owned U.S. Banks.* (1980-11).

Page, Diane, and Neal, Soss M. *Some Evidence on Transnational Banking Structure.* (1980-12).

Weiss, Steven J. *The Competitive Balance Between Domestic and Foreign Banks in the U.S.* (1980-13).

Loeffler, Thomas A., and Longbrake, William A. *Prices Paid By Foreign Interests to Acquire U.S. Banks.* (1981-1).

Department of the Treasury. *Geographic Restrictions on Commercial Banking in the United States: The Report of the President,* 1981.

Edwards, Franklin R., ed. *Issues in Financial Regulation.* New York: McGraw-Hill Book Company, 1979.

Federal Deposit Insurance Corporation. *Annual Report*, 1982 and previous years.

Federal Reserve Bank of Chicago. *Proceedings of a Conference on Bank Structure and Competition*, 1982 and previous years.

Fischer, Gerald C. *Bank Holding Companies*. New York: Columbia University Press, 1961.

Friedman, Milton, and Schwartz, Anna J. *A Monetary History of the United States, 1867–1960*. Princeton, N.J.: Princeton University Press, 1963.

———. *Monetary Statistics of the United States: Estimates, Sources, Methods*. New York: Columbia University Press, 1970.

Ginsburg, Douglas H. "Interstate Banking." *Hofstra Law Review* 9 (September 1981).

Golembe, Carter H. "Our Remarkable Banking System." *Virginia Law Review* 53 (June 1967), 1091–1114.

Hammond, Bray. *Banks and Politics in America from the Revolution to the Civil War*. Princeton, New Jersey: Princeton University Press, 1957.

Heller, Pauline B. *Handbook of Federal Bank Holding Company Law*. New York: Law Journal Press, 1976.

Lapidus, Leonard, and others. *State and Federal Regulation of Commercial Banks*. Washington, D.C.: Task Force on State and Federal Regulation of Commercial Banks, Federal Deposit Insurance Corporation, 1980.

Levin, Jonathan L. "In Search of the National Bank Act." *Banking Law Journal* 97 (September 1980): 741–750.

Redlich, Fritz. *The Molding of American Banking*. New York and London: Johnson Reprint Company, 1968.

Robertson, Ross M. *The Comptroller and Bank Supervision, A Historical Appraisal*. Washington, D.C.: The Office of the Comptroller of the Currency, 1968.

U.S. General Accounting Office. *Stronger Supervision of Credit Unions Needed*. Report no. GGD-83-12 (1982).

______. *Bank Examination For Country Risk and International Lending*. Report no. ID-82-52 (1982).

______. *Bank Merger Process Should Be Modernized And Simplified.* Report no. GGD-82-53 (1982).

______. *Information About Depository Institutions' Ancillary Activities Is Not Adequate For Policy Purposes.* Report no. GGD-82-57 (1982).

______. *Issues To Be Considered While Debating Interstate Bank Branching*. Report no. GGD-82-36 (1982).

______. *Despite Recent Improvements, Bank Supervision Could Be More Effective and Less Burdensome.* Report no. GGD-82-21 (1982).

______. *Formal Supervisory Process For Savings And Loan Associations Should Be Strengthened.* Report no. GGD-81-91 (1981).

______. *Federal Reserve Could Improve The Efficiency of Bank Holding Company Inspections.* Report no. GGD-81-79 (1981).

______. *An Economic Overview of Bank Solvency Regulation.* Report no. PAD-81-25 (1981).

______. *The Federal Structure For Examining Financial Institutions Can Be Improved.* Report no. GGD-81-21.

______. *Federal Examinations of Financial Institutions: Issues That Need To Be Resolved.* Report no. GGD-81-12 (1981).

______. *Despite Positive Effects, Further Foreign Acquisitions of U.S. Banks Should Be Limited Until Policy Conflicts Are Fully Addressed.* Report no. GGD-80-66 (1980).

______. *Federal Supervision of Bank Holding Companies Needs Better, More Formalized Coordination.* Report no. GGD-80-20 (1980).

______. *Banks Having Problems Need Better Identification and Disclosure.* Report no. FOD-89-1 (1979).

———. *Federal Supervision of States and National Banks*. Report no. OCG-77-1 (1977).

Upham, Cyril B., and Lamke, Edwin. *Closed and Distressed Banks*. Washington, D.C.: The Brookings Institution, 1934.

INDEX

A

B

C

D

E

F

G

H

I

O

P

R

S

T

U

W